S0-AFA-335

A CELEBRATION
OF POETS

MIDWEST
GRADES K-3
SPRING 2008

creativeCOMMUNICATION
A CELEBRATION OF TODAY'S WRITERS

A Celebration of Poets
Midwest
Grades K-3
Spring 2008

An anthology compiled by Creative Communication, Inc.

Published by:

creativeCOMMUNICATION
A CELEBRATION OF TODAY'S WRITERS

1488 NORTH 200 WEST • LOGAN, UTAH 84341
TEL. 435-713-4411 • WWW.POETICPOWER.COM

All rights reserved. No part of this book may be reproduced or transmitted in any form or by any means, electronic or mechanical without written permission of the author and publisher.

Copyright © 2008 by Creative Communication, Inc.
Printed in the United States of America

ISBN: 978-1-60050-199-9

FOREWORD

This edition of our poetry anthology is an important transition for Creative Communication. Since our beginning in 1993, we have called our contest "A Celebration of Young Poets." Having worked with student poets for over 15 years, we realized that the writers who have been accepted to be published are not "young" poets. They are poets. Young or old, they are writers who have proven their worth as poets. These are the poets we celebrate.

We also start this year with a new cover for the anthologies. We are excited about this new look and our new logo of a hand releasing stars. Our logo can represent different things. It could be a teacher or mentor releasing a writer to the world through our publication. It could represent the fact that the stars are limitless and these writers are just starting to shine with their potential. We have become the starting point for thousands of writers and we hope each poet continues to make writing a part of their lives.

What is recorded between these pages is unique. It exists nowhere else in the world and is now recorded forever. Take the time to read what these poets have shared. A part of themselves and their world exists in each poem. Savor it. Enjoy.

Sincerely,
Thomas Kenne Worthen, Ph.D.
Editor
Creative Communication

WRITING CONTESTS!

Enter our next POETRY contest!
Enter our next ESSAY contest!

Why should I enter?

Win prizes and get published! Each year thousands of dollars in prizes are awarded in each region and tens of thousands of dollars in prizes are awarded throughout North America. The top writers in each division receive a monetary award and a free book that includes their published poem or essay. Entries of merit are also selected to be published in our anthology.

Who may enter?

There are four divisions in the poetry and essay contests. The divisions are grades K-3, 4-6, 7-9, and 10-12.

What is needed to enter the contest?

To enter the poetry contest send in one original poem, 21 lines or less. To enter the essay contest send in one original essay, 250 words or less, on any topic. Each entry must include the student's name, grade, address, city, state, and zip code, and the student's school name and school address. Students who include their teacher's name may help the teacher qualify for a free copy of the anthology.

How do I enter?

Enter a poem online at:
www.poeticpower.com
or
Mail your poem to:
    Poetry Contest
    1488 North 200 West
    Logan, UT 84341

Enter an essay online at:
www.studentessaycontest.com
or
Mail your essay to:
    Essay Contest
    1488 North 200 West
    Logan, UT 84341

When is the deadline?

Poetry contest deadlines are December 4th, April 7th, and August 18th. Essay contest deadlines are October 15th, February 17th, and July 15th. You can enter each contest, however, send only one poem or essay for each contest deadline.

Are there benefits for my school?

Yes. We award $15,000 each year in grants to help with Language Arts programs. Schools qualify to apply for a grant by having a large number of entries of which over fifty percent are accepted for publication. This typically tends to be about 15 accepted entries.

Are there benefits for my teacher?

Yes. Teachers with five or more students accepted to be published receive a free anthology that includes their students' writing.

For more information please go to our website at
***www.poeticpower.com**,*
email us at editor@poeticpower.com or call 435-713-4411.

TABLE OF CONTENTS

STATES INCLUDED IN THIS EDITION:

Illinois
Indiana
Iowa
Kansas
Michigan
Minnesota
Nebraska
North Dakota
Ohio
South Dakota
Wisconsin

Spring 2008 Poetic Achievement Honor Schools

* Teachers who had fifteen or more poets accepted to be published

The following schools are recognized as receiving a "Poetic Achievement Award." This award is given to schools who have a large number of entries of which over fifty percent are accepted for publication. With hundreds of schools entering our contest, only a small percent of these schools are honored with this award. The purpose of this award is to recognize schools with excellent Language Arts programs. This award qualifies these schools to receive a complimentary copy of this anthology. In addition, these schools are eligible to apply for a Creative Communication Language Arts Grant. Grants of two hundred and fifty dollars each are awarded to further develop writing in our schools.

Arbury Hills Elementary School
Mokena, IL
Jody Diehl*

Atwood Elementary School
Macomb, MI
Karen Brown
Jennifer Donovan
Shawn Kerr*
Colleen Sloan-Kowal*
Ayesha Strait*

Bristol Elementary School
Bristol, WI
Cheryl Fowler*

Broken Arrow Elementary School
Lawrence, KS
Mary VanDyke*

C W Neff Elementary School
Grand Ledge, MI
Sheryl Gorden*

Central Elementary School
Riverside, IL
Katie Meenan*

Charles Hammond Elementary School
Chicago, IL
Glorianna Estela*
Theresa Insalaco
Katie Reiff

Chaska Elementary School
Chaska, MN
Joan Wright*

Cline Elementary School
Centerville, OH
Heather Price
Judy E. Rutherford*
Debbie Smith

Country Meadow Elementary
School
Ashley, IN
Becci Fox*
Laurie Griffin
Ann Owen*
Dawn Passwater*
Cathy Wells*

Coy Elementary School
Oregon, OH
Melissa Collins*

Decatur Classical Elementary
School
Chicago, IL
Mrs. Allegretti
Miss Cohen
Ms. Gingerich
Kimberly Jockl
Nancy Jorbin
Theresa Ludlow
Mrs. Sharping

Deerfield Elementary School
Novi, MI
Mrs. Lee
Rebecca Purcell
Ms. Styles

Detroit Country Day Junior School
Bloomfield Hills, MI
Marie Thomas*

Eastside Elementary School
Constantine, MI
Sheree Sorensen*

Floyd Ebeling Elementary School
Macomb, MI
Jacquelyn Barker*
Mrs. Bettys
Lisa Bruce*
Mrs. Jarzyna*
Mrs. Maul*
M. McIntyre
Stephanie Tonkin
Christine Zatell

Gen George Patton Elementary
School
Riverdale, IL
Mrs. Spearman*

Greenbriar Elementary School
Northbrook, IL
Mrs. Decker
Mrs. Edwards
Mrs. Kowalke*
Mrs. Sanchez
Ms. Schneider
Ms. Shamberg
Mr. Warda
Mrs. Wolavka
Mrs. Wurtzel

H R McCall Elementary School
Waukegan, IL
Linda Garrison*

Hamilton Community Elementary
School
Hamilton, IN
Julie Friend*
LuAnne Letizia*

Hanover Elementary School
Hanover, MN
Jenny Boldt*

Henryville Elementary School
Henryville, IN
Gay Ann Ballintyn*
Mrs. Hodson
Kimberly LaMaster
Dennis Watson*
Melinda Wright

Hillcrest Elementary School
Lawrence, KS
Kathy Bowen
Leellyn R. Tuel

Holden Elementary School
Chicago, IL
Cheryl A. Brewerton
Cheryl Purdy
Alfreda Smith

Holy Redeemer Christian Academy
Milwaukee, WI
Chandra Alston
Colleen Heisdorf*
Marlene Kappel
Laura Steininger*

Hyatt Elementary School
Linden, MI
Diane Hoffman
Becky Joslin
Betsy LaFond
Jennifer Park
Stephanie Rueckert
Marsha Strobel
Terry Tibbits

J C Hoglan Elementary School
Marshalltown, IA
Julie Harvey*

Jackson Center Elementary School
Jackson Center, OH
Diana Centers
Regina Hunsucker

James R Watson Elementary
School
Auburn, IN
Tina Bassett*
Diane Dean*
Ellen Eberling
Denise Hall*
Candace Post*
Lisa Pyck
Susie Samuelson*
Tammy Smith
Kiley Toney*
Pam Warner*
Mr. White

Jefferson Elementary School
Wyandotte, MI
Kristin McMaster*

Kate Goodrich Elementary School
Merrill, WI
Sarah Monti
Lisa Reimert
Rena Sabey*
Angie Zocher

Ladoga Elementary School
Ladoga, IN
Mary Huebner
Janet Vice*

Litchville-Marion Elementary
School
Litchville, ND
Chad Lueck*

Loveland Elementary School
Loveland, OH
John Ernst
Kair Kaser
Andrew Price
Mrs. Shelton

Mable Woolsey Elementary School
Knoxville, IL
Diane Estes*

MacArthur Elementary School
Green Bay, WI
    Mrs. S. Abts
    Roger Drumm*
    Mr. A. Ebeling*
    Kay Knapp*
    Mary Tomasiak*

McKenney-Harrison Elementary
School
    Auburn, IN
        Jane Foster*
        Tim Kindler*
        Nicki Pinnington*
        Jennifer Seiler
        Annie Wing

Meadowbrook Elementary School
Northbrook, IL
    Mrs. Andre
    Ms. Buss
    Mrs. Conrad
    Mrs. Corona
    Mrs. Hitzman
    Ms. Jablonski
    Ms. LaMar
    Ms. Mazzarella
    Mrs. Melnyk
    Mrs. Vivano

Mentone Elementary School
Mentone, IN
    M. Cripe
    Layne Early
    Mrs. Finn
    Staci Revere*
    Vonda Ryman
    Marge Sanders
    Pam Sellers*
    Janie Shriver
    Pam Smith
    Dawn Walker

Michener Elementary School
Adrian, MI
    Ann Cebulski
    Mrs. Yatzek

Midkota Elementary School
Binford, ND
    Pam Adrian
    Larry Tag
    Debbie Walen

Montrose Elementary School
Montrose, MN
    Jenny Boldt*

Noonan Academy
Mokena, IL
    Mary Colbert*
    Cathy Gualandri*

Normandy Elementary School
Centerville, OH
    Mr. Forbes
    Christin Skidmore
    Jan Taylor*

North Intermediate School
Saint Peter, MN
    Mrs. Alom
    Brenda Guappone
    Jo Johnson
    Nina Preheim

Northfield Elementary School
Northfield, OH
    Lisa Bass*
    Ms. Berkley*
    Jen Gruber*
    Ms. Ventre

Orchard Lane Elementary School
New Berlin, WI
    Carrie Boduch*
    Lori San Felippo*

Parkwood-Upjohn School
Kalamazoo, MI
Lee Dodds
Deb Fritz
Barbara Gumpper
Dr. Carol Hogan
Denise Jordan
Kari Strand

Pathfinder Elementary School
Fremont, MI
Carol Dawson*

Patterson Elementary School
Holly, MI
Miss King*

Peck Elementary School
Chicago, IL
Miriam Ali*
Ms. Harris
Kathe Meyers*
Karen O'Connor
Ms. Ramirez
Consuelo Rodriguez
Yesmin Zayed
Doris Zughoul*

Perry Central Elementary School
Leopold, IN
Darlene Davis
Becky Hubert*
Angela Shelby

Phillip May Elementary School
Rochelle, IL
Peg Duffy*
Angela Mahoney*
Mary Zamastil

Queen of All Saints School
Chicago, IL
Liz Adamczyk*

Ramalynn Montessori Academy
Bloomington, MN
JoAnne Murray
Darla Pulles
Cassy Ramalingam
Julie Ryan
Jane Ulwelling*

Rutledge Hall Elementary School
Lincolnwood, IL
Leanne Ellis*

Shorewood Hills Elementary School
Madison, WI
Sandy Rueckert*

Smithville Elementary School
Smithville, OH
Jackie Moomaw
Sandy Workman

Somers Elementary School
Kenosha, WI
Marcy Hyllberg
J. Schantek
Jennifer Van Pamel

St Clare Catholic School
O'Fallon, IL
Diane Giedeman*

St Columbkille School
Dubuque, IA
Cynthia Arenz
Ann Callahan*
Miss Dietzel
Janet Freihofer
Mrs. Murphy

St Michael School
Worthington, OH
Marian Jacobs*

St Paul's Evangelical Lutheran
School
Norfolk, NE
Heidi Rixe*

St Paul's Lutheran School
New Ulm, MN
Marlene Wendler*

St Robert Bellarmine School
Chicago, IL
Sr. Doreen Whitney
Sr. Ann Fanella
Linda Hoffman
Donna Jaconetti
Doreen Whitney

St Timothy's School
Maple Lake, MN
Mrs. Bokusky
Mary Lu Flick

Stocker Elementary School
Kenosha, WI
Ms. Becker
Marie Beronich
Beth Casey*
Meg Fisher
Nancy Granger
Steve Hartfield
Marilyn Siedjak*
Monica Sioco
Margaret Unger*
Ruth Walls*

Strange Elementary School
Kenosha, WI
Beverly Salituro*
Sarah Smith

Suffield Elementary School
Mogadore, OH
Mary Adelman
Mrs. Clason-Grinder
Mrs. Horning
Mrs. Thiry*

Thayer Central Elementary School
Hebron, NE
Yvonne Hoops*

Trinity Lutheran School
Boone, IA
Mrs. Grossnickle
Cathy Sprengeler

Webster Elementary School
Hazel Park, MI
Debbie Dimas
Anita Dupes
Jean Jones
Julie Jones
Sharon Krane
Mrs. Lashbrook
Tammy Scholz
Nancy Tack

Wethersfield Elementary School
Kewanee, IL
Mary Alepra*
Tammy Jackson

Weymouth Elementary School
Charlotte, MI
Paul Murphy*

Woodford Elementary School
Barberton, OH
Mrs. Bowling
Mrs. Carlucci
Sandra Chisnell
Janice Firtha
Mr. Hutchison
Mrs. Lapehn
Karen McGrath
Melissa Midura
Diane Moskos
Melissa Norris
Mrs. Rego
Sharon Sopko
Mr. Stone
Miss Yenchik

Language Arts Grant Recipients 2007-2008

After receiving a "Poetic Achievement Award" schools are encouraged to apply for a Creative Communication Language Arts Grant. The following is a list of schools who received a two hundred and fifty dollar grant for the 2007-2008 school year.

Acadamie DaVinci, Dunedin, FL
Altamont Elementary School, Altamont, KS
Belle Valley South School, Belleville, IL
Bose Elementary School, Kenosha, WI
Brittany Hill Middle School, Blue Springs, MO
Carver Jr High School, Spartanburg, SC
Cave City Elementary School, Cave City, AR
Central Elementary School, Iron Mountain, MI
Challenger K8 School of Science and Mathematics, Spring Hill, FL
Columbus Middle School, Columbus, MT
Cypress Christian School, Houston, TX
Deer River High School, Deer River, MN
Deweyville Middle School, Deweyville, TX
Four Peaks Elementary School, Fountain Hills, AZ
Fox Chase School, Philadelphia, PA
Fox Creek High School, North Augusta, SC
Grandview Alternative School, Grandview, MO
Hillcrest Elementary School, Lawrence, KS
Holbrook School, Holden, ME
Houston Middle School, Germantown, TN
Independence High School, Elko, NV
International College Preparatory Academy, Cincinnati, OH
John Bowne High School, Flushing, NY

Language Arts Grant Winners cont.

Lorain County Joint Vocational School, Oberlin, OH
Merritt Secondary School, Merritt, BC
Midway Covenant Christian School, Powder Springs, GA
Muir Middle School, Milford, MI
Northlake Christian School, Covington, LA
Northwood Elementary School, Hilton, NY
Place Middle School, Denver, CO
Public School 124, South Ozone Park, NY
Public School 219 Kennedy King, Brooklyn, NY
Rolling Hills Elementary School, San Diego, CA
St Anthony's School, Streator, IL
St Joan Of Arc School, Library, PA
St Joseph Catholic School, York, NE
St Joseph School-Fullerton, Baltimore, MD
St Monica Elementary School, Mishawaka, IN
St Peter Celestine Catholic School, Cherry Hill, NJ
Strasburg High School, Strasburg, VA
Stratton Elementary School, Stratton, ME
Tom Thomson Public School, Burlington, ON
Tremont Elementary School, Tremont, IL
Warren Elementary School, Warren, OR
Webster Elementary School, Hazel Park, MI
West Woods Elementary School, Arvada, CO
West Woods Upper Elementary School, Farmington, CT
White Pine Middle School, Richmond, UT
Winona Elementary School, Winona, TX
Wissahickon Charter School, Philadelphia, PA
Wood County Christian School, Williamstown, WV
Wray High School, Wray, CO

Grades K-1-2-3

Note: The Top Ten poems were finalized through an online voting system. Creative Communication's judges first picked out the top poems. These poems were then posted online. The final step involved thousands of students and teachers who registered as online judges and voted for the Top Ten poems. We hope you enjoy these selections.

Top Poem Grades K-3

The Animal World

Oh weasels, ferrets, stoats are three.
Can you name one more, hee hee?

Oh good old frogs can thrive in ponds,
Leaping about amidst the fronds,
Playing a game of look at who,
Wouldn't you like to join them too?

Where is that flying bird the owl?
Maybe he's out in the woods on a prowl.
Isn't that such a marvelous hoot?
It scared the chick back into its coop.

Speaking of chickens, can you hear them cluck?
Maybe they'll have a big stroke of luck.
Did you see their bright colored beaks?
That's because they like to speak.

Where are those funny beasts the sheep?
Oh, there they are taking a leap.
Maybe it's time for them to get a trim.
The sheep's' faces look pretty grim.

I think I named quite a few more.
Now can you name one that can roar?

Gautam Apte, Grade 2
Onaway Elementary School, OH

Top Poem Grades K-3

What Happens at Night in the Art Room

What happens at night in the art room,
It's a mystery, really I know.
The markers go wild telling stories
About what it is like in the snow.
The scissors are cutting the paper.
They're making a really big mess.
The pencils are so very tired,
They just can't join in with the rest.

Jillian Campbell, Grade 2
Detroit Country Day Lower School, MI

Top Poem Grades K-3

Her Story of the Land of the Free

Dear child tell me your story
And I'll tell you mine.
Well dear child I am a statue.
So that being said,
There's not much to say.
But I'll tell you any way.
My land is America so you see.
I am the Statue of Liberty.
My book holds secrets the world doesn't know.
Dear child come with me but bring your family,
I will take you to the land of the free.
Now child give me your tired, your poor, your hungry.
Tell me child your troubles, I will fix them.
The spirits speak stories of your soul.
Dear child what is wrong?
Come to the golden door,
My lamp will light the way for you and for all!

Mollie Elliott, Grade 3
Detroit Country Day Junior School, MI

Top Poem Grades K-3

The Greedy Dog

A large, black dog had a piece of raw meat.
Over a bridge, he ambled with his treat.
He happened to look down
And his face became a frown.
The dog in the water had such a big steak;
Oh, no, there must be some kind of mistake!
"That big piece is mine!"
He said with a whine.
So he barked and he lost;
His meat gone was his cost.
He sagged back to his place,
No more meat in his face.
Moral:
If a steak is in your chop,
Close your mouth so you don't drop.

Ruby Gravrok, Grade 3
Holy Family Home School, WI

Top Poem Grades K-3

Colors

Colors make me happy
And put a smile on my face.
Sometimes they take me
To a happy place.
I love all colors,
Red, orange, yellow, pink, green and blue.
How about you?

Alea Griffith, Grade K
Woodford Elementary School, OH

Top Poem Grades K-3

Wild Horse Racing

Wild horse
racing the wind
running wild and free
galloping
moving all his muscles
ground looking like smeared paint
losing breath every minute
racing the wind
tail flings out behind
soon going to stop and rest
but still going
trying to gallop to
the end of
the valley

Haley Keelan, Grade 3
Greenbriar Elementary School, IL

Top Poem Grades K-3

Spring

S parkly icicles start to drip.
　　Soon we will plan our summer trip.
P icnics are fun, but they have ants.
　　Don't let them crawl up your pants!
R oses are my favorite flower.
　　I water them in the morning hour.
I ce cream is a yummy treat.
　　Eat it fast, it melts in the heat.
N ests are to keep birds warm.
　　Birds like to live on a farm.
G reen grass starts to grow.
　　Soon my dad will have to mow.

Courtney Koeberl, Grade 1
Meadowbrook Elementary School, WI

Top Poem Grades K-3

Springtime

S inging birds in the trees
P retty flowers attracting bees
R ain showers come and go
I ce is gone and so is snow
N ow the trees are budding out
G reen grass growing all about
T oads and frogs call for a mate
I n the sky the sun sets late
M ust be spring with all these things
E njoy the happiness that it brings

Casey Robertson, Grade 2
Robertson Home School, IA

Top Poem Grades K-3

Tulip

Tulip, tulip in my yard,
Is the soil too wet, or is it too hard?
Tulip, tulip, pretty and pink,
Whenever I see you, "How lovely," I think.
Tulip, tulip, I will let you grow,
Oh, how I love you so!

Chloe Sullivan, Grade 2
Carey Ridge Elementary School, IN

Top Poem Grades K-3

Fireworks

Bang, crash, boom!
Colors fill the sky.
The people clap and cheer.
Fizzle, crack, pop!
An explosion of color,
A burst of light,
Splashes and sparkles
Through the night.
The finale booms and bangs and crashes,
Green, gold, and red, it flashes.
Colors fade, there's a moment's pause…
Then a dazzled crowd erupts in applause.

Caroline Walker, Grade 3
Home School, OH

Happy — Sad

My grandma can knit.
My grandma can bake cookies.
But
She has a broken foot.
That is sad.
I can't wait until it's fixed.

Jared Nichols, Grade 1
Strange Elementary School, WI

Shopping

Shopping is fun.
Shopping is great.
Shopping is for shirts.
Shopping is for jeans.
Shopping is for everything in between.

Do you like shopping?

Reagan Hensley, Grade 3
Henryville Elementary School, IN

Winter

The snow falls down on me.
I like to play in the snow.
I like to make a snowman.
It is a wonderful winter too.

The snowflakes are so fluffy and big.
They make everything white.
Like big piles of frosting.
What a pretty sight!

I take my sled upon the hill.
Then came coasting down.
I land in the bottom
In a great big mound.

Duane W. Nissley, Grade 2
Oak Hill Amish School, IN

Tornado

Very dangerous,
Always windy in the sky
Almost killing me!

Kolin Edrington, Grade 3
Henryville Elementary School, IN

Friendship

Mark
Sweet, sensitive
Playing, skating, biking
Best twin in history
Marky

Mary Laken, Grade 3
Somers Elementary School, WI

Homework Rocks!

Homework, you rock!
You keep me up late.
You keep my brain docked at work
when my bedtime is eight.

Homework, you rock!
You act like a charm
and sometimes you make the hairs
fall off my arm.

Homework, you rock!
You won't believe
that even my mom can't
fit you up my sleeve.

Chase Groth, Grade 3
Bentley Primary School, KS

Branden

My brother Branden
fights in the war
a long time
in Iraq
to keep us safe.

Brookelynn Smith, Grade 1
Wethersfield Elementary School, IL

My Brother

My brother
is kind
and helpful
and friendly
I love
my brother!

Kayli Hoad, Grade 2
Pathfinder Elementary School, MI

I Am

I am a collector of cards
I wonder what my great grandpas looked like
I hear my teacher talking
I see my bed a lot
I want to play outside
I am a collector of cards

I pretend to play Pokémon
I feel the table, it is smooth
I touch my glasses that help me see
I worry about losing my Pokémon cards
I cry when I am grounded
I am a collector of cards

I understand that I can't get the board game I want
I say I like Digimon
I dream to see L.A.
I try to get farther on Digimon
I hope to get the board game I want
I am a collector of cards

Jacob Burbach, Grade 3
Kate Goodrich Elementary School, WI

The Guardian of New York

Welcome, welcome to our great country
Where we have mountains, lakes, plains, and rivers.
Here we have freedom.
We make our own choices
And have no one telling us what to do.
You can do lots of things in our country.
P.S. If you can dream it, you can do it!

Damian Runkle, Grade 3
Detroit Country Day Junior School, MI

I Learned

I learned to read, I learned to write,
I learned to tie my shoes in daytime and night.
LEARN, LEARN, LEARN!
I learned to climb, I learned math
I learned times, division and it happened so fast!
I love to learn what can I say?
It is a hobby I do every day!

Maria McGinnis, Grade 3
Willyard Elementary School, OH

Spring

S pring
P ouring shower
R oaring rain
I n the big puddles
N ight storms
G ood rain

R unning in the big puddles
A huge rain cloud
I n the big sky
N ow I feel it's here

Scott Maidens, Grade 3
Deerfield Elementary School, MI

The Dog

I am hairy
I am brown and white
I like to bark
and wag my tail in the air
I like to chase my tail.
My owner is Cheyanne
She is very nice to me.

Cheyanne Genton, Grade 3
Henryville Elementary School, IN

Macee's Furry Puppy

Macee has a furry puppy
Its fur was very curly
And everywhere that Macee went
The puppy acted like a girly!
He rode a limo to school one day.
It was such a sight!
But Macee had a fit
Because it was not right!

Hayley DePriest, Grade 3
Smithville Elementary School, OH

Mudding

Dodge got stuck!
Ford went through the muck.
Chevy went through the creek.
Cadillac got lucky!

Lucas Mills, Grade 3
Mentone Elementary School, IN

Kourtnie

K ourtnie is cool
O utside lover
U sually is happy
R unning and playing
T is my favorite letter
N ever is mean
I ce cream lover
E verybody in my family loves me

Kourtnie Bolton, Grade 3
Atwood Elementary School, MI

Goat

Goat
Big, black
Running, eating, butting
Billy

Hunter Mathiesen, Grade 2
Thayer Central Elementary School, NE

B-ball

Hot sweat,
crowd screaming.

Whistle blowing,
slam dunk!

3 points,
1st quarter,

time out,
injured player.

10 seconds left!
throw it!

5 seconds!
4...3...2...1!

Shoot it,
We won!

We are the champions!!!

Royal Lindsey, Grade 3
MacArthur Elementary School, WI

Me

Mackenzie
Fun, sweet, nice
Daughter of Lisa and Chris Lazarek
Much loved by family and friends
Sibling of Sydney
Wishes of being a movie star
Want to be a professional dancer/doctor
Who is afraid of bears
Who feels good
Who gives greatness
Who would like to go to the Smokey Mountains
Who enjoys playing
Resident of Wyandotte, MI
Lazarek

Mackenzie Lazarek, Grade 3
Jefferson Elementary School, MI

Bailey

Who is my friend?
Bailey
Who doesn't like deer?
Bailey
Who doesn't like puppies?
Bailey
Who likes school?
Bailey
Who likes the merry-go-round?
Bailey
Who likes me?
Bailey
We are best friends forever.

Preston McCrory, Grade 1
Hamilton Community Elementary School, IN

Volcanoes

Red in the air
Shimmering high booms of glare.
Oh so high!
Hotter than the Sun,
Pops lava rocks of fun.
"Run away!" I say
It will catch you right away.

Jordan Nofzinger, Grade 2
McKenney-Harrison Elementary School, IN

Silver
Silver is cool
Silver is on a coin
Silver is on the Statue of Liberty
Silver is on a pencil
Silver is on a door
I like silver!
Dustin Hogan, Grade 2
Bristol Elementary School, WI

I Like Spring
Flowers are here
Baby animals are near
The trees start to bloom
Bees start to zoom
Cody Easter, Grade 2
Ladoga Elementary School, IN

Leprechauns
Leprechaun
sneaky, spy
taking, tricking, spying
a leprechaun is a shoemaker
Elf
Paige Altmann, Grade 2
Stocker Elementary School, WI

I Love You Mama
Roses are red and violets are blue
Sugar is sweet and so are you
You dig through my heart
All the way to the bottom
I love you from head to toe
You are my mama
I love you
I cherish you
You are queen of my world
I love you and you love me
I trust you and you trust me
My eyes are full of water
You are making me want to cry
For I am your daughter
And you are my pride
Cyra Cross, Grade 3
Martin L King Elementary School, IL

Mermaids
Mermaids sing, mermaids dance,
Maybe they have underpants.

They can swim up,
They can swim down,
Maybe they can twirl around.

Fish say hi, and then say bye.
I hope neither of them lies.
Daviana Gonzalez, Grade 3
Lorain Community School, OH

Spring Fun
Spring is fun
Sometimes you can swim
I lay in the sun
It is no longer dim
Austin Williams, Grade 2
Ladoga Elementary School, IN

Moon
Dear moon what is under
your surface.
Do you have stars
around you.
Sometimes I
wonder why
you disappear
and reappear.
One time I saw
You at night
with my grandma
The stars are so bright
and so are you.
I like the
brightness of you.
Can you be
brighter for me?
Moon are
You still
Up in the Sky
When it is morning?
Alexandra Biehn, Grade 3
North Intermediate School, MN

Making Boats
Carving
sanding
adding wood
for a cabin
we're done
try them
float them
in the water
they work
Y A A A A A A
I love making boats!

Evin Aldridge, Grade 1
South Monroe Townsite Elementary School, MI

The Great Iditarod
I ditarod is its name
D ogs wore booties
I t was the first race in 1975
T he dogs are huskies and other outdoor types
A nchorage is where it starts and Nome is where it ends
R oads are not in the race, only trails
O phir is one of the checkpoints
D ogs sometimes get hurt

Jack Durkin, Grade 2
Central Elementary School, IL

Wind
Wind in my fingers, wind in my toes,
Even sometimes it tickles my nose!
It rushes through me with the morning breeze,
with the spring mist I shiver my knees
Spring is wonderful you see,
The crisp air invites me.
From there on, I float in my dreams,
A wonderful fairyland tale it seems.
I feel like a butterfly, dancing as I soar,
Soon my elusion ends, my mom opens the door,
"Katie, it's dinnertime!" I hear her loudly roar.
I say good bye to the wind, my hopes behind,
I eat some pasta, hoping to unwind.
Still as I eat, I think of the wind,
Hoping tomorrow another adventure will begin.

Grace Hamilton, Grade 3
Noonan Academy, IL

Red Eye Tree Frogs

Red eye tree frogs
Stay here
In the rain forest!
In the tree
I see
Your eyes glowing
In the forest.
I am here
In the trees!
Grant Lannin, Grade 2
Norris Elementary School, NE

My House

My house, my house
As small as a mouse
Smaller than a mall
Smaller than all
But it was ate
By mouse Kate
All my bowls
All had holes
My mouse hole
Lead to a pole
I don't remember
But remember members...
Don't let a big mouse
Eat your small house.
Blake Lanter, Grade 3
St Clare Catholic School, IL

March

Spring starts!
Lucky clovers
St. Patrick's Day
Breezes blowing
Fun in the sun!
Longer days
Greener grass
I turn older
My cousin's birthday
Fun in the pool
I love March!
Angela Peterson, Grade 2
Queen of All Saints School, IL

The Night and the Moon

The night and the moon,
look magnificent together,
but beautiful apart.
The night and the moon,
remind me of a loon,
flying in the deepest, darkest sky.
The night and the moon,
goes beyond the sky,
and anything that can fly.
The moon itself,
seems like a never-ending light,
while the night remains,
like the deepest ocean,
is always at a great height.
A night without the moon,
or a moon without the night,
would make my heart sorrow until tomorrow.
Mohammad Butt, Grade 3
Islamic School of Greater Toledo, OH

Happiness Is...

Happiness is going to Grandma Weaver's house,
Getting pears off trees,
Going to get food from Las Limas,
Going out to eat,
Reading books,
Making cookies,
When it is my birthday,
Going to football practice,
Going to basketball practice,
I love football,
Happiness is awesome!
Nick Johnson, Grade 1
Hamilton Community Elementary School, IN

Penguins

They can swim.
They can eat fish.
They can slide on their bellies.
They live in a rookery.
They can huddle together.
They can stay warm.
Lee Reed, Kindergarten
McKenney-Harrison Elementary School, IN

Island of Hope and Tears
Island of hope, island of tears,
Island of love it also appears,
Immigrants come here,
To our land oh so dear.
It's called Ellis Island,
It's your land and my land.
Come here, to this place,
Have no disgrace.
Here it is that you can be free,
Lady Liberty also waits for thee.
Please trust me,
For there is much more to see,
In the great land called America.

Sophia R. Hausch, Grade 3
Detroit Country Day Junior School, MI

Hersheys
I see millions
I mean MILLIONS
Of dreamy, creamy Hersheys.
I ask Dad,
"Can I have one?"
He says,
"No, no, and no!"
I beg,
"Please, please, please?"
He says,
"No, no, and no!"
"I'll pay."
"Oh, Fine."
Now it's all mine!

Trevor Conrad, Grade 2
James R Watson Elementary School, IN

White
Ghosts
Bones
Snow
Paper
Birds
Stripes
I love white!

Corbin Davis, Grade 1
James R Watson Elementary School, IN

Dogs
Howl at the moon
Little horse
Walk
Four legs
Pointy nose
Bark
Dogs
Michael Hamrick, Kindergarten
Northfield Elementary School, OH

Dogs
Dogs love to play with humans
And with other dogs
They chase cats
They are man's best friends.
Mitchell Farnham, Kindergarten
Ramalynn Montessori Academy, MN

The Greatest Spring Ever!
I watch flowers in spring
And I like to sing in the hay
I like to play all day
Spring is a fling
Devin Woodcock, Grade 2
Ladoga Elementary School, IN

Swings
I like swings
they're cool
and you sit on them
and you jump off!
Isaac Nurmi, Grade 2
Pathfinder Elementary School, MI

The Life of a Spaghetti Noodle
I am a noodle.
I move by wiggling,
My enemy is the fork.
Oh so bad *I hate* the fork!
I can't stop thinking about the fork.
I shall rest in peace for now.
RIP
Nathaniel Santana, Grade 2
Hosford Park Elementary School, IN

Tooth
Once I had a tooth
It wiggled,
And wobbled,
And tickled,
And jiggled,
But once I bit an apple
Instead of a tooth there was a hole.
Jared Lindstrom, Grade 2
Patterson Elementary School, MI

My Stupid Dog
My dog is so stupid
that when I call her name
she looks the other way
Riley Krim, Grade 2
Pathfinder Elementary School, MI

Buzz
The buzzing bee
Stung someone on the knee.
Buzzing bee
Get away from me!
Olivia Lehrke, Grade 2
Stocker Elementary School, WI

Pink
Pink is for juicy bubble gum!
Pink is for fancy poodles!
Pink is for gourmet cake!
Pink is for fluffy pillows!
Pink is for lipstick!
I love Pink!!!
Emily Houtz, Grade 2
Bristol Elementary School, WI

Winter Wonderland
Winter wonderland
Crunching in the sparkling snow
Sparkling snow is pretty
The wind is blowing hard
I hear the breezes blowing loud
The crows are chirping
Victoria Vollmer, Grade 3
Midkota Elementary School, ND

Buzzing Bees

Bees are buzzin' all around
All around the little town
Right and left
Up and down
Mommy bees, daddy bees,
Brother bees, sister bees
Even baby bees,
All the bees in bee world like to buzz everywhere

Carlie Parrish, Grade 2
Arbury Hills Elementary School, IL

Spring

S ounds of birds chirping like a little orchestra.
P ainting in the nice weather is a good thing to do.
R ain falling into flower pots and rain gauges.
I nside you can open your windows you can feel the nice breeze on your face.
N ow it's spring you can play in the water if you have a hose.
G reen leaves start to grow on your trees and your flowers.

Michael Moy, Grade 3
Peck Elementary School, IL

Winter's Feelings

Winter feels like cold slapping my face with all it's fury
Freezing my feeling buds.
Winter sounds like the wind howling at my bedroom window.
Winter tastes like the snow freezing my taste buds.
Winter looks like you are walking on top of the clouds.
Winter smells like kids next door, drinking hot chocolate.

Juliano Tamburino-Schmitt, Grade 2
C W Neff Elementary School, MI

On the Bus

I see snow falling and
Twinkling like diamonds from the sky.
On my way to school,
I hear the bus go "beep, beep, beep"
And it's a long bumpy ride.
Smelling the gas from the bus,
Makes me think that I hope we don't break down.
At least it feels cozy and warm
Sitting by my friends.
Do you feel the cold?

Austin Outlaw, Grade 1
Eastside Elementary School, MI

I Am a Football
I am a football,
People throw me,
People kick me.

I am a football,
People jump on me,
People throw me on the ground.

I am a football,
People kick me for a field goal,
People throw me to people.

I am a football.
Keith Wright, Grade 3
Mentone Elementary School, IN

My Dog
My dog
I love my dog
My dog
I feed my dog
My dog
I love my dog so much!
Rashmi Acharya, Kindergarten
Ramalynn Montessori Academy, MN

Love
Love is beautiful.
Love is romantic.
Love is loving.
Tell me
Is love all of those things?
Kaylee Johnson, Grade 3
Kyle Trueblood Elementary School, KS

My Dog Buddy
Buddy is my little dog,
He likes to play on the log.
He chews on a squeaky ball,
And loves to chase it down the hall.
He always follows me where I go,
And he likes to help me row.
Bradley Robinson, Grade 1
Monroeville Elementary School, OH

What I Don't Need
I don't need Brussel sprouts.
I don't need broccoli.
I don't need homework.
I don't need stinky socks.
But I do need family.
Alexis Hooker, Grade 3
Woodford Elementary School, OH

Dragonflies
Dragonflies fly by
Flying, gliding, and soaring
Amazing insects!
James Brosnan, Grade 3
St Robert Bellarmine School, IL

Blue
Blue is for tasty blueberries
Blue is the best of all: Dallas Cowboys
Blue is the baby's eyes
Blue is a blue balloon
Blue is a whale
Blue is for wet blue water
I love blue!
Breanna Scherer, Grade 2
Bristol Elementary School, WI

I'm Getting a New Puppy
I'm getting a new puppy.
He's going to be so much fun.
I hope he's going to be fluffy.
I'll take him for a run!
Sara Williams, Grade 1
Meadowbrook Elementary School, IL

Piglet/Pig
Piglet
Soft, fun
Playing, sleeping, running
Mom, inside, pen, outside
Drinking, eating, snorting
Strong, fast
Pig
Dani Addler, Grade 1
Ladoga Elementary School, IN

Haunting

Haunting is when I am in the basement.
Haunting is when I am in the basement. alone.
I go to the basement to get some nails.
The door smacks open.
The stairs squeak like a monster.
I see some bats flying and
some spiders crawling.
The walls feel like snake skin.
It was slimy.
The floor is like quick sand and I am sinking.
I see Wolfman.
I see Frankenstein and Lake Monster.
They're coming for me.
I wonder who made monsters.
I don't like monsters.
Good thing it's in my dream.
Haunting is being in the dark.

Rey Medrano, Grade 2
Michener Elementary School, MI

My Cat

I like my kitty.
He likes to play.
My cat likes to play
With me sometimes
And my cat likes to jump
With me.
Cats, cats, cats.

Kaylen Stankovic, Kindergarten
McKenney-Harrison Elementary School, IN

Soccer

Kick, kick and run, run, run,
Everything about soccer is fun, fun, fun!!
Come on let's go get off your feet.
We're a team no one can beat.
We run and run around the field
It's almost like we cannot yield.
I'm sorry to say but the game is over today,
My team won because it's 83 to 1.
I'm also sorry to say you have to leave,
I hope this game was to your please.

Mary Ott, Grade 3
MacArthur Elementary School, WI

Sneaky the Chameleon

The animals can't see the chameleon
Because he is camouflaged.
Sneaky where are you?

David Gonzalez, Grade 1
Stocker Elementary School, WI

Cookie! Cookie!

Cookie! Cookie!
I love you a lot,
You're big and round,
Chewy and good.
I cook you and eat you,
Oh, I can't get enough,
Cookie, cookie
You're yummy stuff!

Lauren Bower, Grade 1
Northfield Elementary School, OH

My Friend Sydney

Sydney
is funny
smart
a good writer
most of all
a great
best friend

Lindsay Horton, Grade 2
Pathfinder Elementary School, MI

Rain Rain

Rain rain I love the rain.
How it makes me want to play.
How it falls on the ground.
It makes puddles all around.

Paige Bird, Grade 3
Weymouth Elementary School, MI

Trees

Trees? Why did you bring up trees?
I mean we see trees everywhere.
I wish there were no more trees.
Wait! I do want trees so I can breathe.

Riley Beel, Grade 3
Valentine Elementary School, NE

Parents

My mom gets me food
and feeds me
and I feed her too
and now I have to
take care of her
'cause she doesn't feel good.

Preston Anthony, Grade 2
Pathfinder Elementary School, MI

Bowling

Bowling is cool
I like it
Ball
Pins
Bowling

Marcus Macesich, Kindergarten
Northfield Elementary School, OH

Hawaii Is So Beautiful!

It is so beautiful!
I wish I could go,
On an airplane.
It will be a little bumpy.
I won't care when I get there.

Arianna Henry, Grade 1
Strange Elementary School, WI

Spring Is Here

Riding my bike
Those I like
I ride at the park
And hear dogs bark

Jordan Crist, Grade 2
Ladoga Elementary School, IN

Best Friends Ever

Friends are fun to play with
You can have more than one
It's really fun to have more than one
You can play with everyone
It's fun to have friends
Because you can take them anywhere

Cassandra Marc, Grade 2
Arbury Hills Elementary School, IL

Coco

C oco is a good dog.
D ad gives Coco a walk through the fog.
E aster is Coco's favorite holiday.
F eed Coco we always do, she eats her food then she'll lay.

Johnathan Chesney, Grade 3
Jefferson Elementary School, MI

Skateboarding Turtles

Skateboarding turtles are so cool.
Doing flips, manuals too when they fall they go in their shells.
They get hurt then they bleed.
They need Band-Aids all over their knees.
They yell "Mommy it's broken I need some Motrin."
When they get their Motrin they have to sit for five hours.
That's why they have pools.
Once they get better they do 50-50 grinds and kick flips.
Skateboarding turtles are awesome.

Aaron Ferdinande, Grade 3
Floyd Ebeling Elementary School, MI

Soccer

On a hot summer day, first game of the year
I was on defense, and my team and I were ready to win!
I huffed and I puffed, the whistle blew.
Chase the ball! coach yelled,
Stole, passed, shot, and we scored a goal!
Yellow kick, said the ref.
Emily you rest, Sara go in! Grabbed my water bottle
and began to drink, gulp, gulp, gulp
Coach starts yelling defense!
Emily in, Amber out.
Falcons scored 1 to 1.
Beep, beep,
Switch, Rachel, Amber, Emily,
Now let's score a goal!
Grabbed my water and began to drink, gulp, gulp, gulp,
Switch, beep, beep, 20 minutes left of the game,
Sara in, Sophie out, Dana in, Amber out, blue kick
Whistle blew, kick, dribble, pass, shoot, score
We scored another goal, 2 to 1,
10 seconds left of the game!
3 to 1, game over! We won!

Sara Stieber, Grade 3
MacArthur Elementary School, WI

Got Milk?

Moo, moo, brown cow
Can I have some milk, now?
Yes, yes, yes, you can
Do you have a pail or pan?
Yes, yes, yes, I do
Now can I milk you?
Ruth Konzen, Grade 1
Wild Rose Academy, WI

Snow Fort

Snow fort
Protective, fun
Hiding, blocking
Needed in snowball fights
Snow fence
Matthew Adams, Grade 3
St Michael School, OH

A Bear Dream

Once a bear
Came to me
When I was up there
In the tree

Then I jumped
Out of the tree
And he came
Right at me

And I shot him
So he would
No longer
Come at me
Samuel Jay Schrock, Grade 3
Oak Hill Amish School, IN

Leaves

When we went out to gym,
We made piles of leaves.
When we threw them
Up in the air,
I felt like I was a leaf, too.
Kiara Luna, Grade 1
Holden Elementary School, IL

My Sister

Who bugs me when I do my homework?
Sister.

Who thinks 10 plus 10 equals 11?
Sister.

Who smells like a flower?
Sister.

But, I love her very much.
Adriyanna Juarez, Grade 1
Strange Elementary School, WI

The Patriot Soldiers

See the Patriot soldiers go
Across the dark midnight snow.
They go to meet the horrible foe
with the cold winds that blow.
The Patriot soldiers never stop
Even with the bitter winds.
They know many will die,
But they know they must try.
They know America must be free.
The Patriot soldiers are valiant and strong.
Caleb Harris, Grade 3
Lions of Faith Academy, IN

Little Brother

I have a little brother
that he is so curious he goes in my room
and grabs my things.
But I still love him so much.
He's my favorite brother
in the whole world.
Karina Villasenor, Grade 2
Peck Elementary School, IL

Snow

Cold
Frostbite
Snowpants
I like snow.
Matthew Anderson, Grade 1
James R Watson Elementary School, IN

Springtime
The happy bunny hops
While an acorn nut drops
The rain starts to fall
I hear my mom's call
When I'm in the house
I'm cozy and warm
When the sun comes up
I'm out the door
Springtime fun
Has just begun

DeLyna Hadgu, Grade 3
Decatur Classical Elementary School, IL

Snowman
White snow
Carrot nose
Coal mouth
Three balls
Hat
Scarf
Mittens
Sticks for arms

These are all the things you
need to make a snowman!

Lucas Mason, Grade 1
James R Watson Elementary School, IN

Monster Jam
Monster Trucks crush cars.
Monster Trucks race fast.
Monster Trucks have names like
Grave Digger and El Toro Loco and
Raf and Batman and
The Thing and Wolverine

Nikalys McKean, Grade 2
Country Meadow Elementary School, IN

Cat
Sometimes my cat bites
Sometimes he begs
But no matter what, I still love my cat

Eve Zweifel, Grade 2
Madison Central Montessori School, WI

Cheer

Cheerleaders do stunts.
Stunts are pyramids,
and we also do flips,
and cartwheels.
We do round offs.
Shouting is what we do.
Back bends are the hard ones.

Emma Swader, Grade 3
Henryville Elementary School, IN

My Tutu

I wear my Tutu everywhere.
I wear my tutu in the park.
I wear my tutu in the school.
I wear it in the pool, oops!
I think it got wet!

Ally Gardner, Grade 1
Henryville Elementary School, IN

Spring

Spring is here, spring is here.
It's a favorite time of year.
Now that all the snow is gone,
I can finally mow the lawn.
All the bees will sit in hives
while butterflies awake the skies.
All the flowers start to grow.
Some in fact will grow in rows.
Most of which I am very fond
Ducks will love all the ponds.

Emily Milobar, Grade 3
Floyd Ebeling Elementary School, MI

My Sister

My sister can sometimes be mean,
But her room is always clean.
My sister can sometimes be loud,
But she can act gentle as a cloud.
My sister is so smart,
And I love her with all my heart.
My sister can sometimes be kind,
A sister like this is hard to find.

Kassidy Kascht, Grade 1
Strange Elementary School, WI

Keeper of the Mon"keys"

I used to have a lousy job
as Keeper of the Keys,
Now that I've got common sense
I'm training my mon*keys*.

Sam Boeder, Grade 3
St Paul's Lutheran School, MN

Riding My Bike

I like to ride my bike
and sometimes hike.
I go down the road
faster than a toad.
I sometimes go over a jump
because I hit a bump.
With the wind in my face
and I'm happy to go place to place.

Preston Kussow, Grade 2
Zion Lutheran School of Wayside, WI

If I Were a Flower…

I would see the tall grass.
I would hear the loud wind.
I would smell other flowers
I would feel people touching me.
I would taste my food.
I would do nothing.

Kayla Reisch, Grade 2
Stocker Elementary School, WI

Kittens

Kittens are cute and cuddly.
But sometimes they are mean.
They love to play.
But if you scare them,
They will run away.

Carley Palmer, Grade 2
Woodford Elementary School, OH

The Seasons

I love the summer.
I hate the winter and fall.
I love the spring too!

Kristen Medrano, Grade 3
Weymouth Elementary School, MI

Brandy

I have a dog. Her name is Brandy.
Brandy bites me a lot. Brandy is playful.
She has lots of toys. Brandy eats Beneful dog food.
Our dog is one year old.
She is brown and black and white.
She has a pink collar. Brandy sleeps on my mom and dad's bed.
She likes to go for walks.
We're taking her to Tennessee.
My grandma's dog's name is Brandy too.
I hope Brandy is okay in the car.

Bobby Moore, Grade 3
West Park Community School-Cleveland, OH

Snow

I like to hear the crunching snow underneath my feet and toes,
It glitters in the sun.
The air and breeze is so cold, gentle snow comes down.
Snow is coming from heaven,
the snow is like little angels from above,
tall hills I sled down again and again.
I never want the snow to go.

Annie Huguelet, Grade 3
Noonan Academy, IL

Zachary Williams

Zachary
Smart at math, nice, happy, funny
Son of Mike and Steph
Lover of toy cars, parents, playing
Who feels class is too long, weekends are too short
Who fears my sister, school, my dad
Who would like to see Africa, Hawaii, Canada
Resident of Indiana, USA
Williams

Zachary Williams, Grade 2
Country Meadow Elementary School, IN

Beautiful Butterflies

Beautiful butterfly lives in the lonely air.
Butterflies make me forget the things I learned over there.
The butterflies are beautiful and white
They make me think of something quiet.

Nereida Orozco, Grade 3
Levan Scott Academy, IN

I Can't Clean My Room

I can't clean my room!
My feet are swelling.
My toenail is falling off.
My brain is hurting.
I think I have a cough.
I'm afraid of the spiders under my bed.
I can't find the key to my door.
I'm too tired.
I have lots of homework.
What? Today is a school day?
Yeah! Bye!

Lauren Skaggs, Grade 3
Smithville Elementary School, OH

As Delicate as Gold

Gold
White gold
Sapphire blue
no one is as
beautiful as the
true
you
it's light
it's the beautiful
Wright.
Yes Mrs. Wright
is the beautiful, beautiful light
as beautiful as a necklace
as delicate as gold
she is pretty
she is witty and very nice too
I bet you wish you had a teacher
like her
I am stuck to her like glue.

Eden McCauley, Grade 3
Henryville Elementary School, IN

My Shoe

I think my shoe is made of fabric.
The fabric travels and travels
And travels and travels
Until the fabric is dirty.

Karson Hastings, Grade 2
Orchard Lane Elementary School, WI

I Am Ice Cream

I am ice cream.
With chocolate
Ready to be eaten.
With chocolate syrup.
Waiting for mouthwatering faces.
Frozen like a freezer.
I am ice cream.

Joseph Alspaugh, Grade 3
Mentone Elementary School, IN

Red

My favorite color is red
My head is red, my head gets red
when I am nervous
I get a lot of red erasers too
My mom has a red hat,
My sister has a red sock
My other sister has a red book bag
Red is the first color of the rainbow
Only I forgot my first sister has
red lipstick to buy

Anahy Marquez, Grade 2
Peck Elementary School, IL

The Dog

Dogs sleep all the time
Dogs go outside all the time
But dogs need inside time too
And jump for bones too.

Ryan Ramalingam, Grade 2
Ramalynn Montessori Academy, MN

My Dad

snoring
like thunder
crashing down
raining so
hard
I am
so tired
of hearing
snores

Shelby Mott, Grade 2
Pathfinder Elementary School, MI

Colors

Red is watermelon that makes me happy.
Green is the grass that is so grassy.

Brown is the dirt where the buffalo roam.
Blue is the ocean's cool own foam.

Black is a dark, spooky night.
Purple are the mountains that are so right.

Pink is a great wink!
Silver is an ice rink.

What do colors mean to you?

Ryan Mayhew, Grade 2
Detroit Country Day Lower School, MI

Chase

Chase is awesome,
Chase likes football,
Chase likes to run,
Chase likes to push the merry-go-round,
Chase likes to play with his friends,
Chase likes to be on the monkey bars,
Chase likes to count to 100,
Chase likes to count backwards,
Chase likes pepperoni pizza,
Chase likes hot dogs,
Chase likes sports,
Chase likes playing Xbox,
Chase loves these things.

Christian Reichhart, Grade 1
Hamilton Community Elementary School, IN

Army

I'm proud a lot
of soldiers' sacrifice.
This life in war to
keep our country safe.
From bad guys,
People in war should be respected
at all times even in war and home.
Have a great world!

Thaddeus Crump, Grade 3
West Park Community School-Cleveland, OH

Monster Truck

My monster truck could pull.
Instead, it smashes,
and crashes.
It will crash by the ramp,
on the really tall lamp.
Sometimes it can flip.
Big foot would trip.
Grave Digger and Bigfoot will fight,
with all their might.
One is at night.
The fight will be tight.

Omar Shaheen, Grade 1
Islamic School of Greater Toledo, OH

My Mom Is Happy

My mom is happy
Happy day,
Happy time,
Happy adventures,
Happy rhymes,
Happy day mom.

Hannah Lewallen, Grade 1
Mentone Elementary School, IN

Girl

girl
wears dress
likes to run
likes to jump too
girl

Naxi Galvan, Grade 3
Phillip May Elementary School, IL

Piglet/Pig

Piglet
Soft, playful
Playing, running, sleeping
Mom, barn, pigpen, cage
Yard, mud, wild, outside
Eating, hunting, sunning
Strong, large
Pig

Lillie Boyer, Grade 1
Ladoga Elementary School, IN

Vacation

D riving up mountains
E veryone
N ever ending fun
V ery hot
E at pie
R elatives

Shawn Ast, Grade 3
Kyle Trueblood Elementary School, KS

Rainy Days

Rainy days are wet.
Some are cold.
Some make noise.
Some are quiet.
I splash in puddles…
After the storm is gone.

Kyrsten Reilly, Grade 1
Strange Elementary School, WI

Pretty Little Bird

Pretty little bird
Sitting on a branch
Singing sweet songs.

April Arlington, Grade 3
Atwood Elementary School, MI

Puppy/Dog

Puppy
Fun/cute
Sleeping, playing, jumping
Outside, hiding, doghouse, woods
Eating, hunting, sunning
Fast, big
Dog

Thomas Richardson, Grade 1
Ladoga Elementary School, IN

Spring Weekend

Birds chirping in the distance.
Trees blowing simple shadows.
The suns rays beat down,
warmth on the cold chilly earth.

Jack Trainor, Grade 3
Deerfield Elementary School, MI

Wonderful Words of Hope

I look up at her when we are floating past in the ship,
I ask my mama,
"Who is she?"
"That is Lady Liberty," she replies.
As we get to the harbor I ask my sister,
"Why is she there?"
"She is welcoming us immigrants to the new land."
I stand there in awe,
She seems to say to me,
"I am the Statue of Liberty,
Your welcome and your hope to this new land,
Where the streets are paved with gold,
Where you can be free with many new things to open up to.
Your guidance is in my hands,
You can trust and believe me and..."
She stops,
And suddenly all of my questions are answered.
Now I am an American.
Her words still echo in my head!

Gabrielle Hooper, Grade 3
Detroit Country Day Junior School, MI

Midnight Ride

At night I can hear my grandpa's horses
Running around under the moonlit night.
Making beautiful noises that sound like a lullaby

Bridger Field, Grade 3
North Intermediate School, MN

When You're Asleep

In your bed, fast asleep,
your eyes are closed, but your mind still flows
inside your head, your mind really rolls.

But on the outside, you're really still,
you do not move, you do not squirm
like a little worm.

Inside your mind, it can be scary,
it can be pleasant or very crazy,
but when you wake up, your thoughts are all gone,
vanished.

Lauren Carstensen, Grade 3
Stetsonville Elementary School, WI

School

School is fun,
You can run
in gym,
School is cool,
There are lots
of rules,
no running,
no humming too.
We go to Mass,
We pray and sing,
The bell in church
goes ding, ding,
We also do math
and spelling,
and you can even do
storytelling
School

Grace Koh, Grade 2
Queen of All Saints School, IL

Dog/Gabe

Dog
Furry, white
Playing, cuddling, sleeping
He likes to eat snow
Gabe
Nadia Miller, Grade 2
Coy Elementary School, OH

The Fog

The fog
It's thick
It's very dangerous too
And I would pay five dollars
Just to get through.
Christian Kinzie, Grade 3
Anita Elementary School, IA

Summer

The hot summer day
It burst into flames so bright.
Light, fun, wonderful, hot.
Chandler Cairatti, Grade 3
St Clare Catholic School, IL

Rainbows

Rainbow, rainbows

Rainbows are pretty.
Rainbows are cool.
Rainbows are way up
In the sky.

Rainbows, rainbows,
I like rainbows!
Madison Arnold, Grade 1
James R Watson Elementary School, IN

Snow Monster

Snow monster
Snow monster
White and black
HUGE and humongous
It eats little snow monsters
It lives in snowy caves
That never melt
It is a dangerous cave
It never is destroyed
The power bounces back
At the person
Isaiah Kalaau, Grade 2
Country Meadow Elementary School, IN

Roller Coasters

Highs and lows
Fun and excitement
Fast and slow
Sometimes a headache
The dark lands,
Become light lands
Sometimes height depends,
Or even age, to go on
Girls and boys
Grandparents and parents
No matter what gender
These bouncy rides,
Are mostly at fairs
And they bring excitement to the whole world
Sanjana Kumar, Grade 3
Madison Central Montessori School, WI

My Invention

Some day I want to make a robot
Whose metal won't burn near anything hot.
It will do hard math and go to Neptune,
I hope I can make this contraption quiet soon.

It could carry things inside its brain,
Movies! Books! And exciting games!
Maybe I'll make a robot some day.
Right now, I'd rather go outside and play!

Nathaniel Scholl, Grade 3
Decatur Classical Elementary School, IL

Ulysses S. Grant

ULYSSES S.
18th President
Fighter, general, strategist
Who loved swimming
Who believed we could win the Civil War
Who wanted the war to end
Who said, "The South must surrender"
GRANT

Larissa Wagner, Grade 2
Our Lady of Lourdes School, WI

Winter

Fun snowballs,
King and queen snow angels,
Fun skiing on the ice,
Frostbite,
It is cold!

Kaylee Towle, Grade 1
James R Watson Elementary School, IN

Christmas

I am Christmas.
I celebrate Jesus' birthday.
I like the ornaments put on my tree.
I also like it when Santa comes
and puts presents under my tree.
It even tickles me when an angel or star
is put on my highest branch.
I am Christmas.

Evan Weaver, Grade 3
Mentone Elementary School, IN

Ashley
A wesome
S miles a lot
H ilarious
L aughs a lot
E xcellent
Y oung as a cub
McKenzie Nalband, Grade 3
Atwood Elementary School, MI

Stars
Stars in the sky,
Stars in the sky,
Laying down at night,
Getting ready for the moon,

The moon says to the stars,
Good night,
And I love you.
Mi'Lynda Candelario, Grade 3
Lorain Community School, OH

Fun!
Homework and pencils
Paper and teachers
Really too much fun
Children tying their sneakers
Playing and laughing
I'm starting to drool
Fun! Fun!
This makes school
Calista Cherches, Grade 3
Montrose Elementary School, MN

Fishing
I like to go in the morning.
And my dad told me a warning.
We fish until dark.
Sometimes it's in the park.
I wish I caught a fish.
To put him on a dish.
But I still had fun.
With my dad in the sun.
Mykayla Rasmussen, Grade 2
Zion Lutheran School of Wayside, WI

Curiosity
Curiosity killed the cat.
But something brought him back.
So kids be aware of that.
Something brought him back.
Remember that.
Teanna Smith, Grade 3
Woodford Elementary School, OH

The Five Senses of Spring
I see blue birds
I hear the waves
I smell corn
I taste ice cream
I feel that new animals are coming
That's the stuff that comes in spring
Abril Anoyli Lozada, Grade 3
Woodside Elementary School, MI

The Sun
So high up and bright
Very hot and relaxing
Yellow, real quiet
Maverick Hillman, Grade 3
Mable Woolsey Elementary School, IL

Halloween
Candy treat.
Faces meet.
This holiday is really neat!
Curfews past.
It's a blast!
I wish it would last.
Brooke Black, Grade 2
Patterson Elementary School, MI

Puss
I am a puss climbing.
I feel hungry when I'm climbing a tree
I love climbing!
I can see birds at the top of the tree.
I can hear a dog barking.
I'm a puss climbing.
Michael Kirk Bendix, Grade 2
Ramalynn Montessori Academy, MN

Winter

Winter tastes like snowflakes falling to the ground.
Winter sounds like wind blowing.
Winter smells like hot chocolate.
Winter looks like a white frosting field.
Winter feels like snowflakes and just snow too.
I like snow a lot because you get to play in it
And jump in it and sled on it,
And make snowmen.
You can shovel your back yard.
I shovel my Grandma and Grandpa's back yard because
It has a lot of snow.

Kassandra Parisian, Grade 2
C W Neff Elementary School, MI

Winter

Winter tastes like snow spinning in the air, landing on my tongue.
Winter looks like angels everywhere.
Winter feels like warm cozy hands by the fireplace.
Winter sounds like wolves howling at the moonlight, on the hills.
Winter smells like my bunny's warm fur.
I love winter.

Eric Brand, Grade 2
C W Neff Elementary School, MI

Snow

We're having fun in the snow,
But this year there isn't very much, you know.
When the snow gets very deep,
We can sled down hills that are steep.
After a couple of days,
School will close down
And no alarm clock will have to sound.
And now we all have to go back to school, you know.
Because there isn't very much snow.

Emily Flamion, Grade 2
Perry Central Elementary School, IN

Blue

B lue oceans, Pacific and Atlantic
L ike rain so gentle
U ltimate like Blue Dragon of the Skies
E xhibit. It's the star of India, the largest blue star sapphire

Clayton Leng, Grade 2
South O'Brien Elementary School, IA

Stars in the Sky

Stars in the sky sounds like pie.
Stars in the sky always like to cry.
Try to make a little pie.
Good bye baby sky, you're my little pie.
Let's go try some apple pie.
Stars in the sky make me cry,
Have a try of apple pie.

Michelle Bear, Grade 2
Midkota Elementary School, ND

Basketball

I like Basketball.
It is fun getting a slam dunk
To win the game.

Kris Guinn, Grade 1
Henryville Elementary School, IN

Valentine's

One two
Candy
Three four
Hearts
Five six
Cards
Seven eight
Rose
Nine ten
Start again

Bobby Houtz, Grade 2
Mentone Elementary School, IN

Basketball

B ouncing the ball
A thletic
S wish
K nocking the ball
E xercise
T all baskets
B all to dribble
A ll around the court
L ike the sport
L earn drills

Braxton Robertson, Grade 3
Henryville Elementary School, IN

I Am in a Dream

My room is lit with
my thoughts.

Everything is warm
and cozy.

I hear my fan blowing
against my
window shade.

I see all my
stuffed animals
and feel like my
room has come
alive.

It feels like I am
In a dream,
because everything
is just
right.

Camilla Bjelland, Grade 3
North Intermediate School, MN

Spring

S unshine outside
P icnic at the park
R ock climbing
I 'm riding my bike
N ight outside
G rass to walk on

Kassity Simpson, Grade 1
Southwood Elementary School, IN

My Goat Named Float

I had a goat,
His name was Float.
He likes floating in the lake.
He has a friend named Snake,
who lives in the lake.
They splash and play all day,
in May on a hot, hot day.

Alyssa Uttech, Grade 1
Rock Ledge Elementary School, WI

My PlayStation 2

My PlayStation 2 is fun to play
Sometimes I put some things out of my way
I can't play unless I ask
Or I lose my PlayStation 2 task

Zach Lockwood, Grade 3
Woodlawn Elementary School, KS

Spring

The green grass, the fresh smell.
I like to hear the bunnies hop.
Sunny day please make the flowers grow
as tall as they can grow.

Isela Breceda, Grade 2
Holden Elementary School, IL

Mallory

Pray for lungs.
Pray for hope.
Pray every day.
Pray to God.
Pray to Mallory.
Pray for breath.
Pray for oxygen.
Pray for joy.
Pray for Mallory.
Believe in Mallory.
Believe in hope.
Believe in miracles!
Don't believe in death today.

Isabel M. Virgen, Grade 2
Decatur Classical Elementary School, IL

Spiderman

Spiderman Spiderman is cool.
Spiderman is awesome
Spiderman
Swing all around swoosh!!
Swoosh!!.
Spiderman.
Spiderman
Spiderman he will web
You up woosh!!!

Lucas Baumgartner, Grade 2
Country Meadow Elementary School, IN

The Solar System

The solar system is very important
Also Ms. Darl taught us
I like Earth and the sun
Because they're shiny
Even the planets are a family.
Aavni Varadbam, Kindergarten
Ramalynn Montessori Academy, MN

Hot Dogs

Eat them with ketchup.
Eat them with mustard.
Don't eat them with custard.
Hey, they're dogs not hot dogs.
Don't eat them with ketchup.
Don't eat them with mustard.
They're hot, but they're dogs.
Gene Keiber, Grade 3
Valentine Elementary School, NE

What Flies in the Spring Time?

What flies in the spring time?
It is not a fly or a bee.
It is nice and colorful.
It flies high in the sky.
It has big wings.
It is a butterfly.
John Aguirre, Grade 2
Peck Elementary School, IL

I Like to Eat

Food
Yummy, delicious
Savoring, cooking, amazing
Food is great!
Eat
Brandon Erickson, Grade 2
Stocker Elementary School, WI

My Dog Stanly

My dog Stanly is special
I loved him a lot.
But now he is in dog heaven.
Isaiah Barends, Grade 2
Pathfinder Elementary School, MI

Plums! Plums!

Plums, plums
I love you a lot.
You're sweet and juicy,
Delightful and delicious.
I eat you and demolish you,
Oh, I can't get enough,
Plums, plums
You're fabulous stuff!
Katie Urich, Grade 1
Northfield Elementary School, OH

Alligator and Me

I love being an alligator
There's so much fun stuff to see.
If you were an alligator
I'm sure you'd feel like me.
Gilberto Salas, Grade 2
Holden Elementary School, IL

Basketball

Pass, run down the court
Pass again
Throw it at the basket
Oh, no! You missed.

Other team gets the ball.
Try to get the ball.
Where's our luck?
Brandon Fogle, Grade 1
Woodford Elementary School, OH

My Little Brother

My little brother is like no other
When it comes to being a boy!

He's full of excitement
He makes me happy
And fills my day with joy!

From day to night
We sometimes fight
It's a brother and sister thing.
Georgia Oberg, Grade 2
Stocker Elementary School, WI

My Room

My room is very messy
My room is very comfy
My room is always the same
My room is where my sister and I sleep
My room is very dark sometimes
My room is my favorite place to be
My room is where I think things out
My room is full of ribbons, trophies, and medals
My room is filled with books to learn from
My room is where I will remember my grandma always
My room I love I just love it!!!!!!!!!!!

Joanie Sandstrom, Grade 3
Meadowbrook Elementary School, IL

Summer

Summer is not a bummer.
In the summer, I love to swim in our pool.
In the pool, it is very cool.
The summer is very hot!
In the summer, my family and I ride bikes and take hikes.
In the summer, my aunt drives her hummer.
In the summer, we have barbeques.
I love barbeques.
My uncle loves them, too.
We have a ball until it is fall.

Taylor Miller, Grade 3
Woodford Elementary School, OH

Sunshine

Today we had a Sunshine play,
It started up at eight,
The curtains came up perfect,
The letters weren't so great.

S was Terra, she came, but showed up late,
U was Billy, he just never came.
N was Katie, she was out with flu,
S was Grant, but he was at a game.
H was Shelia, she wouldn't leave her home,
I was John, but he was left alone.
N was Maya, she's out with her dad and fame,
And I was **E** , the only one that came!

Sarah Smith, Grade 3
Henry W Longfellow Elementary School, IL

Rain

Clear and delightful
rain,
Cold or warm
rain,
Rain on trees
on leaves,
on my sister,
and me,
Rain
Falling from
the sky.

John McMahon, Grade 2
Queen of All Saints School, IL

Cupcakes

Cold
Creamy chocolate,
Sweet
Sugar sprinkles,
Tasty
Terrific treat.

Andy Wehrmeister, Grade 2
Queen of All Saints School, IL

Late for the Bus

I missed the bus
I made a fuss!
So I had to walk to school
On my way I saw the bus
I saw Sally and May
Then I ran
I was late to school anyway.

Olivia Marquette, Grade 3
St Timothy's School, MN

Hawaii

H ot
A loha
W aves
A wesome
I ncredible
I sland

Jack Imesch, Grade 3
Burr Elementary School, MI

Investigators

Intelligent
Fantastic spies
Camouflage clothes
Intelligent gear
But most of all
My dad!!!

Seth Draper, Grade 3
James R Watson Elementary School, IN

The Old Skeleton

Lying on a rock under the ocean
Seaweed sticks to the body
Never moving an inch
Sharks bite at the body
Divers never notice

Alex Reiten, Grade 3
Litchville-Marion Elementary School, ND

Zane

Zane is my little brother.
He died because he was very, very sick.
I remember the days I played with him.
Now my mom has a new baby.
She named him Lane
To remember our little brother Zane.
We love you so much.

Lucas Allen, Grade 2
James R Watson Elementary School, IN

When School Is Over

I won't miss homework.
I won't miss math.
I won't miss the bus.
I won't miss getting up at 8:00 in the morning

I will miss my teacher Mrs. Strait.
I will miss my friends.
I will miss hot lunch.
I will miss my art teacher.

Summer will be fun for one and all.
See you at school when it turns to fall!

Julia Baker, Grade 3
Atwood Elementary School, MI

Sun

S un is shining.
U nder the light,
N ature is so bright.

Gavin Booser, Grade 2
Jackson Center Elementary School, OH

Sharks

S uper fast
H uge
A ttack
R azor sharp teeth
K illers
S neaky

Tyler Holwerda, Grade 3
James R Watson Elementary School, IN

Hilton Head

Swimming in the deep ocean
Swish, swoosh
Salt water burning in my mouth
Swish, swoosh
Gathering sand for a castle
Swish, swoosh
Diving like a dolphin in the waves
Too
Far
Away
From
My
Mom!

Jacob Samuelson, Grade 2
James R Watson Elementary School, IN

Monkeys

Swing by vines
Like bananas
Brown, gray, black
Loud, quiet
Nice, mean
Monkeys are cool
Jump from branch to branch
oo-oo-ah-ah

Hannah McAfee, Grade 1
James R Watson Elementary School, IN

Mean Brother

Chasing me
around the
house
with a
plastic
baseball bat.
Up
the
stairs,
chasing
me
everywhere!
Bang
Ouch
I'm Telling Mom!!!

Rayana Secrest, Grade 2
Waterloo Elementary School, IN

Spring

S occer teams playing
P ools are full
R iding my bike
I ce cream cones dripping
N ine o'clock is dark
G et outside

Dante Gennaccaro-Archer, Grade 2
Stocker Elementary School, WI

Basketball

Basketball is my favorite sport.
I like to run down the court.
Preston plays baseball with me.
We shine like glee.

Brevin Wendland, Grade 2
Zion Lutheran School of Wayside, WI

Making Cookies

I made some cookies.
Hard and soft and round and tough.
I like to eat them best of all.
Make them anytime,
Free for all!

Emma Neil, Grade 2
Onaway Elementary School, OH

The Vampire

The vampire!
Black hair, green face,
Big teeth, red eyes,
Red lips, too creepy.
Don't think I'm going
Trick-or-treating!

Rachel Flory, Grade 3
Smithville Elementary School, OH

Cats

Cats
Furry, soft
Running, cuddling, clawing
Cats like to run around.
Animal

Zachary Johnson, Grade 2
Stocker Elementary School, WI

My Rabbit

My rabbit takes care
of her babies
day and night
by the garage
so they will not die.

Erik Streitmatter, Grade 1
Wethersfield Elementary School, IL

What Can I Do?

"What can I do, Mom?"
"You can go upstairs and play."
"But Dad is upstairs, Mom."
"Can you get a book?"
"Thank you, Mom."

Austin Sutherland, Grade 1
Woodford Elementary School, OH

Captain

My dog loves to sleep.
My dad cares for him.
He goes to the office
and barks at the doorbell.
He sleeps in the kitchen.

Jaden Ma, Kindergarten
Ramalynn Montessori Academy, MN

Two Front Teeth

When my mom was just a little girl
She went to her Nina's house with her friend Shirl

Her two front teeth were as wiggly as can be
But not ready to come out yet, said she

Nina grabbed her and said to Uncle Ted
Let's rip her teeth out, right out of her head

They grabbed her and yanked out her poor teeth

She did not know what to do
but then her Nina told her that it's as good as new

She walked out of their house and prayed to the Lord
All she could think to say was, "Your tortillas are like cardboard!"

Kelsey Lentz, Grade 3
St Clare Catholic School, IL

Spring

S hining sunflowers glow during the afternoon.
P urple are the tulips and red are roses.
R ivers flow through the forest.
I ce cream is cold so is snow.
N ephews are boys and nieces are girls.
G rass grows when it stops raining.

Austin Wegner, Grade 2
Stanton Elementary School, NE

Robots

Robots are smart like a fox.
Some think they're a scorpion
Attacking in the desert
Humans were fighting back
Against the robot
One human called in reinforcements
The humans never knew who led the attack
The attack was to hack the system
They were looking for an artifact
That was the one and only Allspark
It was just the beginning of the end
Of a war that started on a planet called Cybertron

Samuel Kelly, Grade 3
Woodlawn Elementary School, KS

Flowers

F antastic petals
L oving smells
O utstanding shapes
W ow! Are they cool?
E xcellent colors
R oses are my favorite!
S o nice to smell

Kallie Snowtala, Grade 2
Stocker Elementary School, WI

Me

As cute as a button
As soft as a pillow
As yummy as a cupcake
As good as God
As lovable as a horse.
I like me.

Avery Wiersema, Grade 2
Pathfinder Elementary School, MI

I Love Living!

Living is so fun.
I love living!
You should look in the past
And remember what you've done.
I love living!

Katarina Kovac, Grade 3
Atwood Elementary School, MI

Cheyanne

She is nice, sweet and very friendly.
Then she plays with me at recess.
That's why Cheyanne is my friend.

Chrissy Schubnell, Grade 3
Henryville Elementary School, IN

Games

G ames are cool.
A nalogue stick.
M y games only.
E veryone plays a lot.
S weet games rock.

Jon Petrucci, Grade 3
Atwood Elementary School, MI

Ladybug

It is very small
See it flying in the sky
Ladybug galore!

Adam Krajewski, Grade 3
Little Red Elementary School, WI

I Am a Hummer

I am Hummer.
People sit in me while
I do all the work!

I am a Hummer.
Sometimes I have televisions
and sometimes I don't.

I am a Hummer.
I have four doors…
it's kind of like having four arms.

I am a Hummer.

Derek Hunsberger, Grade 2
Mentone Elementary School, IN

Summer

As summer lurks
On in and
Kids start to jump
And play
On a nice warm day
Coming
Day after day

Grace Atter, Grade 3
Montrose Elementary School, MN

Talking

I
  love
    to
      talk
TALK! TALK! TALK!
But now the talking has to end
Because my grades are low again.

Olivia Feger, Grade 3
Henryville Elementary School, IN

Home

H omes, homes
O nly people
M y mom and my dad live in my home.
E xcellent home

Ally Smith, Grade 1
James R Watson Elementary School, IN

Pickles

I am a pickle.
It's coming
Oh! No!
The mouth!
It's like surgery without anesthesia

Bye! Bye!
Crunch!

Carolyn Vadney, Grade 3
James R Watson Elementary School, IN

Bailee

Bailee, the Lab, she is my pet,
She loves to get wet,
Her color is yellow,
Crazy she was, now she is mellow.

Food is her thing,
A bone she wants us to fling,
She loves to play fetch,
Wow, our girl can really catch!

Bailee has a big bark,
She'll never turn down a walk at the park.
Bailee is cool, she is fun,
As for a friend, she is a loyal one!

Lindsay Chaney, Grade 2
Crissey Elementary School, OH

Blue

I love blue paper.
I love blue crayons.
I love blue markers.
I love BLUE!

Ryan Nash, Grade 1
James R Watson Elementary School, IN

Collecting Rocks

When I was a little kid
(about 5)
I collected rocks.

Until my mom
Threw them away
In a box.

Then about 20 years later
I was on my own.
That meant
I could collect rocks
And mom would
Leave me alone!

Aleksander Sasha Noah Levesque, Grade 3
Shorewood Hills Elementary School, WI

School

Sister Colleen in not mean
She is the nicest person
I've ever seen
I love you, you love me
I love school as you can see
I go to school every day
We go on field trips and ride on hay

Tikayla Clinton, Grade 2
Holy Redeemer Christian Academy, WI

I Can't Get Up

I can't get up!
The light isn't working
My alarm broke
The dog is on me
I'm stuck in the sheets
It's too cold
The boys are hitting me
I think I'm getting sick
My leg is broke
My ankle is twisted
I think I have the chicken pox
What? We're leaving for a birthday party?
Let's go!

Tori Hackworth, Grade 3
Smithville Elementary School, OH

The Wild Desert

Periwinkle blooms overflow a wild desert field
Winds blow unremarkably shiny tumbleweeds glistening in the sunshine
Greater roadrunner sits lazily, staring straight ahead

Coyote gives a long, strong, hungry howl
Cottontail freezes and silently looks all around
In disbelief cottontail stares right into the eyes of golden eagle

Risking his fur, he runs for it
Streaking past broad-tailed hummingbird and gecko
Hearing the bird of prey right behind

Panicking, he bounds faster —
Just in the nick of time
Saved by shelter

All of a sudden
Everything is quiet

Nothing moves
In the wild desert

Lianna Kowalke Reinwald, Grade 2
Prairie Crossing Charter School, IL

The School Bus

The school bus
Noisy
Kids are crazy
The bus
Goes flying
No seat belts
Every time it stops
I go flying!

Kaylee Stiffler, Grade 1
South Monroe Townsite Elementary School, MI

Blue

Blue looks like my sister's eyes.
Blue smells like a stinky t-shirt.
Blue tastes like salty sea water.
Blue sounds like a bluebird singing a cool song.
Blue feels like a sponge when I scrub the floor.

Jacob Adams, Grade 2
Will Carleton Academy, MI

My Dog

My dog is a hog.
My dog chases frogs.
He likes to eat.
He likes to drink.
He likes to lie near the silver sink.
He's white and brown and
sometimes I take him to town.

Andrew Sigmund, Grade 2
Waterloo Elementary School, IN

Renni

R eally likes Sunny (pet dog).
E ats candy
N ice
N eat
I ce cream!

Renni Wieman, Kindergarten
Medford Elementary School, WI

My Dad Snores

My dad
Snores like
Thunder and lightning.
It's a pain.
Now I can't sleep.
And I hate it.

Brianna Perez, Grade 2
Pathfinder Elementary School, MI

Fish

I have two fish.
They sleep and they eat…
And eat and eat.

Emily Nightingale, Grade 1
Bristol Elementary School, WI

Bowling

If you go bowling
it's really, really fun
you'll see a lot of people
that are bowling
and having fun.

Lauren Medina, Grade 3
Henryville Elementary School, IN

Deer

Deer live in the woods
Eat corn, apples, and salt blocks
White tail flips fast.

Jacob Henry Miller, Grade 3
Little Red Elementary School, WI

Spring Rain

Spring is a time of year
When lots of rain comes
It falls on the ground
It reminds me of snowflakes

Alyse Todd, Grade 2
Ladoga Elementary School, IN

Panda Bears

Black
White
Cute
Bamboo
Bears

Daniel Cody, Kindergarten
Northfield Elementary School, OH

Spring Can Be Fun

I see spring.
I smell bees buzzing around.
I smell wet trees.
And flowers coming back up.
I see my allergies
are coming back again.
I can have fun anytime in spring.
Because spring is the best.
Spring can be fun.

Hunter Hoff, Grade 3
H. R. McCall Elementary School, IL

The Sun

The sun is bright.
The sun is light.
The sun is yellow, orange and red.
The sun is hard to look at.
The sun is a pretty sight.

Michaela Kerr, Grade 3
Atwood Elementary School, MI

Happiness Is…

Happiness is fun,
it is playing with my friends,
it is so fun,
it is more fun when there is
outside recess,
it is really fun when my mom
plays with me,
it is passing math facts
and getting good grades,
and NOT going to the principal.

Kobie Naus, Grade 1
Hamilton Community Elementary School, IN

Monster Trucks

The trucks are loud
Monster trucks are huge
Monster trucks jump over cars
They get trophies

Nathan Immel, Grade 3
James R Watson Elementary School, IN

Rain

Drip, drop
Rain is falling
Drip, drop
Now it's storming
BOOM BANG!
Drip, drop
Can you hear the storm?
Drip, drop
Yes
Drip, drip
I'm scared now
Drip, drop.

Jerika Adams, Grade 2
Country Meadow Elementary School, IN

Cats

C uddle like a fur ball
A cute bundle of joy
T oo cute for me
S o like a cutie pie

LaTosha Banks, Grade 3
James R Watson Elementary School, IN

My Grandparents

She bakes cakes.
She comes to parties.
She loves us.
Grandma Stork

Sewer
She bakes cookies.
She has a garden.
Grandma Williamson

He has a few horses.
He likes to drive a truck.
He lives in the country.
Grandpa Stork

He had a farm.
He had kids.
He died.
Grandpa Williamson
Mitchell Williamson, Grade 1
Anita Elementary School, IA

A Warm Sea Night

My warm sand bed
Is like a blanket
To comfort me.
I hear the sea talking.
it is a drum booming
While saying,
"Go to sleep"
As the sea sings
Me a lullabye.
Sophia Schmidt, Grade 2
Norris Elementary School, NE

My Pet Turtle

My pet is slow
and green as a bean.
It's round
and has four feet.
And it eats leaves.
It needs clean plants.
Betzayda Vergara, Grade 2
Peck Elementary School, IL

European Conquerors

We marched in battalions.
We were solid and never gave in
To those we were ordered to destroy.
We conquered more of Europe than Hitler
With forces formed in Italy.
We overthrew barbaric Germany and Egypt
And many countless others.
We were indestructible for so long
With weapons forged by the greatest smiths —
The best the world ever knew.
We had many different strategies,
The best army of our time,
For our generals were the smartest.
But we were conquered.
It was a sad fate —
The end comes to all great things.
Robbie Kleibohmer, Grade 2
Broken Arrow Elementary School, KS

Tan

Tan looks like sand on the warm beach.
Tan smells like maple syrup.
Tan sounds like shiny pennies tinkling.
Tan tastes like toast in the morning.
Tan feels like leaves in the fall.
Everett Blonde, Grade 2
Will Carleton Academy, MI

The Sky

Did you know the sky was so beautiful?
When I look up, I dream of being in the sky.

I dream of being the sky,
I dream the clouds are vanilla ice cream.

I love the way the sky and clouds are
When I die
I will float to the sky.

I will have a grave under the sky
While I lie in my grave
I will have a happy day.
Tianna Harrison, Grade 3
Gen George Patton Elementary School, IL

Spring

S pring is here
    it's the best time of the year.
P laying children are having fun.
    And can you see the beautiful sun?
R ed, blue, yellow flowers all around.
    Do you hear the spectacular sound?
I am so excited that spring is here.
    I could hear a pack of birds chirping in a tree that is near.
N ext time it rains, go outside.
    You might see a rainbow by your side.
G reen is the color I mostly see.
    Because of all the grass and green trees.

Oscar Hernandez, Grade 3
Peck Elementary School, IL

Soothing Sea

I went under sea one day, it was oh so wonderful!
I heard the sound of coral drums.
I felt the soft soggy sand.
I saw the bubbles popping from my little bits of breath.
I felt good and relaxed from an enchanting aqua sound
When it was time to say goodbye to the wonderful friendly sea,
It shook a wave and took me to dry land.
I went to my room and there, on my desk, was a piece of coral.

Keena Du, Grade 2
Meadowbrook Elementary School, IL

Statue of Liberty

I look over you with freedom and love and I say,
"Give me the rejected,
And I will accept them with my golden torch of freedom."
I am the symbol of freedom for all who come,
Who were saying, "This wonderful land where can it be?"
"It is said that a woman stands lighting the way to freedom."
This beautiful country…I am so very proud to live in!

John Pearson, Grade 3
Detroit Country Day Junior School, MI

Spill

When my drink is at the table I knock it over
and it spills like 100 drinks filled with ice cubes and water.
Oh no, the water got my sock wet.

Tyler Pierce, Grade 3
Hyatt Elementary School, MI

Summer

No school!
Swimming
Soccer catching frogs
Playing in the sun.
I like summer!

Nate Tillery, Grade 2
Pathfinder Elementary School, MI

Summer

"no school"
staying up
twenty-four hours
laying in the grass
sometimes fishing
with my uncle
and his girlfriend
playing at Fremont Lake
playing with my cousins
sweating like crazy
I love summer.

Dominique Rumsey, Grade 2
Pathfinder Elementary School, MI

Dogs

I love dogs
Bad dogs
Soft dogs
Good dogs
Mad dogs
Any kind of dog

A dog in a house
A dog with a collar
A dog with a hat
A dog that slobbers
I love dogs.

Sleeping dogs
Happy dogs
Smiling dogs
Eating dogs
I love dogs.

Deja Wilson, Grade 2
Stocker Elementary School, WI

School

In school
there are noisy kids that hum
and shout
but it's still okay.
We have pencils
that are pointy
and squeaky
when you write.
At recess time some people
stomp, stomp, stomp
when they chase, and
hop, hop, hop
when they play hopscotch.
They yell for fun, but when they go in
they say "awwwww"
because they had so much fun.

Wendy Zhu, Grade 2
Meadowbrook Elementary School, IL

My Balloon

It was a hot and sunny day,
but my balloon floated away!
I wanted it to stay and play,
but now I lay and say
Is it that way my balloon floated away?

Zach George, Grade 3
Ramalynn Montessori Academy, MN

Pandas

Pandas are...
black and white.
Pandas...
live in China.
Pandas eat bamboo.

Tiffani Fisher, Grade 3
Henryville Elementary School, IN

Candy

Candy is so sweet.
I think it is a yummy treat.
Sometimes it creates greed.
Come and have some fun with me!

Katelyn Miller, Grade 2
Zion Lutheran School of Wayside, WI

Raccoons

Raccoons are sneaky.
Raccoons are like ninjas.
Raccoons are tricky.
But there is one raccoon that does not steal.
Stuffed animal ones!

Alex Stevenson, Grade 1
Woodford Elementary School, OH

The Bear

I see a big, brown bear at the zoo.
I hear the awesome, furry bear roaring at me.
I smell the bear eating a fish with his claws.
That fish must taste good.
It's funny to see that bear eat.

Joshua Connelly, Grade 1
Eastside Elementary School, MI

Snow

Snow is great
Snow is fun
Snow is white
You can run in it
You can get four-wheelers stuck
You can sled behind four-wheelers
Wwweeeeeermmmmm!
Got to go…Dad's stuck again
He really likes that snow
I have to get the four-wheeler
Wwweeeeeeeemmmmmmmm!
Go Dad, you got stuck anyway
I love snow
Do you!

Jonah Webb, Grade 2
Country Meadow Elementary School, IN

Spring

S unflowers blossom in the sun.
P urple flowers bloom in gardens.
R ed rainbows are safely in the sky.
I nsects come out of the mud.
N ice green grass is growing in yards.
G iant worms are on my driveway.

Jack Vogel, Grade 2
Stanton Elementary School, NE

Things I Like
I like to talk,
I like to sing,
I like to do most everything,
I like to play,
I like to bike,
I'd like to take a big long hike,
I like to eat,
I like to nap,
I like to annoy my sister Pat!
Elijah Jost, Grade 3
Woodlawn Elementary School, KS

Lindsay
her eyes are
sparkly blue
her hair is
soft and smooth
she's smart
as Mrs. Dawson
I like her.
Sydney Ensing, Grade 2
Pathfinder Elementary School, MI

Yellow
Yellow looks like Michigan.
Yellow feels like the hot sun.
Yellow smells like dandelions.
Yellow sounds like Michigan fans
cheering during a football game.
Yellow tastes like bananas.
Joshua Case, Grade 2
Coy Elementary School, OH

Kristin
Kristin is nice, she's small, cute,
she has blond hair, she's good,
her number in school is 11,
and Kristin is special because
she's nice, cute, smart, pretty,
she can remember things,
she wears her hair in a pony tail,
I like her for who she is.
Jordyn Motsinger, Grade 3
Henryville Elementary School, IN

The Dogs
My friend Louisa and I love dogs.
She likes big dogs.
I like almost all.
I like short and tall.
The big and the small.
I like them all.
Except the Puli!!!
And I don't like the droolly!!!!
Vera Wall, Grade 2
Pope John XXIII School, IL

Cow
Spotted, big
Eating, drinking, running
Holstein
Jaymee Hibbs, Grade 2
Thayer Central Elementary School, NE

Games
I like games
You can win you can lose.
I like games.
There are fighting games,
There is Halo 3.
It is really fun!
But the thing I can't do
Is buy those games because
I don't have an Xbox 360.
Kaleb Hayes, Grade 1
Henryville Elementary School, IN

Jump Jump Fall
Jump
Jump
Fall
Jump
Jump
Fall
Down on
the ground
if you get hurt
don't do it any more
Ian Paige, Grade 2
Pathfinder Elementary School, MI

Wolves Are Here
Wolves are scary
Wolves are black
Oh no help
I hope there's hope
It is near me
There's a thorn bush
I will hide behind it
I'm safe and I am home

Drew Hereld, Grade 2
Jackson Center Elementary School, OH

Under the Lunch Table
Under the lunch table, you will find
An open door to go behind.
Watch your step! It's very bumpy.
The piles of food could be lumpy.
As long as you have lived
People have been
Sticking their food under here back then.
Like gum and grapes,
Potato scraps,
Macaroni,
And bologna,
Cherries, berries,
And strawberries.
This may have put you in a hungry mood,
But please do not eat this smelly, old food.

Alyssa Fanella, Grade 3
Sleepy Hollow Elementary School, IL

Colors
Red
Purple
Green
Black
White
Brown
Orange
Blue
Yellow
Pink
I like colors!

Alexis Monroe, Grade 1
James R Watson Elementary School, IN

Fall

fall
leaves blow
red and orange
really cool
fall

Joey Carter, Grade 3
Phillip May Elementary School, IL

Squids

Squids, squids
everywhere
swimming around
the ocean square.
Look out squidy,
here comes Mr. Sperm Whale.

Jacob Romero, Grade 2
Waterloo Elementary School, IN

The Farm Dog

A dog that lives on a farm
Might want to do harm
But this dog is tame
Tame without being lame
If you make a growl
It really will not prowl
All it does is sit
Won't hurt you the slightest bit
Sit by its side
Watch it with pride
Dogs usually make me want to flee
But this one's okay with me

Emily Silber, Grade 3
Rutledge Hall Elementary School, IL

Mom and Dad

Mom
Lovely, pretty
Smiling, hugging, helping
Mother, provider, parents, father
Runner, worker, listener
Strong, muscular
Dad

Mikayla Masching, Grade 3
St Clare Catholic School, IL

Spring

Spring, Spring,
it's finally here.
So I'll hang my coat up really high
and say bye, bye.
And now it's time to play,
see you on the way!

Sarah Patton, Grade 3
Deerfield Elementary School, MI

The Star

Bright star at night
flashing yellow light.
You are so bright above my roof.
Good night little star, good night.

Anthony Gonzalez, Grade 2
Holden Elementary School, IL

Dolphins

Dolphins are very good at tricks
They can also swim in the water
They can jump in the air
They are very cool.

Christian Ceurvorst, Kindergarten
Ramalynn Montessori Academy, MN

My Family Likes

My dad
likes dogs.
My mom
likes work.
My brother
likes rated M games.
And I
like my family.

Isaac Hisle, Grade 3
Henryville Elementary School, IN

The Dog and Frogs

There was a dog
Who liked to chase frogs.
One day he got stuck in muck.
So he never had any luck.

Annie Ashley, Grade 2
Ramalynn Montessori Academy, MN

My Chew Boy

My puppy is named Socks
He likes to eat and go on very long walks
He likes to steal socks and toys
He loves to play outside
He loves to snuggle with my daddy
He loves to make new friends
He loves to chew on things
He loves to sleep in my bed
He loves to watch the sunset with me

Veda Cobb, Grade 2
Broken Arrow Elementary School, KS

Cats

My cat is fat.
I don't know why?
Maybe he ate too much.
Or he did not exercise.
Like he was supposed to do
every morning and night.
Or he took a nap like
he was not supposed to do.
Or he ate a cookie.
Hey who ate a cookie?
Tigger did you eat the cookie?
Meow?
Of course you did not.

Brett Harguth, Grade 2
MACCRAY West Elementary School, MN

Sun

S o big, so bright,
U nseen at night,
N ever so bright at night.

Andrea Allenbaugh, Grade 2
Jackson Center Elementary School, OH

Dogs

Dogs like to go running
Dogs like hiding
Dogs like digging
Dogs like eating
Dogs like sleeping

Topanga Hine, Grade 2
Country Meadow Elementary School, IN

Sports Are Fun

Sports are fun,
Sports are cool,
Football and baseball,
Hockey and basketball.
You can play them
any day
and any time.
Patrick Hardy, Grade 2
Queen of All Saints School, IL

Leaves

In and out I see
leaves come down.
Just like bats,
they fly around.
Henry Chen, Grade 1
Holden Elementary School, IL

Crystal

Crystal
Big, cheerful, pretty
Shivering, convincing
Melts at the end of winter
Frosty's wife
Anna Sabatino, Grade 3
St Michael School, OH

Me

John
A student
At Burr Elementary
During the day
Because I need to learn
John Minicuci, Grade 3
Burr Elementary School, MI

My School

Loud
Hungry
Tired
Work, work, work
I wish I could go home.
Macey Panaro, Grade 1
Bright Elementary School, IN

Summer

I like summer
You can play
You can ride your bike
You can play baseball
You can play basketball
You can play football
You can play kickball
You can look at the sky
Donovan Greer, Grade 2
Holy Redeemer Christian Academy, WI

The Moon

Hello moon,
How do you get so bright?
I look out the window and I see half of you
moon.
How do you get a full moon?
I like how you give us light in the dark.
So it won't be too dark.
Cinthia Parras, Grade 3
North Intermediate School, MN

Happiness Is...

Going on vacation,
Riding your bike in the summer,
Having a new puppy,
Playing with your friends in the summer,
Happiness is all around the world.
Katie Catterall, Grade 1
Hamilton Community Elementary School, IN

Turtles

Turtles move slow.
Turtles move fast.
Turtles move on land.
Turtles move underwater.
Sea turtles, Painted turtles,
Small turtles, large turtles.
SNAP! SNAP! SNAP!
Ow! Ow! Ow!
How can I forget
Snapping Turtles!
Ethan Bailey, Grade 2
James R Watson Elementary School, IN

Colors

Aqua and turquoise reminds me of the big, blue sea.
Black and gray makes my day very lonely.

Orange and yellow brighten up my day.
White is the snow on a winter day.

Dark blue and purple makes me feel sad.
Red and bronze makes me feel mad.

Light blue is the ice we use to skate on.
Brown were the plains where Indians hunted on.

Green and gold are the colors that make people rich.
Silver are the dimes and quarter we use to buy with.

What do colors mean to you?

Christopher Soo, Grade 2
Detroit Country Day Lower School, MI

A Girl Named Shiyla

This poem is written by an eight year old girl,
one with blonde hair but not with one curl.
The boys flock to her by dozens and masses,
just to check out her cool, hot pink glasses.
Her teacher's name is Murphy, who doesn't have a flaw,
which is way better than a teacher who has Murphy's Law.
Her favorite animal is the buzzing bumblebee,
she goes to class at night to learn her karate.
This little girl's unique name is Shiyla,
it's the end of the poem so I have to say bye-ya!

Shiyla Bower, Grade 3
Weymouth Elementary School, MI

The Colors of My Summer

Green were the trees that gave me shade.
Pink were the flowers that now are leis.
Teal was the color of the water in the bay.
Black was the car that drove me all the way.
Brown were the horses that ate all the hay.
Clear was the glass that I broke and I paid.
Blue is my face because I didn't say,
White was the cross that I prayed with every day.

Maggie Sheerin, Grade 3
St Clare Catholic School, IL

Horse
Running on the plains
Keeping on beat with the wind
Running wild and free.
Jordan Lynch, Grade 3
Henryville Elementary School, IN

My Cousin Will
My cousin Will,
He's only three.

I wonder, will he be like me?

My cousin Will,
In Kindergarten he will be,

I wonder, if my best pal he'll be?
My cousin Will!
Kendra Hummer, Grade 2
Waterloo Elementary School, IN

No More School
Summer!
School's out
No more
vomiting
at lunch!
No more
teachers!
We won't have
a boring life
No more math
homework!
No more buses
Ding Dong
School's out!
Gage Guzman, Grade 2
Pathfinder Elementary School, MI

Wind
Chilly with a push
Can't see it woosh right through
With tenderness and might
Hannah Sunderland, Grade 3
Mable Woolsey Elementary School, IL

Kittens
Cute
Meow
Milk
Kittens
Ashley Sobczyk, Kindergarten
Northfield Elementary School, OH

I'm Allergic to Cheese
I'm allergic to cheese,
it makes me sneeze.
So get my medicine will you please.
Hunter Kula, Grade 1
Trinity Lutheran School, IA

My Dog, Ren
My dog Ren smells like "wet dog."
He looks old and tired.
Sometimes he sounds like a dying frog.
Ren's a collie with colors of coal black,
walnut brown, and snow white fur.
He's a medium size dog that I love.
Megan Boyd, Grade 3
Emerald Elementary School, MI

Imagine Me
Imagine me, a leaf.
Falling from the dark blue sky.
Landing on a brown tree branch.
Dancing fast and creeping down.
Getting stepped on.
Imagine me, a leaf.
Frankie Torres, Grade 2
Michener Elementary School, MI

Nighttime
Night
Scary, black
Cooking, eating, sleeping
Cooling, warming, nearing, sunrise
Awakening, changing, leaving
Bored, tired
Day
Allison Silvestrini, Grade 3
St Clare Catholic School, IL

Time

The pendulum swings while the clock rings
without a doubt time is running out.
The day had ended and has depended
on the sun whose job is done.
The day was splendid but has ended,
shimmering light turning into night.

Richard Colwell, Grade 3
Medford Area Elementary School, WI

Spring

The roses are growing and the violets too
but where do you see all the birds flying to
It takes a lot of hours to smell the flowers.
I jump and jump but I feel on a big old lump.
We went on the slide and then we went inside.

Maureen Varela, Grade 2
Peck Elementary School, IL

Soaring Eagle

The eagle soars past
A snowy arctic mountain
Searching for its prey.

Bumjun Park, Grade 2
Shorewood Hills Elementary School, WI

Easter

Easter
People think Easter is
About Easter eggs
And Candy
But it is all about
JESUS!

Lindsey Armitage, Grade 3
James R Watson Elementary School, IN

Soccer

S occer is a scream to me
O h, and soccer it hurts sometimes
C rying may happen
C uts and scrapes also
E verybody thinks this will be easy
R ight, I think not! It will be hard.

Alaina O'Neill, Grade 3
Kyle Trueblood Elementary School, KS

Snakes

Whenever you see a snake,
you'll hear the earth quake.
Whenever you see a snake,
you'll shake.
A snake slithers and crawls.
He climbs up the walls.
A snake in a tree,
wouldn't scare me!

Dayton Priebe, Grade 1
Rock Ledge Elementary School, WI

I Am Sledgehammer...

I am sledgehammer
Hear me smash
I am sledgehammer
Hear me kill
I am sledgehammer
Hear me smash tables
I am sledgehammer
Hear me hit
I am sledgehammer
Hear me smash chairs

Todd Cornett, Grade 2
Mentone Elementary School, IN

The New School

I am going to a new school
It has a pool
It is made of bricks
But I like sticks
I got six people in my group
Some like to snoop in my group
But I do not snoop
I like school.

Simon Willard, Grade 3
St Timothy's School, MN

I'm Glad

I'm glad I have cats,
I'm glad I have a brother,
I'm glad I have my mom and dad,
I'm glad I have fish!

Blake Wandmacher, Kindergarten
Ramalynn Montessori Academy, MN

Homework

Homework!
You have to do a lot of work.
I do not like it, but I have to do it.
Homework!

Jared White, Grade 3
Atwood Elementary School, MI

Megan

M y name is Megan
E xtra helpful
G ymnastics lover
A nice person
N ever gives up

Megan Wandmacher, Grade 3
Atwood Elementary School, MI

How I Feel in Spring

I feel hot and sweaty.
I feel shocked.
I feel sad in spring.
I feel wind also.
I feel excited in spring.
That's how I feel in spring.
People probably feel like me
or maybe they don't feel like me.
Either way we all feel
something in spring.

Jacob Chagoya, Grade 3
H. R. McCall Elementary School, IL

Owls

So silent
On very
Swift wings
That's why
It gives voles
Nightmares
Like a flying Ninja
Talons
Are the swords
That are being
Drawn in attack.

Austin Engelhardt, Grade 2
Orchard Lane Elementary School, WI

Marshmallows
Chewy
Sticky
White
Sugary
Yummy
O-o-o-o-o-o!

Steven Green, Grade 1
South Monroe Townsite Elementary School, MI

If I Were Queen of the World
I'd stop the wars and say, "Wars no more!"
and give gold to people who are poor.
I would put people that are bad
with wrestlers who are mad!
I would buy several pets
and check them with vets.
When I shop at the mall.
I would have a ball.
I'd buy a rabbit, a gerbil, a hamster, and a dog,
I would not want to buy a hog.
I'm going to buy me a castle decorated with jewels,
and ask my guards to follow my rules.
I'd give my people 100 pieces of gold,
and a stuffed animal that they can hold.

Trianna Destiny Rodriguez, Grade 3
JFH Educational Academy West, IL

Green
Green looks like art paper.
Green smells like flowers out of the garden.
Green tastes like an apple out of the orchard.
Green feels like squishy Play-Doh.
Green sounds like a pretty bird singing outside my window.

Sarah Huff, Grade 2
Will Carleton Academy, MI

Iditarod
The iditarod is a cool sport, cool sport, cool sport,
And dogs love it, dogs love it, dogs love it,
Mushers are in a rush, in a rush, mushers are in a rush,
Dogs race in the snow, in the snow, in the snow,
Dogs race in the snow!

Averie Robertson, Grade 2
Central Elementary School, IL

Gum

Chewy
Bubblicious
Spicy like a pepper
Yummy, yummy, in my tummy
Gummy
Lauren Schneider, Grade 3
Atwood Elementary School, MI

Musical Weather Report

We're in the garage.
Tom plays his tuba.
Tina plays her trumpet.
"Thunder!" we yell.
Philip plays his flute.
Wilma plays her whistle.
"Rain!" we yell.
George plays his guitar.
Betty plays her banjo.
"Wind!" we yell.
Daniel plays his drum.
Hildagard plays her harp.
"Lightning!" we yell.
Herman plays his harmonica.
Violet plays her violin.
"Sun!" we yell.
Kaeli Rowan Heins, Grade 2
Meadowbrook Elementary School, IL

Red

Red is my favorite color
I found a red flower on my dress
to wear to the party
Today I found a pair of red shiny shoes
and a red butterfly in the sky flying
Jocelyn Camacho, Grade 3
Peck Elementary School, IL

Splish Splash

Splish, splash went the rain.
Splish, splash went the mist.
Boom, boom went the thunder.
And then the lighting was very noisy.
Ryan Cotler, Grade 2
Meadowbrook Elementary School, IL

I Am Me...

I am a nice boy who likes
Baseball and wrestling.

I am me.

I have a baby brother and a sister.
My dad's name is Griffin.

I am me.
Peyton Tucker, Grade 2
Mentone Elementary School, IN

Bad People

Hustling and running,
asking for money.
What are they going to do?
They have to do something.
Hiding and stealing,
shooting and killing,
getting sent to prison.
Beating up people,
turning their hearts black,
Why won't they pray?
The earth will shake.
The sun will rise.
Heaven will praise.
Markeith LaFranté Taylor Jr., Grade 3
Earl M Lawson Elementary School, KS

Arizona

Arizona
Very hot
Almost never rains
Has lots of pools!
Desert
Laurel Repshas, Grade 3
Atwood Elementary School, MI

Blossoms

Blossoms grow and grow
Blow in the wind, blow and blow
Then float far away
Taylor Creek, Grade 3
Mable Woolsey Elementary School, IL

Buddy
Buddy, please, oh please move!
You're smaller than me
But I still can't see.
Please, oh please, will you move for me?

Christopher Calabrese, Grade 3
Atwood Elementary School, MI

Turtles
Shiny, hard
Smooth, round
Snappy, muddy
They live in the pond.

Jaguar Clifford, Grade 2
Country Meadow Elementary School, IN

A Dog Named Jacky
My dog is black
My dog likes to chase cats
Then he gets tired
So he rests for two hours

Christopher Sykes, Grade 1
Holy Redeemer Christian Academy, WI

The Amazing Iditarod Race
I t's from Anchorage to Nome
D ogs like running in the race
I n every dog there is a tracker
T akotna is close to the starting line
A laska is where it starts
R unning for the dogs is tiring
O n the track the ice might crack
D ogs have booties on

Samantha Doornebos, Grade 2
Central Elementary School, IL

Dogs
Dirty dogs
Get all wet.
They run all over
All the time.
YUK!
He slobbered on me!

Kyler Price, Grade 2
James R Watson Elementary School, IN

Snowball Fight

Snowball fight
Dangerous, hard
Packing, throwing, dodging
Don't get hit in the face
Winter fight
Samuel Laird, Grade 3
St Michael School, OH

Fall

Fall is here
I fear the deer
I feel the cure
The leaves are ready here
The leaves are falling
I heard my mom calling
I wanted to go to the mall
But, I had a phone call.
Carrie Ogram, Grade 3
St Timothy's School, MN

My Best Friend

Play
Have fun
My best friend.
Great
Love her
My best friend
Natalie
Loves me
My best friend.
Play
All the time
My best friend.
Deann Martin, Grade 1
Bright Elementary School, IN

Miso

Miso
Hyper, cute
Eating, sleeping, playing
She is color blind
Girl
Eliza Dowd, Grade 2
Pope John XXIII School, IL

Monkeys

silly monkeys
loud monkeys
quiet monkeys
nice monkeys
friendly monkeys
mean monkeys
oh
no
help
me
Kaitlynn Slaven, Grade 1
James R Watson Elementary School, IN

My Dad

Nice
Plays with me
Works
Helps me
I love my dad!
Hailey Poff, Grade 1
James R Watson Elementary School, IN

Roses Are Red

Roses are red
Violets are blue
Daisies are white
Moon flowers are purple
Sugar is sweet
So are all of you
Haleigh Smith, Grade 2
Country Meadow Elementary School, IN

Bees

Bees like to buzz around your head
Buzz!
Buzz!
Buzz!
You hear that buzzing everywhere you go.
Watch out for that bumblebee
Right in front of your face.
WATCH
OUT!
Andrew Novak, Grade 2
Country Meadow Elementary School, IN

Yellow

Yellow looks like two stars twinkling up in the sky.
Yellow feels like cuddling up with a soft blanket.
Yellow sounds like someone crumpling up manila paper.
Yellow smells like a brand new banana from the store.
Yellow tastes like biting into a big juicy pineapple.

Grace Gadwood, Grade 2
Will Carleton Academy, MI

Apples

Bright, red, shiny and yummy too.
A kind of food very healthy for you!
It is also a fruit that I like to eat.
But just make sure you wash them before you eat.

Caroline Walsh, Grade 2
Onaway Elementary School, OH

Pink

Pink looks like beautiful flowers in the spring.
Pink smells like strawberry cake after it comes out of the oven.
Pink tastes like pink food coloring when it is stale.
Pink sounds like paint on a piece of paper.
Pink feels like the sky in the summer when it is nighttime.

Hanna Korn, Grade 2
Will Carleton Academy, MI

Colors

Green reminds me of grass in the field.
Silver is the color of a knight's shield.

White, the color of a plane.
Red, the Red Wings have a lot of game!

Yellow means yield on the road.
Brown, the color of a toad.

Oceans, where the dolphins swim in the deep blue.
The color of aqua is a very nice shoe.

Orange is the color of a juicy grapefruit.
Black is the color of a big boot.

What do colors mean to you?

Matt Lamb, Grade 2
Detroit Country Day Lower School, MI

Red-Eyed Tree Frog
It hops
It hops a lot
It blends in well
Frog
Isaiah Warren, Grade 1
Henryville Elementary School, IN

Cubs Baseball
"Play ball!" says the ump.
It hits the mitt.
"Strike one," says the ump now.
Felix Pie hits a shot.
Back…back…it's gone.
Home run!!!
The Cubs win!
What a game!
The crowd goes wild. Ahhhhhh!
It's the playoffs now.
Evan Barnes, Grade 2
Meadowbrook Elementary School, IL

Grandma
Who loves me?
Grandma!
Who gets us up early?
Grandma!
Who takes us to the doctors?
Grandma!
Hope Terry, Grade 3
Henryville Elementary School, IN

Max
Jumping
and
running
and
barking
but
he
is
still
good.
Tyler Young, Grade 2
Pathfinder Elementary School, MI

What Sports Will I Do?
I might play football or wrestling.
Or hockey or soccer or basketball
Or baseball or Chinese dodgeball
Or I might race.
Emmanuell Smallwood, Grade 1
Woodford Elementary School, OH

Lizard
My lizard is a boy
With lots of joy.

His name is Spike
that doesn't ride a bike.

He is a baby
that doesn't have one rabbi.

He likes a lot of light
but doesn't like to fight.
Danika Nacy, Grade 3
Atwood Elementary School, MI

I Am Snow
I am snow.

You see me coming from the sky.
You see me on the ground.

I am snow.

You make snowmen out
of me and igloos too.

I am snow.
Asia O'Connor, Grade 2
Mentone Elementary School, IN

Raw Cake
I made a cake
That I didn't want to bake
So I ate it raw!
It tasted so bad.
Sheridan Thorp, Grade 2
Ramalynn Montessori Academy, MN

Spring

S pring is coming again.
P laying in the rain.
R ain coming down the window pane.
I nsects coming again for the spring.
N ests are getting built again.
G arden flowers growing.

Jasmine Pantoja, Grade 3
Peck Elementary School, IL

Aren't I

Aren't I going to be in a coffin someday?
Aren't I going to die someday?
Aren't I going to be in a cemetery someday?
Aren't I going to be buried some day?
Aren't I going to Heaven?

Justin Lange, Grade 3
Kyle Trueblood Elementary School, KS

Sunset

The sun starts to set tonight.
To me it is a pretty sight.
All the colors are so bright.
Orange, red and yellow
Make a pretty light.

Micajah Rippy, Grade 3
Bradie M Shrum Upper Elementary School, IN

Spring

S ounds of wind chimes fill the air
P lay in the sun let's have some fun
R ainbows in the sky it seems like they fly
I nsects fly in the air
N o wearing hats, gloves and jackets
G reen leaves growing in the trees

Jesus Flores, Grade 3
Peck Elementary School, IL

Ice Cream

I like ice cream
It's good for my body
It makes me act funny
Ice cream is the best!

Tyrone Ward, Grade 2
Holy Redeemer Christian Academy, WI

Candy! Candy!
Candy, candy
I love you a lot,
You're yummy and tasty,
Chewy and gummy.
I love you and eat you,
Oh, I can't get enough,
Candy, candy
You're wonderful stuff!
Samantha New, Grade 1
Northfield Elementary School, OH

Sled
S liding down the hill
L ike to go sledding
E very day you play
D o you have a cool sled
Eric Hume, Grade 2
Mentone Elementary School, IN

Mouse
At the dawn of day
a sleepy mouse is wakened
by the hawk's deep cries.
Christian Baer, Grade 3
Chantry Elementary School, IA

Dinosaurs
Dinosaurs, dinosaurs
Lived long ago
Some were big
Don't you know.
Some were bad
Some were nice
Some lived where
There's lots of ice.

I wish they could visit…
    but talk to them…

I would have to be
Way up high
In a tree!
Jason Nevel, Grade 1
Woodford Elementary School, OH

My Goofy Dog
I have a dog,
That sits on a log.
She always gets sad,
But then she gets glad.
When she wags her tail,
She helps get the mail.
Then she plays with her cap,
Next she goes to eat my map!
Keyanna Kail, Grade 1
Monroeville Elementary School, OH

Karate
Punch
Kick
Fight
Num chucks
Staffs
Bamboo swords
Breaking boards
Dojo
High block
Low Block
Karate!
Josiah Somkit, Grade 2
Waterloo Elementary School, IN

Nathan
I have a brother named Nathan.
I am as happy as can be.
He is cute as can be.
In two more years, he'll be three.
He loves to give kisses,
He misses me when I leave.
We love each other!
Ashley Korb, Grade 3
Atwood Elementary School, MI

My Two Cats
I have two cats,
They are really fat.
They snag you when you're sleeping,
They go outside and are creeping.
Abi Roeder, Grade 1
Monroeville Elementary School, OH

Spring Is Here!
Spring is here!
The air is changing all around us.
Easter has past.
The warm air is coming fast.
Beautiful flowers and trees are blooming.
The sun is shining warmer and warmer.
Days are going past slower and slower.
Even though we get a lot of rain,
these days in spring are not the same.
My favorite part is that animals and insects come out.

Scarlett Fryer, Grade 2
Brimfield Elementary School, OH

Summer
Summer is here summer has come!
We all eat ice cream Yummy! Yum! YUM!
Goodbye snow on the ground.
Hello! Summer all around town.
No more sledding, snowboarding, or snowball fights.
Now it's swimming, beaches, and lots of kites.

Erin Gallagher, Grade 3
Walls Elementary School, OH

Noodle
I have a poodle her name is Noodle.
Noodle loves to doodle.
Noodle is all white.
She hates to fight.
Her best friend is a pug.
She does not drink out of a bowl, she drinks out of a mug!
Her buddy is a bunny.
She is funny.
She does not have a favorite sport.
But she loves to build forts.
Her favorite song is "Hot Cross Buns."
She thinks it is lots of fun.
Noodle did a doodle in her sleep.
Her doodle was a sheep.
Then the next night she did a doodle of a bug.
When she woke up that morning she named it Dug.
That afternoon she got scared of a farm!
But that farm had no harm.

Sydney Burdick, Grade 3
Greenbriar Elementary School, IL

Dinosaur the Chihuahua

Dinosaur the Chihuahua is really little,
With a great big mouth.
He chews on a bone.
He has a good color on him.
His color is brown.

Valicity O'Connor, Grade 1
Stocker Elementary School, WI

Spring

Spring there,
Spring here,
Spring everywhere!
See it — flowers blooming
Hear it — bees buzzing
Feel it — soft grass
Smell it — beautiful flowers
Spring there
Spring here
Spring everywhere!

Tatum Pencek, Grade 3
Suffield Elementary School, OH

My Sister and Me

My sister is Jahkila.
She is 8 years old.
She is my twin sister
and I love her.
We look the same.
We wear the same clothes too.
And we wear the same hair style.
We play together
I love my sister very much.

Jahleiah Woods, Grade 2
Parkwood-Upjohn School, MI

Summer

S unny
U mbrellas
M oths
M emories
E agles
R unners

Nicholas Perch, Grade 2
Arbury Hills Elementary School, IL

Crackly sand
like ice breaking
surrounding snowy mountains
that look like clouds

Jordyn Phipps, Grade 3
Greenbriar Elementary School, IL

Summer Is Fun

December is a bummer,
I like to play in summer.
I like to swim in my pool,
I like to stay at school.

Rachelle Schuller, Grade 1
Monroeville Elementary School, OH

Spring Fun

Spring is here
School is almost done
Baseball begins
Now its time for fun

Ty Williams, Grade 2
Ladoga Elementary School, IN

The sun goes down
Making a path of light
On the deep blue sea

Michael Weller, Grade 3
Greenbriar Elementary School, IL

Patriots

Patriots let nothing stand in their way
to let their country live with
joyfulness and happiness

Scott Wenzel, Grade 3
Greenbriar Elementary School, IL

Playgrounds

Playgrounds are cool
And you are too.
But I like playgrounds
Because you can play on them a lot.

Savannah Durbin, Grade 1
Henryville Elementary School, IN

Bubbles

Bubbles here
Bubbles there
Bubbles can go anywhere
They go up high
They go down low
Sometimes they don't know where to go
They can see there up so high
I think they're even above the sky
They're up, up, up in outerspace
Some might even have a race
But then the bubbles drop
And suddenly they POP!

Tara Tischer, Grade 2
Arbury Hills Elementary School, IL

First Graders

We work, we play
We love to draw
Together we can do anything
Yes we can!
We love our teacher
We love our friends and
We love first grade!
Hurray!

Jennifer Blohm, Grade 1
James R Watson Elementary School, IN

Twisty!!!

Twisty twist!
Twisty likes peanut butter sandwiches
He is in trouble
Crash!
His name is Twisty Twist!
His only friends are Squidley and Pincher!

Jazmen Truelove, Grade 2
Country Meadow Elementary School, IN

Rain

R ain is so wet and the sound is splashy
A duck enjoys the rain
I will leap through the puddles
N o playing outside

Gracie Fortman, Grade 2
Central Elementary School, IL

Iguana

I have an iguana that is
in the dinosaur family.
It is green, It drinks water
and plays all day
and it eats healthy
and dances all day.
It jumps up and down
in its cage.

Miguel Corona, Grade 2
Peck Elementary School, IL

Murray the Dog

I have a dog named Murray.
She is very furry.
My dog always chews
on my new shoes.

Alexis Johnson, Grade 1
Trinity Lutheran School, IA

It's Raining

The sky is gloomy.
The grass is damp.
The people have umbrellas.
It is raining outside.

Natalie Pedziwiatr, Grade 1
Holden Elementary School, IL

The Football Game

I went to a football game.
The players were really lame.
I caught the football.
But I ended up in the hospital.

Jacob Sterenberg, Grade 1
Trinity Lutheran School, IA

Snowball

Snowball
Round, frozen
Making, throwing, playing
Pressed and rolled
Together
Soft Ball

Andrew Sanderson, Grade 3
St Michael School, OH

Two Mice

Are mice nice? Yes, they are nice.
Do they roll dice? Yes, they do roll dice.
Do they have lice? No, they don't have lice.
Can they hold dice? Yes, they can hold dice.

Seth Wiler, Grade 2
MACCRAY West Elementary School, MN

Where Your Imagination Takes You

Your imagination takes you,
to a world, far away.
To Paris, London, Canada, the moon, Lebanon,
or even a world of inventions.
Your imagination,
can take you anywhere.

Mohammed Shaheen, Grade 3
Islamic School of Greater Toledo, OH

Color

Red is raspberries and race cars.
Orange is oranges and open bags of Doritos.
Yellow is yarn and young chicks.
Green is grass and gross slime.
Blue is blueberries and book covers.
Purple is prom dresses and paints.
Black is black eyes and bad guy masks.
Brown is buffalos and bacon.
Pink is popping bubble gum bubbles
and pages in my book.

Rachel Warner, Grade 3
Holly Elementary School, MI

Seasons of the Year

Spring is a wonderful time of the year
there is nothing to worry about, nothing to fear.
Winter is the coldest one, playing
in the snow is so much fun.
Fall has so much colorful trees,
most kids love to play in the leaves.
Summer has the hottest days,
you can swim around in many ways.
That is why I love the seasons of the year.
Each one is different, each one is near.

Julia Moroz, Grade 3
St Catherine of Siena School, IN

Spring

S un is so bright and warm.
P ink, blue, red, yellow, green and purple flowers are so beautiful.
R ainbows with different colors look so pretty in the sky.
I ce cream bells ring, ring.
N o more wearing boots, hats, coats, and scarfs.
G reen leaves are growing on trees.

Crystal Marquez, Grade 3
Peck Elementary School, IL

Moonlight

Moonlight glistens like a river in the moonlight.
A soft, whispering sound, like the Amazon rain forest.
As white as freshly fallen snow, whiter than a bunnies fur.
Beauty, and glory, all in one captured scene. Light as can be.
Soft as an angels glow. lifted with dignity, and love.

Amanda Smit, Grade 3
Atwood Elementary School, MI

Girls

Girls think they are so pretty.
Girls think they have to get their nails done.
Girls think they have to be so pretty for their boyfriends.

Josh Metzger, Grade 2
Woodford Elementary School, OH

Colors

Lavender are the flowers in the meadow.
White are the clouds in skies that blow.

Indigo is the fierce thunderstorm at night.
Yellow is the sun that shines so bright.

Light blue is the sky during the day.
Spring green is the grass that makes me want to play.

Brown is the chocolate that tastes so good.
Pink is the color of my coat and hood.

Gold is the money that makes people rich.
Black is the dark color of the mean witch!

What do colors mean to you?

Heather Zimmerman, Grade 2
Detroit Country Day Lower School, MI

Spring Is Blue

There are blue flowers
They get watered by spring showers
The blue sky is big
I see a bird carrying a twig

Jared Remender, Grade 2
Ladoga Elementary School, IN

Color

What is red?
Red is an eraser
Red is a nice, fast car
What is blue?
Blue is the ocean
Blue is a dark sky

What is green?
Green is the leaf on a tree
The grass is green
What is yellow?
Yellow is the warm, hot summer sun
Yellow is a pencil
Yellow is my mom's favorite color

What is pink?
Pink is my sister's favorite color
Pink is a nice glass of pink lemonade
on a hot summer day
What is black?
Black is my dad's favorite color
Black is a color of a fish
Black is a mat

Ben Henke, Grade 3
Kate Goodrich Elementary School, WI

Stuffy

As soft as a mouse.
As soft as a bunny.
As soft as a cat.
As soft as a bird.
As soft as my favorite
Stuffed animal
Stuffy.

Kiona Leeman, Grade 1
Rock Ledge Elementary School, WI

Bunnies

Bunnies hop and hop
Digging homes in the dirt
Jumping and playing

Ayrika Gooley, Grade 3
Mable Woolsey Elementary School, IL

In the Spring

In the spring I see ponds.
In the spring I hear birds.
In the spring I smell pine trees.
In the spring I feel relaxed.
In the spring I can see, hear
smell and feel outside.

Ashley Lewis, Grade 3
H. R. McCall Elementary School, IL

What Is Baby Blue?

The sky is sweet baby blue
The water is wet baby blue
A baby boy wears a baby blue shirt
A hat is happy baby blue
The rain is drippy baby blue
I love Baby Blue!

Payton Armbruster, Grade 2
Bristol Elementary School, WI

Spring

S unflowers are growing.
P uddles are growing big.
R ed tulips are blooming.
I nteresting flowers are big.
N ip air is coming out.
G reen grass is growing tall.

Tenna Beel, Grade 2
Stanton Elementary School, NE

Baseball

In the spring I play some baseball.
It is not hard at all.

I catch the ball in my mitt,
I get a hit!

Tyler Andrews, Kindergarten
Bristol Elementary School, WI

The Statue of Liberty

The Statue of Liberty was a sign,
A sign of freedom for many eyes.
Over the sea their eyes rolled,
To see their only destiny,
Out of their captivity.

It was a great sight to see,
The great, one and only,
Statue of Liberty.
And so we say thanks to thee.

Some deported, some denied,
Some with great illness,
Who took it in stride
They all had to be strong,
All those months on a boat,
But to see you,
Was like being lifted afloat.

Since seeing you then was a great relief,
Even seeing you now
Makes some people cry their belief.
You are extremely wonderful...
Our Statue of Liberty.

Ailsa Bentley, Grade 3
Detroit Country Day Junior School, MI

Jayla

J umbo cakes
A pple eater
Y ummy food
L ove my daddy
A dorable

Jayla Anderson, Grade 2
Holy Redeemer Christian Academy, WI

Green

Leaves
Trees
Crayons
Grass
I love green.

Haley Button, Grade 1
James R Watson Elementary School, IN

Sledding

Big hill
Going down
Fast
Spinning
Big air
Crashing
Flipping
Having
Fun
I love
Sledding
Sledding is fun!
Christian Cartner, Grade 2
Patterson Elementary School, MI

Penguins

Feathers thick and thin
Flightless birds can swim and walk
Penguins lay big eggs
Steven Wang, Grade 3
Weymouth Elementary School, MI

Turtles

Turtles
Are
Slow
And
Swim
Walk
Turtles
James Olsen, Kindergarten
Northfield Elementary School, OH

School

Oh school
Oh school
I hate school!
So school
Could you please close
So I could stay home
and play my
PlayStation 2.
James Whitten, Grade 2
Pathfinder Elementary School, MI

Snowflakes

Falling in my hair,
Different, white, pretty, and small
Catch them on your tongue.
Ana Larson, Grade 2
J C Hoglan Elementary School, IA

Rock Collector

I like to collect rocks.
They are soft and flat.
They are really cool.
I have lots of rocks.
Trevor Coyle, Grade 1
Henryville Elementary School, IN

Football

Football
Being Q.B.
Throwing it out and catch
Running in the field and awesome
Touchdown
Callaway Bird, Grade 2
Congress School, MI

Kittens

I love kittens
Smooth kittens
Silky kittens
Soft kittens
Fluffy kittens
Any kind of kitten.

A kitten in a basket
A kitten in a box
A kitten in a shed
A kitten with socks
I love kittens.

Sleeping kittens
Running kittens
Swinging kittens
Napping kittens
I love kittens.
Kate Graffen, Grade 2
Stocker Elementary School, WI

I Don't Want to Go to School

I don't want to go to school,
I am sure it won't be cool!
I will go outside and play today,
Or I will learn math, what's an array?
The teachers don't let us talk in the hall.
One teacher's mean, and really tall!
Her name is Miss Lacy, she's not polite,
She eats like a pig, what a sight!
The gym teacher makes us run 3 miles a day.
Tomorrow she'll let us run two, Hooray!
There's one thing that's good in this dreadful place,
The music teacher's nice with a beautiful face!
So you don't believe my really cool poem.
I'll make another one that you can show them.
Then you'll be really extra furious.
I'll be grounded and you'll be victorious.
But please don't take me to school!

Cole Winston, Grade 3
Henry W Longfellow Elementary School, IL

Loving

Loving is when I feed my dog Lo-La.
Loving is when I feed my sweet dog.
Loving is when I give my dog a warm hug.
Loving is when I give my dog a kiss on her wet nose,
just like when my mom gives me a kiss.
Loving is when I give my dog a soft pillow.
Loving is when I let her outside to go to the bathroom.
Loving is when I play Frisbee with her.
Loving is when I give her a warm bath, as warm as a blanket.
Loving is when I give her water.
Loving is when I give her a ball to play with.
Loving is when I train her.
Loving is when I hope she knows I love her.
Loving is when I will cry when Lo-La dies.
Loving is when I worry she will choke
on her food because she is so small.
Loving is when I whisper in he ear, "Don't cry, please."
Loving is when she dreams a wonderful happy dream.
Loving is when I wonder if she knows I laugh
at her when she plays with Kinya.
So, do you love your fluffy dog that much?

Navi Turner, Grade 2
Michener Elementary School, MI

Summer

Summer appears with
licking ice cream
no school,
when the sun comes out
when grass starts to grow
when the Fourth of July comes.

Olivia Morley, Grade 3
Northfield Elementary School, OH

Colton Coyote

Colton Coyote howls every night.
Colton Coyote eats rabbits.
In the morning he runs in the woods.
Now he goes to coyote school.

Colton Casper, Grade 1
Stocker Elementary School, WI

Football

The sound of the Q.B.
calling a huddle
playing in the snow
and playing in the rain
jumping and yelling
when you score a touchdown

Shane Phillips, Grade 3
Henryville Elementary School, IN

Apples

Juicy
Healthy
Yummy
Red and green
Circles
Apples

Tommy Vetrovsky, Kindergarten
Northfield Elementary School, OH

Trucks

Colin likes trucks
but they cost a lot of bucks
Mom says she will pay
as long as he will play

Shayleigh Smith, Grade 3
Weymouth Elementary School, MI

Winter

It's so cold outside
We need to go inside
I will play soccer
No not outside
It's so cold
Stay inside

Zachary Helm, Grade 2
Patterson Elementary School, MI

I Can't Do My Chores

I can't do my chores because
My hand fell asleep
My stomach hurts
It smells too bad
There's too much dust on my glasses
My favorite show is on TV
I just coughed, I must be sick
My friend is coming over
What's that?
We're leaving for Myrtle Beach?
Ok, I'll be done in 5 minutes.
Goodbye

Emerald Huffman, Grade 3
Smithville Elementary School, OH

Sharks

S uper fast
H ungry almost all the time
A fraid of them
R ubber
K ings of the sea
S ome are a silver color.

Hayden Viers, Grade 3
Henryville Elementary School, IN

Water in the Puddle

It is dirty.
This is a good place for a birdy.
A boy splashes the pool,
to go to school.
First it was hot,
then it was cold.

Wileed Mathkour, Grade 1
Islamic School of Greater Toledo, OH

Alexis
I have a friend
Her name is Alexis
She lives in Texas
She drives a Lexus

Lindsi Johnson, Grade 2
Jackson Center Elementary School, OH

Louisiana
My family cooking my favorite food
The wind blowing on my face
Crawfish boiling
Sweet crawfish and crab going in my mouth
Soft sounding jazz music

Makenzie Roth, Grade 3
Smithville Elementary School, OH

Embarrassing
Embarrassing is falling off a skateboard.
I see my good skate shoes slip off.
I hear the board slam on the ground
I smell the dry pavement.
I touch the long rail
I taste blood on my lip

Landon Smith, Grade 3
Litchville-Marion Elementary School, ND

Flowers
Flowers are beautiful
They smell good
They need water
They grow big
Flowers

Autumn Heath, Kindergarten
McKenney-Harrison Elementary School, IN

Buffalos
Buffaloes graze on all the days,
Including spring and fall,
They look for food all day long,
Sometimes they find nothing at all,
Their big furry bodies may slow them down.
So they take a rest down on the soft ground.

Nick Marietti, Grade 3
Noonan Academy, IL

Collecting Gems

Collecting gems
is really fun,
green and sparkling,
yellow and shiny,
clear and round,
blue and square,
heart-shaped,
You should try it.
Grace Gleason, Grade 2
Queen of All Saints School, IL

My Wild Brother

My brother is very wild.
My sister is very mild,
and I'm just a normal child.
Ty England, Grade 2
Trinity Lutheran School, IA

Football

Football
Cool, awesome
Tackling, passing, running
Down the field for the win
Aggressive game
Brian Zapior, Grade 3
St Michael School, OH

Snowboard

Snowboard
Hard, slick, wide
Skimming, bounding, landing
Coordination keeps you safe
Snowslider
Drew McQuade, Grade 3
St Michael School, OH

Tigers/Animal

Tigers
Scary, furious
Scratching, killing, eating
In the jungle
Animal
Anthony Harper, Grade 2
Congress School, MI

Fairies

Some are pink.
Some are rainbow.
Some are yellow.
Fairies!
Jessi Gerke, Kindergarten
McKenney-Harrison Elementary School, IN

The Cheer Day

Hot summer day,
First time,
I'm scared.

People around me encouraging me.
Trying, but can't.
I try several times, all railed.

I go back in a week,
I try, I succeed!
Yeah!

That's how I got my back-handspring

Along the way, my courage helped a lot!
I'm so proud!
Hailey Weyenberg, Grade 3
MacArthur Elementary School, WI

This Is What I Think Spring Should Be

Spring is here
Spring is here
It's time to go
outside.
RECESS!
It is spring
It is time to have
a BBQ
Can you see it?
Spring is here
Spring is here
Time for spring break
This is what spring
should be.
Kayla Pounds, Grade 3
H. R. McCall Elementary School, IL

Fatherless Heart

My heart is lonely and full of despair,
not having a father to hold me or care.
His image is a sudden blur,
that my mind erases and concurs.
His face seems appealing, but then again strange;
his voice seems familiar but then again estranged.
My heart races when I think he'll one day appear,
the day he'll hold me caress me and show me, he cares.
I hope for the day he'll feel remorse, for being away for so long;
for not having enough courage to come back soon.
On Father's Day I wish he were around
to tickle and play games and carry me around.
To enjoy a nice Father's Day dinner would be so nice
where we can talk about school, work, and friends
and plan our next event one step at a time.

Priscilla Cisneros, Grade 3
Peck Elementary School, IL

Daniel

My hair is like golden sun,
My eyes are like clear sky and clear water, because they are blue.
My arms are like a bruised up apple.
My heart holds love that is as warm as the color gold of the sun.
I live in a house and eat lots of spaghetti with meatballs.

Daniel Danecker, Grade 1
JFH Educational Academy West, IL

Caring

Caring is when I have to watch my brothers.
My mom or dad asks me to watch my brothers.
I have to wrestle.
I have to sit with Cristopher on the couch and entertain him
or he will cry or scream.
I'll go mad if I have to watch three little boys forever.
J.J. will say sorry and Cristopher will go to sleep
and Santino will watch Sponge Bob.
Mom and Dad come back and say, "Good job."
I wonder if I'll ever stop watching J.J., Cristopher and Santino.
I would rather go to Brooklyn's house than stay at home
watching all of my brothers.
My brothers are as wild as monkeys in a jungle.
Caring is when I have to stay home with my wild brothers.

Maria Pace, Grade 2
Michener Elementary School, MI

The Funny Easter Bunny

The Easter Bunny gives you eggs.
But, I know one that gives you socks for your legs.
He gave Ashley a stone, he gave Alex a bone,
and he gave Jill a pine cone.
Joel wanted a basket, but instead he got a casket.
That's the Easter Bunny I know.

Dane Kocinski, Grade 2
Crissey Elementary School, OH

Gymnastics

Cartwheels
Round-offs
Cat walks
Cat leaps
I did
Gymnastics
I love gymnastics!

Lucie Harmon, Grade 1
South Monroe Townsite Elementary School, MI

Kids

Kids are cool kids are fun
kids like to play all day long
they like to play on the swing
jump on the beds and do everything
do you like to play soccer,
whooshing through the winds, feel the breeze
do you like to ride on a bike
go around the town do anything you like
do you like to play the games that I like to do
like basketball, soccer and volleyball too
Do yo like to play hockey on the ice and in the skates
and try to make a goal also
Do you like to do Tae Kwon Do hi-ya!

Annie Murphy, Grade 3
Noonan Academy, IL

Dancing

Dancing and prancing and running around.
Jumping and leaping right off the ground.
I wear tap shoes to ballet shoes to jazz shoes and galore.
At the end of the day I want more!

Sophie Dominguez, Grade 3
MacArthur Elementary School, WI

Goosebumps

Goosebumps are scary.
Goosebumps are exciting!
Goosebumps are fun to read.
Goosebumps are my favorite.
I love Goosebumps!

Troy Hickman, Grade 2
James R Watson Elementary School, IN

French Fries

French fries are
munchy and crunchy
They are
Good
good
Good
good
Goooood!
And if they are called
French fries
Shouldn't they be made from
FRENCH people?

Jill Kuhn, Grade 2
Country Meadow Elementary School, IN

The Dog That Adds When He Is Mad

I have a dog,
That sits on a log.
When my dog gets mad,
He starts to add.
When he gets too sad,
He bites my silly dad.

Carley Helmstetter, Grade 1
Monroeville Elementary School, OH

School

School is exciting
School is awesome
School is interesting
School is torture
I'm just kidding...
School rocks, but
ONLY in the summer!

Austin Osterhout, Grade 2
James R Watson Elementary School, IN

Football

I tackle. I win.
I
   Like
     Noah
      He...
Is
  On
  My
    Football
     Team.

Tanner D. Peterson, Grade 1
Bristol Elementary School, WI

Grandma's House

When it's warm and sunny,
I like to be there at noon,
To hear the cows moo
And see the chickens run,
While I play in the hay.
I will go there next summer,
And that makes me warm inside!

Patricia Murczek, Grade 3
St Robert Bellarmine School, IL

Zachary

Z enner is my teacher
A lways smiles
C an run fast
H elps people
A nice kid
R aces
Y ellow things are nice!

Zachary Breneman, Kindergarten
Medford Elementary School, WI

Air Balloons

High in the sky,
I can see them fly,
Oh my!
There so high.
I wave goodbye.
I wish I could fly.

Megan Weyers, Grade 1
Rock Ledge Elementary School, WI

Colors

Pink is the color of a flamingo.
White is the color of the puffy clouds.
Gold is the color of a shiny trophy.
Red is the color of blood.
Green is the color of the grass.
Blue is the color of the sky.
Copper is the color of a penny.

Do you like colors?

Kyle Konath, Grade 3
Atwood Elementary School, MI

I Don't Know Why

I don't know why
My cat is acting funny.
He kind of looks like a bunny,
I don't know why
My brother is
Hopping
Like a kangaroo.
I don't know why
My dad is trying
To fly
My mom wants
To eat a cow and
I am purple from head to toe.
    I
    Don't
    Know
    Why.

Evan Sadowski, Grade 2
Orchard Lane Elementary School, WI

Pizza, Pizza

Pizza, pizza
I love you a lot,
You're tasty and yummy,
Healthy and good.
I love you and love you,
Oh, I can't get enough,
Pizza, pizza
You're yummy stuff

Matthew Balishin, Grade 1
Northfield Elementary School, OH

I Love You Mom

I love you Mom and that's all I'll say.
So please Mom, I'm begging you, please don't move away.
I'll be a wreck, I will be very sad.
I love you Mom.
I love you so much!
I guess there is no stopping you.
So I will just say, I love you Mom and goodbye.

Marisol Ruiz, Grade 2
Bristol Elementary School, WI

I Like Spring

I like spring
I like spring
I see fat squirrels,
bees, robins and the clear blue sky
I like spring
I like spring because I like to walk my dog
I like spring
I like spring because I feel hot, playful and excited!

Brian Rivera, Grade 3
H. R. McCall Elementary School, IL

St. Patrick's Day

Gold, Irish, rainbows, shamrocks,
leprechauns, fun, pots, treasures, emeralds,
green, magic, strong, super, bright,
Ireland, powerful, shout, glee, lands, fairies,
dance, parades, elves, charms, folks, celebrations,
discovered, customs, flying, heroes,
forest, silk, awesome

Kayla Prather, Grade 3
Henryville Elementary School, IN

Spring

S pring is fun and exciting it's when the groundhog comes out of hiding
P laying in spring is a world of fun all the time I see kids having fun
R obin birds are singing and flying I love it when they sing their nice lullaby
I ce is a really good thing because spring is a really hot thing
N ights of spring are really dark but you could hear owls walking
and making their sounds
G oing outside in the spring seeing the flowers spring in the air
it's a beautiful thing to see

Alyssa Trujillo, Grade 3
Peck Elementary School, IL

My House

My house is huge.
My house is on a hill.
The color of my house is bright red.
The rooms are big.
My family is happy in the house.
I love my house.

Nilson Leka, Grade 3
Atwood Elementary School, MI

Spring

S ummer isn't here
P retty flowers
R elaxing season
I sn't snowing
N ot foggy
G reen grass

Ethan Tgiros, Grade 1
Floyd Ebeling Elementary School, MI

Ian

Ian
green eyes
likes to play
brother Keagan no sisters
soccer is my favorite sport
has a brown dog named Toby

Ian Cronkright, Grade 3
Barhitte Elementary School, MI

My Friend

I know a friend that I can always trust,
Morning, evening,
Day, night,
And all around.

When I need a friend,
I can always go to him.
He's a friend I can count on.
He is always there for me
When I need him.

His name is Mason R.

Evan Goldberg, Grade 2
Meadowbrook Elementary School, IL

A Cardinal

I saw a cardinal
It was so still
I thought it was pretend
Until it moved
It was redder than the one
My mom has on the ledge

Clea Hatzigeorgiou, Grade 1
Meadowbrook Elementary School, IL

Cats

Cats
White, brown
Eat, purr, sleep
It hisses when it's sad.
Pet

Porsha Hightower, Grade 3
Prospect Elementary School, OH

Sports

Playing games,
Outside
Inside
Racing
Tennis
Soccer
Softball
Sports are fun.

Andrew Alcazar, Grade 2
Queen of All Saints School, IL

The Mad House

A pig goes oink
A wolf goes howl
A rat goes squeak squeak
A dog goes ruff ruff.
But there is a cow that goes
Moo Moo Moo!!!
THAT'S ENOUGH!
Oinking, Howling, Squeaking, Barking,
And mooing!
Said the farmer
Geez this a mad house.

Joseph O'Bryan, Grade 3
Henryville Elementary School, IN

Happiness Is...

When I see my brother at school,
The basketball Shoot-out,
Playing with my cousins at school,
Climbing the rock wall,
School is cool!

Cole Boyd, Grade 1
Hamilton Community Elementary School, IN

Homework Excuses

It was ran over by a truck,
Someone threw it in the dump,
Then was invaded by a duck,
And landed with a thump!

It fell out of my bag,
On the way to school,
Then was abducted by aliens,
It was really cool!

It was put together,
By a camel from Egypt,
He was so desperate,
So decided to eat it!

My dad didn't know,
But cooked it on the grill,
I didn't cry in fright,
But it sure was a thrill!

It flew in the air,
And landed on a plane,
And was dropped into the zoo,
It landed in Malibu.

Avery Yalowitz, Grade 3
Decatur Classical Elementary School, IL

Family Pet

Dog
Great Dane
Black and brown
Big
I like my dog!

Carson Smith, Grade 1
James R Watson Elementary School, IN

The Fly
Once there was a fly.
He flew up in the sky.
And fell in a pie.
Hanna Sobhani, Grade 2
Ramalynn Montessori Academy, MN

Little Black Snake
Little black snake
Looks like a worm.
Slithering through the dark night.
Doug Childers, Grade 3
Lorain Community School, OH

The Sights I See in Spring
I see sunshine
shining on the earth.
I see birds all around
while I lay on the ground.
I see flowers growing
from the ground.
But today
don't make a frown.
Alex Sanchez, Grade 3
H. R. McCall Elementary School, IL

Dolphins
Dolphins jump
I can jump
Dolphins dive
I can dive
Dolphins eat fish
I eat fish
Dolphins can swim fast
I can swim fast too!
I like dolphins
Summer Dubrow, Grade 1
Webster Elementary School, MI

Baseball
Jackson likes baseball.
He loves to pitch the baseball.
Pirates are the best.
Jackson Hajer, Grade 2
Central Elementary School, IL

Snakes
Snakes can be 35 feet long
and they eat deer, ducks
and other mammals
and they are very dangerous animals
they are an endangered species.
Dominic Sobhani, Kindergarten
Ramalynn Montessori Academy, MN

Daphne the Puppy
Daphne the puppy runs really fast.
She licks her paws to keep them clean.
She's really fun and she's really cute!
I love Daphne the puppy!
Madison Rios, Grade 1
Stocker Elementary School, WI

Sisters
Sisters fight, sisters kick.
Sisters hate, sisters love.
Sisters talk, sisters scream.
Sisters hurt, sisters heal.
Sisters help, sisters tell secrets.
Sisters are always there for
each other…when least expected.
Halley Johnson, Grade 3
Henryville Elementary School, IN

Jobs
Michael says a NHL hockey player
Is what he wants to be.
Kyle would be a wrestler,
And Matt would go to China.

I'd like to be a soccer player man
And score a lot of goals.
I'd kick my soccer ball up in the air
And then eat ice cream that's good.

I score a million goals,
As many as I could.
And I would give free pops
To everyone who's nice.
Jason Bour, Grade 3
Atwood Elementary School, MI

The Last Soccer Game
On the hottest July day,
It was the
Last soccer game of the year.

I started on offense.
Whoooo!!! Sounded the whistle.
All the kids run
After the ball.

The referee blows the whistle for the quarter.

All kids charge for their water bottles,
And start to chug,
It was 5 minutes for break,
Then back in.

Whoooot!!! Sounded the whistle.
Number 12 was the kicker,
All kids run to get the ball,
And 10 scores right before the sound of a whistle.
And at last it was 1 to 2
We lost the game!

MacKenzie Zambon, Grade 3
MacArthur Elementary School, WI

Colors
Lime green is a popsicle on a hot summer day.
Green reminds me of a meadow when I'm running far, far, away.

Black are the scary knights that are fighting.
Red is hot fire! What a bright sight!

White is the sparkling snow falling from the sky.
Orange reminds me of a pumpkin pie.

Turquoise is the shining sky.
Gold are flying angels going by.

Yellow is the hot sun.
Brown is a hamburger with a bun.

What do colors mean to you?

Sam Ferber, Grade 2
Detroit Country Day Lower School, MI

Spring

S unshine is coming.
P ink tulips are growing pretty.
R ainbows are sparkling in the sky.
I ce is melting on the ground.
N ice weather is hot.
G iant worms are out everywhere.

Hannah Heppner, Grade 2
Stanton Elementary School, NE

Foods

Pizza,
Ham,
Hotdogs,
Turkey,
Cake,
Cupcakes,
Cookies,
Brownies,
Easter eggs,
I love food!

Caleb Baird, Grade 1
James R Watson Elementary School, IN

The Lady from Spain

There once was a lady from Spain,
Who came to the USA for rain.
She slipped in a puddle,
And broke her knuckle,
And now she's in a lot of pain!

Karthik Jasty, Grade 2
Detroit Country Day Lower School, MI

Swimming

I love to swim,
All freeform.
Not in a ring,
It doesn't have to be warm.

Dive and swirl,
Jump off of the diving board.
Twirl, twirl, twirl,
You don't need a surfboard.

Sheila Loosevelt, Grade 3
Decatur Classical Elementary School, IL

About Me

Emma
Short, fast
Running, balancing, listening
Loves to do gymnastics
Friend

Emma Jane Rohrer, Grade 2
Pope John XXIII School, IL

Happy

I am happy and
you are happy.
All of us can be happy.
If I am happy
you can be happy,
lots of people can be happy.

Miranda Ferrel, Grade 2
Holden Elementary School, IL

Trinity

Trinity, Renata
Nice, friendly
Lets me use her hair stuff
She is my friend and amazing
Friends

Renata Arias Garcia, Grade 2
Congress School, MI

My Cat

Prrr
Meow
I love her
Soft
Cute
My cat

Alex Williams, Grade 1
Bright Elementary School, IN

The Party

Get off the seat
Move your feet
Here's the beat
Get your treat.

Luke Stadts, Grade 3
St Clare Catholic School, IL

Life

Life is amazing,
but sometimes it's hell,
and sometimes it's heaven.
But always remember,
that you're a winner in life.
We have good people,
bad people.
We got different races,
and you have to respect them,
like they respect you.
Life will always be your best friend.

Larissa Ingram, Grade 3
Cityview Performing Arts Magnet School, MN

Tia and Grandma

Grandma likes cooking,
Tia likes playing,
Grandma likes cleaning,
Tia likes ruining things,
Grandma likes walking,
Tia likes running,
Grandma likes computer,
Tia likes watching TV,
Grandma wears red and pink T-shirts,
Tia wears red and green sweaters,
Grandma likes sleeping,
Tia likes barking,
Grandma likes the quiet,
Tia likes noise,
Tia is my best friend!

Alexandria Baysinger, Grade 1
Hamilton Community Elementary School, IN

Pizza

Thin
Thin
Crust
add the cheese, add the sauce
don't forget the pepperonis go
Down
Down
On the pizza!

Michael Wells, Grade 2
Country Meadow Elementary School, IN

I Am the World

I am the world.
Countries and states fall on me.
Water rushes on me.

I am the world.
People walk on me.
I have lava running in me.

I am the world.
The equator burns me.
Water cools me down.

I am the world.
Some places are hot some cold.
Fish cutting into my creeks.

I am the world.
Sydney Schaeffer, Grade 3
Mentone Elementary School, IN

Men and Fish Are Alike

Men and fish
are alike.
When they open their mouths
they get into trouble,
they say unknown words
that we can't understand.
When fish open their mouths
they get snagged by a hook!
That's how men and fish are alike.
Alex Mott, Grade 3
Weymouth Elementary School, MI

Animals

Animals
Animals play
Animals eat, sleep
Animals come in sizes
Animals are mammals
Eat, drink
Animals
Cute
Josie Rogers, Grade 2
Webster Elementary School, MI

Spring Is Nice

Honey is sweet
Berries are juicy
Mmm, Mmm, Mmm

Watch the flowers blooming
Crickets are creeping in the bushes
Shh, Shh, Shh
Riley Flores, Grade 2
Stocker Elementary School, WI

Rain

Rain
Storms
Rain
Thunder
Rain
Lightning
Rain
Wet
Rain
Puddles
Rain
Sprinkles
Zachery Howard, Grade 2
Patterson Elementary School, MI

The Puppy

Cute little puppy
barking at his master's door
wants to come in now.
Regina Gravrok, Kindergarten
Holy Family Home School, WI

The Best State

North Dakota is the best,
It's better than the rest.
It's where wheat and sheep are sold
And rodeos with bulls so bold.
I love to be in North Dakota.
I guess all farmers do...
That's why I wrote this poem
To tell all of you!
Michael Temple, Grade 2
Temple Christian School, ND

Dear Little Snow

Dear little snow, you look warm
Like a blanket, but,
When I go
Outside I feel really
Cold.

Oh little snow, oh beautiful snow
You're as white and as fluffy as the
Clear fluffy clouds.
Oh little snow don't go away
Cause
The kids still want to play.
Little snow I remember when I used to
Make snowmen, have snowball fights,
And made snow angels.
Do you need to go?
Oh little snow please tell me when you get an answer.

Heather Smith, Grade 3
North Intermediate School, MN

Soul Mate

My soul mate would be a modest wolf of gray
A companion for night, a companion for day
An amazing animal with fuzzy warm fur
And when I am down he would be the cure
What gleaming light would shine in his eyes
I see in my life, he would be the surprise
Once he touches my heart with his warm, gentle paw
I couldn't stand being apart; it would feel too raw
How I long for a soul mate just like him
As I stare at the sky on my balcony rim

Alexa Robertson, Grade 3
Rutledge Hall Elementary School, IL

Rainbow

R ed is the first color of the rainbow.
A mazingly beautiful.
I t is very pretty.
N ot always do you see a rainbow after it rains.
B eautiful.
O range is a color of the rainbow.
W ater helps make a rainbow.

Ben Lulich, Grade 2
Central Elementary School, IL

Snow Storm

B itter cold
L arge chunks
of snow and
I ce. It
Z ips and
Z aps all
A cross the
R oad in the
D ark night.
Rachel Patris, Grade 2
Meadowbrook Elementary School, IL

Snow

Snow is cold.
Snow is clean.
When it's warm,
Snow is wet.
Ivan Mathew, Kindergarten
Ramalynn Montessori Academy, MN

Jumping Rope Is fun

J umping rope is for our heart
U p and down and up and down
M y jump rope is purple
P umping up my heart

R eady to jump rope
O utside I am jumping rope
P eople like to jump rope
E very day I like to jump rope
Madison Haywood, Grade 2
Woodford Elementary School, OH

Winter

Winter makes me think of ice cream.
Ice cream makes me think of snow.
Snow makes me think of snowmen.
Snowmen make me think of people.
People make me think of friends.
Friends make me think of fun.
Fun makes me think of my birthday.
My birthday makes me think of winter.
Mara Peppin, Grade 2
Cedarcrest Academy, MN

Dogs

I love dogs
Soft dogs
Little dogs
Big dogs
Brown dogs
Any kind of dog.

A dog in a car
A dog in a house
A dog with the teacher
A dog with a mouse
I love dogs.

Black dogs
Brown dogs
Swimming dogs
Growling dogs
I love dogs.
Michael Saldana, Grade 2
Stocker Elementary School, WI

The Rat

I see a rat
it has a hat
his name is Matt
and that is that.
DamiAnne Piehl, Grade 3
Weymouth Elementary School, MI

Cookies

Cookie, cookies, cookies
Ring, ring, ring.
Out comes the cookies
With a ring-a-ling ling.
Yummy, yum, yum.
I like cookies.
Crunch, crunch, crunch.
Cookies, cookies,
I like cookies.
chocolate chip is the best.
Down the hatch
So good to eat.
Mason Wetley-Traver, Grade 1
Strange Elementary School, WI

Spring

The sky is blue,
The grass is green.
I'm so glad
It's finally spring!

Haylee Anderson, Grade 3
Bradie M Shrum Upper Elementary School, IN

Green

G rass swaying in the wind,
R eaching out to grab a green leprechaun.
E ach and every green thing is precious.
E xtinct green things are precious too.
N ature.

Madeline Elliott, Grade 3
Holly Elementary School, MI

Space

Mercury
the sun
Jupiter
Pluto
Asteroids
A comet
Venus
I-O
Saturn's rings
Earth
Mars
Uranus
Neptune
Olympus Mods

All these things make space awesome!

Joseph Platt, Grade 1
James R Watson Elementary School, IN

My Dog Alley

My dog Alley is really sweet
she's playful, funny and also neat.
She likes to jump
she likes to bark
she is my puppy no matter what.

Alyssa Wells, Grade 2
Country Meadow Elementary School, IN

The Moon and the Sun
The moon is like a balloon.
And is cool like a loon at noon.
At night the moon sings a cool tune.
And soothes a baboon.
Anish Aggarwal, Grade 2
Ramalynn Montessori Academy, MN

Dog
In the bright sun light
a dog outside digs a hole
for a bone to share.
Makayla Hunt, Grade 3
Chantry Elementary School, IA

My Dog and Me
Dog,
friendly, silly,
crying, jumping, loving
me sister dog, virtual dog
hyper, smart
Logan
Logan Shipe, Grade 2
Wethersfield Elementary School, IL

April
April is my birthday.
Animals come out from burrows.
Trees are growing leaves.
Flowers are blooming.
April is a lively month.
Nights are cool.
Come on let's play.
Trevor Willcuts, Grade 3
Valentine Elementary School, NE

What if the World Was All Water?
What if the world was all water?
Would we turn into fish?
Would we still drive cars?
Would we need a lot of sun
so the water could evaporate?
But, what if the world was all water?
Payton Pooler, Grade 3
Willyard Elementary School, OH

My Friends
My friends are sweet
They like to eat
They are neat.
My friends like to take a seat.

My friends run fast.
They like to pass.
They like to hug.
They drink out of a jug.

My friends like to fall
Also they run in the hall.
My friends like to sin
Also they like the lost and found bin.
Morgan Scheiber, Grade 3
St Timothy's School, MN

Sprained Ankle
I once sprained my ankle.
And on the next day,
I went to the hospital
to get an X-ray.
Chloe Henderson, Grade 3
Kyle Trueblood Elementary School, KS

Cub/Bear
Cub
Soft, cute
Playing, eating, crawling
Cave, sleeping, wild, swimming
Growing, running, hunting
Cuddly, funny
Bear
Mariah Crispin, Grade 1
Ladoga Elementary School, IN

Snowflakes
Snowflakes
Cold, tasty, white
Falling, sticking, melting
Snowing weather keeps me smiling.
Snowday
Grace Morris, Grade 3
St Clare Catholic School, IL

What I Love About You
I love the way you smile at me,
I love your face.
I love your smile, it makes it final that I love you so.
I love your face, it shines with grace so beautiful and proud.
I love the way you talk to me, it makes me feel so good and safe.
When you talk, you lock me up in your stories.
I love the way you skip rocks on the lake with me.
I love you.

Mya Lee Hanson, Grade 2
Cedarcrest Academy, MN

Blue
I think blue is dark and scary.
Sometimes though, it can be light and airy.
Blue is like our country on the flag that matches the sky.
Blue matches wide open spaces like the Earth and the ocean.
Blue is like spring and robin's eggs and Easter.
Blue is my favorite color!

Samantha Hughes, Grade 2
Bristol Elementary School, WI

When School's Over
I won't miss the loud, short outdoors time.
I won't miss thinking that it's Monday when it's Sunday.
I won't miss busy days.
I won't miss morning stuff.

I will miss Mrs. Fanning.
I will miss having entertainment at my table.
I will miss odd math.
I will miss late lunch.

Summer will be fun for one and all.
See you at school when it turns to fall!

Peyton Bainbridge, Grade 3
Atwood Elementary School, MI

The Fourth of July
Independence rains from the sky. Fireworks look like bolts of light. On the
Fourth of July I feel so good when fireworks crackle all night. A burst of purple
a burst of red a burst of green right over my head. Throughout the country we
celebrate this day. Our country's independence all night and all day.

Philip Anderson, Grade 3
Madison Central Montessori School, WI

Bugs

Bugs are cool to me!
Caterpillars, butterflies...
Creepy, crawly bugs!
Anna Stork, Grade 2
Anita Elementary School, IA

Frogs

F un frogs
R olling in the sun
O utside frogs
G arden hoppers
S pring frogs
Grace Marshall, Grade 1
Parkwood-Upjohn School, MI

Mittens

Mittens
Furry, silky, colorful
Warming, shielding, guarding
Your hands will never shiver
Hand warmers
Kara Pavliga, Grade 3
St Michael School, OH

Bunnies

Bunnies are cute and sweet
Bunnies are nice and neat
They're funny
They're bunnies
And I have two
Cute sweet
Nice neat
Funny bunnies
Cassandra Magana, Grade 3
Peck Elementary School, IL

Snow Plow

Snow plow
Enormous, awesome
Waiting, plowing, pushing
Blade for shoving snow aside
Snow pusher
Daniel Cobb, Grade 3
St Michael School, OH

Green Finger

Green finger, from sugar candy.
Green finger, is not so handy.
Green finger, is totally ugly.
Green finger, is so smudgy.
Green finger, can't wash it off.
Green finger, makes me cough.
Green finger,
Green finger,
Green finger,
Disappear!
Natalie Swanson, Grade 3
Greenvale Park Elementary School, MN

Horses

You can **H** ave lots of fun with them.
They're **O** utstandingly good jumpers.
They love to **R** ace against others.
There' **S** a lot you can do on them.
They **E** at apples and carrots.
They're **S** o much fun!
Allie DeRubertis, Grade 3
Noonan Academy, IL

Happy

Happy is when I catch a baseball.
When I'm happy I like to hit the baseball.
I cry when I get hurt.
I wonder all about what I will dream.
Maybe I'll dream about being a big hitter.
I will hear like a mouse.
I will play all day.
I will see like a bird.
I will catch the ball!
Happiness is playing baseball.
Drake Lansdell, Grade 2
Michener Elementary School, MI

Winter Is Here

The air is cold
The snow is whiter than a polar bear's fur,
It is whiter than my pearly whites
Snow covers the ground like a blanket.
Griffin Hader, Grade 2
Patterson Elementary School, MI

The Mall

Everything is there!
Pizza Hut
Panda Express
Come with me.
Eat and chow down!

Landry Kiser, Grade 2
McKenney-Harrison Elementary School, IN

My Dogs

I love my dogs.
I have four of them.
One is at my dad's house,
Three are at my mom's.
I love my dogs!

Tyler Reed, Grade 2
James R Watson Elementary School, IN

Leprechaun

I once met a leprechaun from Skock.
Every day he fell off the dock.
But whenever he saw the clock,
then he would go back to the dock.
That strange little leprechaun from Skock.

Christopher Brewer, Grade 3
Somers Elementary School, WI

Hockey

H it the puck.
O ut on the ice.
C oaches shouting to the team.
K eys help coaches open lockers.
E quipment keeping people safe.
Y ell for the people who score and win!

Samuel Weiss, Grade 2
Meadowbrook Elementary School, IL

April

A couple of ants march, march, march.
P airs of them go looking for lunch.
R unning all over but not too much.
I see them all over.
L ook, let's go for cover!

Paul Farlow, Grade 3
Southwood Elementary School, IN

Summer

S un shining in the sky
U nderwater games
M ovies are awesome
M eeting friends
E ating ice cream
R unning in the grass
Jannelle Rodriguez, Grade 2
Stocker Elementary School, WI

Funky Monkeys

Orange and brown bodies
With super long tails
And weird hair
That is super fluffy
Dancing around the tree
In crazy outfits
Doing the chicken dance
With lollipops in their hair
Charlie Evans, Grade 3
Broken Arrow Elementary School, KS

My Dolly and Me

I take my Dolly to school,
We jump into the blue pool.
I wish I could stay at school,
So I can rule the school.
Jordan Blackford, Grade 1
Monroeville Elementary School, OH

Chickens

Feathers, orange beaked
Laying, flying, running
Chickens protect their eggs
From foxes and other animals
Chick
Chandler Nennig, Grade 2
Stocker Elementary School, WI

Halloween

A dark loud night
Freaky, screaming, horrifying
A fun haunting holiday!
Alejandra Hermosillo, Grade 3
Jane Addams Elementary School, IL

The Eagle Soccer Game

It is 5 to 3.
Kick,
split, splat.
My team wins!

First place!
My own trophy!
So much fun!

Dad, Mom,
Grandma, Grandpa
clapped.
Took lots of pictures
of my team.

Eagle soccer rules!
Max Dahlin, Grade 3
MacArthur Elementary School, WI

Snowy Day

When you go outside
On a snowy day
You can see the snow falling
On the ground.
You can hear the trucks driving by.
You can feel the wind blowing
In your face.
You can feel the snow.
You can taste the breeze.
I like a snowy day.
Amber James, Grade 1
Woodford Elementary School, OH

What's in the Closet?

Green and furry mean and striped
What do you know!
It has three ears.
I used to pass with fear.
But, now I pass with my bat
I will open it later.
Well what do you know?
It's just my shirt, my scarf, and my hat.
LeAnna Venner, Grade 2
Patterson Elementary School, MI

Winter

Winter's tornado wind is fierce.
It rushes my hat off and howls in my ear like an owl.
The wind makes a noise, t-s-s-s!

Ben Hoskins, Grade 2
C W Neff Elementary School, MI

Family

Here is my dog running from my kitchen to my living room,
like he's a horse on a race track.
You can hear the jingling of his collar, like a bell.
His feet thump, thump, thump, but he is a very light little dog.

Here is my sister looking in the cupboard for something to eat.
I hear crackling like the crackle of the bag of chips.
The bag of chips was sour cream and onion.

Here is my dad making bacon in a frying pan.
One side is crisp and the other side is still fresh, not crisp.
Then he flips the bacon with a spatula.
He smells the crispy fresh crispy bacon.

Here is my mom making her bed. She puts the lightweight covers on first.
Then the comforter, that is very heavy.

Claire Thompson, Grade 3
North Intermediate School, MN

Bunny

B unnies are born in spring
U nder the tree the bunny is born
N eeds fur to survive the winter
N eeds white fur in the winter for camouflage
Y ou can buy bunnies at Petsmart

AJ Meindl, Grade 2
Central Elementary School, IL

Winter Fun

Winter tastes like hot chocolate on a cold winter day.
Winter sounds like the wind blowing a tree back and forth.
Winter smells like buttered popcorn on movie night.
Winter looks like snowflakes falling from the sky.
Winter feels like snow falling on my house.
Winter is fabulous!

Stephanie Gray, Grade 2
C W Neff Elementary School, MI

My Daddy-O

Daddy-o
He's nice
I love him
I'm his brown-eyed girl!!!
He's the best
He's cool!
Daddy-o

Shayna Cunningham, Grade 2
Webster Elementary School, MI

Postcard

Tropical, hot sandy beach
Dusk, sun setting
Late at night
Water rushing, night bugs singing
Seagulls flying overhead,
Colors roaming everywhere,
Stars beaming in the sky
Swimming, dancing
Next week!

Alyssa Billman, Grade 3
Coulee Region Christian School, WI

If You Look in a Book

If you look in a book
I'll promise you will find
Whatever you wish of.
I just
Promise, promise
Promise, promise
Whatever you are
Looooooking forrrrrrrr
Will come to you
I just promise.

Olivia Gauthier, Grade 2
Patterson Elementary School, MI

Spring Has Come

When the snow melts
Flowers start to bloom
I know that it's spring
I shout hooray

Chyanne Davis, Grade 2
Ladoga Elementary School, IN

Flowers

I love flowers
Pink flowers
Red flowers
Sun flowers
Yellow flowers
Any kind of flower.

A flower that is small
A flower that is big
A flower that is purple
A flower by a pig
I love flowers.

Growing flowers
Blooming flowers
Pretty flowers
Orange flowers
I love flowers.

Sophia Parra, Grade 2
Stocker Elementary School, WI

Adults

No adults allowed!
Could I put them in a cloud?
They're always so loud.
No adults allowed!

Sarah Ceurvost, Grade 2
Ramalynn Montessori Academy, MN

Shark

A quick meat eater
It has great, sharp, pointy teeth
Large and great white sharks.

Crimson Long, Grade 3
Henryville Elementary School, IN

Wondering to Jump

What is down there
Should I jump
Will I get hurt
Wondering, wondering
Should I do it?

Alicia Riehle, Grade 3
Greenbriar Elementary School, IL

Salami

I like salami,
I like salami,
It's hot,
It's my favorite,
I like my dad's salami,
It comes from deer,
I love my salami!

Ethan Wilson, Grade 1
Hamilton Community Elementary School, IN

Jordan

J umping in my bed I do
O reos are sweet to me
R ed is a pretty color
D rink pink juice
A pples are good
N uts are too!

Jordan Underwood, Grade 3
Holy Redeemer Christian Academy, WI

Summer Hot Days

Summer is here,
Right now!
Let's have some fun
And dance around.
What should we do?
Cold days are through.
Hopscotch, jump rope, run around,
do somersaults on the ground.
How about hide-and-go seek?
I won't peek.
You go hide.
I'll be over here.
Don't hide near.
Now we are done.
Let's have some more fun.
There he is.
Let's catch him.
I want ice cream now.
Does this stuff really come from a cow?!
I have to go.
I had fun playing in the sun.

Savannah Meadows, Grade 2
Meadowbrook Elementary School, WI

Rain

It sprinkles.
It thunders.
Scary Lightning.
Lightning toasts the TV.
Then when it's done
There's a rainbow
Pretty colors
Mom says
And
Dad says
When will the rain come again?
Elizabeth Vailliencourt, Grade 2
Patterson Elementary School, MI

Family/Together

Family
Kind, peaceful
Loving, laughing, playing
We like spending time together
Together
Jimmy Davis, Grade 2
Coy Elementary School, OH

Tick Tock Tick Tock

Tick tock tick tock
The chiming of the clock
The hands point throughout the day
To tell me when it's time to play
It tells me when to work and clean
At night it tells me when to dream
Tick tock tick tock
The minutes passed
Tick tock tick tock
School's out at last
When you go home to a clock
I guarantee you will hear
Tick tock tick tock
But when you go to bed
Because you were such a sleepy head
The pictures of clocks fill your head
You also hear the sound
Tick tock tick tock
Luke Conover, Grade 3
Noonan Academy, IL

The Nut

Looks
Like it
Is falling
From the

Fading
Sky
Amber Deardorff, Grade 2
Orchard Lane Elementary School, WI

Sharks

Sharks, sharks, sharks
Why do they eat a lot?
Why do they eat meat?
Why are they so mean?
Why do they swim so fast?
Sharks, sharks, sharks
Joshua Keller, Grade 1
Strange Elementary School, WI

Water

Fresh water falling
Falling into the ocean
Can see through water
Matthew White, Grade 3
Atwood Elementary School, MI

Fish

I had 7 fish.
2 dies.
Then I had 5.
Then 5 fish dies.
Now I have no fish.
Brandon W. Smith, Grade 1
Bristol Elementary School, WI

My Dog

My dog's name is Bandit.
He is big and nice.
He likes to play with me.
He makes me so happy.
I love my dog Bandit!
Ashley Clelland, Grade 1
Strange Elementary School, WI

Clouds

Clouds are gloomy they make me sad
Sometimes they are very bad
When it rains on a sunny day they come in anyway.
I do not like clouds at all
But sometimes I like them very small.

Chris Kaminski, Grade 3
Noonan Academy, IL

I Like

I like milk
    I like hot chocolate
I like the sun
    I like the stars
I like cows
    I like horses
I like deer
    I like bears
I like something but you will not like it
    I like something too but you will not like it
I like swimming
    I like swimming too
Yes I do
    I pick swimming too!

A.J. Holder, Grade 2
Hillcrest Elementary School, KS

My Chinchillas

Eat raisins
Like raisins
If you cuddle with them
You will not stop
Thinking about them!

Jack Ryder, Grade 1
South Monroe Townsite Elementary School, MI

Winter

W atching television
I ce skating
N ice warm cocoa
T urning the clocks back
E clipse on February 21, 2008 at 10:27 p.m.
R eceiving Christmas gifts

Zach Metzger, Grade 3
Woodford Elementary School, OH

Clifford

He's red
He's big
He's bigger than you
It's Clifford
And Emily Elizabeth
She loves him!
Arf! Arf!

Molly Graham, Grade 1
Bright Elementary School, IN

School Rocks

S weet
C ool
H ot toys on recess
O utrageous
O utgoing
L earn cool things

R ocks
O utstanding
C ool teachers
K icking soccer fields
S weet gym

Emily Waltrip, Grade 3
Hyatt Elementary School, MI

Frog

Frog
Slippery, slimy
Swimming, jumping, biting
Different colors and sizes
Cool

Jake Bundy, Grade 2
Congress School, MI

Snowstorm

Snowstorm like a giant magnet
Picking up snow
And throwing it
Down.
BOOM!
CRASH!!

Carson Ellerbrake, Grade 2
Norris Elementary School, NE

The World of Hope

Welcome to America
The freedom to the world,
People come to this place
To honor the family of the U.S.A.
Friend or foe, they come to this land,
Island of Hope, Island of Tears,
This land of freedom awaits you,
As long as my torch is raised,
It shall be open to all immigrants
That come to this very land.

Julia Chebbani, Grade 3
Detroit Country Day Junior School, MI

Happiness Is…

Happiness is…
When we're at school,
When we're at recess.
When we're at lunch,
When I get to ride my bike,
When I get to play with my friends,
When I get to ride my four-wheeler,
When I get to go with my friends,
Happiness is…

Brock Petre, Grade 1
Hamilton Community Elementary School, IN

Sunset

The sun sets behind the hill.
The moon rises.
The stars twinkle in the sky.
And the clouds turn blue and dash away.
And a shooting star shoots upon the sky.
And the water shines blue.

Alexandra Premo, Grade 2
Hyatt Elementary School, MI

Superman

Superman
Cape, powers
Fighting, flying, saving
Superman fights the villains
Superman

Kevin Sanchez, Grade 3
Charles Hammond Elementary School, IL

My Little Hand*

My hand is small
But my heart is big.
I'm growing up that is true.
But I will spend time with you.
I will grow up and have a family of my own.
But I will have you in my heart forever.

Lauren Bryan, Grade 1
Wethersfield Elementary School, IL
*Dedicated to my mom

Snowboarding Fun

My lucky snowboard,
Racing Mom and Dad,
Seeing who would win the downhill race.
BOOM! I ran into a snow fort!
CRASH! I ran into a tree!
Dad in front, Mom in second, I am last.
I try to catch up, now I am in 2nd place.
Mom is now last.
Dad is still in front of me.
I turn and turn to the jump,
Whoosh! Now I am in front. I win!!!
Now comes my Dad and then my Mom.
I am proud of myself.
My parents are proud of me too.
It is not about winning,
It is about having FUN!
And so is your family.
Now it is time to go home.
We had a great time.
My Dad said, that we would come back soon.
Snowboarding! It was real fun.

Austin Roberts, Grade 3
MacArthur Elementary School, WI

Spring

S unshine shines down at me.
P uddles are very big.
R abbits hop! hop! hop high!
I ce cream melts when the sun is shining.
N ip of the air I smell.
G rass grows so so high.

Amiah Francis, Grade 2
Stanton Elementary School, NE

Red

Red is like a shiny red apple.
Red is a bunch of cherries.
Red is a nice juicy strawberry.
Red is a big bouncy ball.
Red is a big bunch of raspberries.
I love red.

Kathryn Perri, Grade 2
Bristol Elementary School, WI

Stars

So beautiful so high
Twinkling in the sky.
Like little light bulbs
in the Sky
I wish I was
One in the sky.

Maia Tilly, Grade 2
Hillcrest Elementary School, KS

My Missing Tooth

I have a baby tooth
I wiggled my tooth
Nothing happened
I bit an apple and
My tooth wiggled and wiggled and
My tooth came out.

Isabella Barnette, Grade 2
Patterson Elementary School, MI

Sweet Peach

Roses are red
Violets are blue.
I'm sweet as a peach
And so are you.
I love to sing I love to do,
But most of all I love YOU!

Jane Frank, Grade 2
Central Elementary School, IL

Water

Water is fun
you can spray it at someone
you can even jump off a diving board

Haley Isenhath, Grade 3
Weymouth Elementary School, MI

Rain

Raindrops filling the sky
watching and watching
as you go by

Matthew Lauerman, Grade 2
Orchard Lane Elementary School, WI

Roses

My mom likes to smell roses
today the flower is bright
and pretty roses smell beautiful
flowers are my favorite.

Esha Aggarwal, Kindergarten
Ramalynn Montessori Academy, MN

Nintendo

N eat to play
I nside fun
N ever get up
T wo times as fun
E xercise your thumbs!
N ot challenging
D o not get up!
O n at my house.

Louis Roederer, Grade 3
Henryville Elementary School, IN

Softball

The ball flings across the field
Sounds clearing the air
Feet stomping around the field
Noises screaming
Someone calls out
The sound of a ball going in the glove
I love to play softball

Salena Garrett, Grade 3
Henryville Elementary School, IN

Bears

Big sharp claws to scratch,
Sneaking up for some honey
Good and delicious.

Tydor Kang, Grade 2
J C Hoglan Elementary School, IA

Imagine Me

Imagine me, a scarecrow.
Scaring the crow.
Standing on a stick.
If the wind blows me,
I will move back and forth, from side to side.
Made of straw, a farmer's hat and farmer's clothes.
Scaring blackbirds and crows at night
so they don't eat the vegetables.
That's my job!
Imagine me, a scarecrow.

Jonathan Jimenez-Trejo, Grade 2
Michener Elementary School, MI

I Wonder What It's Like to Grow Up?

At night in bed, I lay down in the biggest, darkest bedroom.
I think about myself when I get older,
I tried to go to sleep, but I cannot go to sleep,
I am too excited
Until I grow up
I draw pictures, I eat things, I scream
I cried last week, I danced, I played, I bit my nails
I'm reaching, I'm desperate,
My seeking, wanting to grow up
I dress up in my mom's clothes, but
I do not fit in her clothes
Maybe, I will not grow up
I don't want to be an adult
There is too much responsibility
My mom can handle things
But, it's just too hard for me
I ask my mom, "Do I look older?"
She said, "No!"
I feel happy
I do not want to grow up because I like myself the way I am.

Chyna Jones, Grade 2
All Saints Academy, OH

Friends

When you look at a friend you see not a person
but a graceful human being capable of anything and beyond.
When you look at a friend you see
love, compassion, and a kind gentle person.

Kate Bennett, Grade 3
Houdini Elementary School, WI

The Magic Pencil

I found a magic pencil,
that was stuck in a rock.
I pulled and I pulled,
and it just wouldn't unlock.
I got an idea.
I said a magic word,
and it came free.
I drew a picture
and it came to life!
What a cool pencil!

Henry Van Ess, Grade 1
Rock Ledge Elementary School, WI

What Will I Do?

What will I do?
I will play checkers.
No!
I will play in the backyard.
No!
I will play with my friends.
Yes!

Kolbie Lange, Grade 1
Woodford Elementary School, OH

Jesus

Jesus died on the cross
Because I was lost
When Jesus died, I cried
I am asking Him to come back
Because He is a good friend
Ask Him to come
To be a good friend again

Joseph Slaughter, Grade 3
Martin L King Elementary School, IL

School

S cholastic
C omputers
H omework
O n the playground
O nly nine more years
L unch!

Anya Malchie-Inman, Grade 3
Atwood Elementary School, MI

Butterfly

Pink. Blue. Green.
Butterfly's flying swiftly
Through the bright air
Showing off her wings.
Making swirls of colors
And beautiful sights.

Teidra Fuson, Grade 3
Emerald Elementary School, MI

Fall

Fall fall the best time of all
Watch the leaves fall.
Squirrels gather nuts.
And keep them in their huts.

Chris Mathew, Grade 3
Ramalynn Montessori Academy, MN

Spring

Spring is here
Spring makes flowers
Spring is great
Spring makes jeans turn into shorts

Austin Black, Grade 3
Suffield Elementary School, OH

Koze

There once was a monkey named Koze.
He loved to swing with little Rosey.
They flew from tree to tree,
While they ate bananas and cream.
When the sun went down,
Their smiles turned to frowns.
But they knew the next day
They would play, play, play!

Christy Swierczynski, Grade 2
Sleepy Hollow Elementary School, IL

Harvest Season

Dry and fun
Farming, picking, hauling
Goes to the elevator
Harvest Season

Danielle Carney, Grade 3
Mable Woolsey Elementary School, IL

Pal

I have a dog; his name is Pal
The cool thing about him is he has a penpal!
When he was young
he got stung
Once we thought he had rabies
but the other dog had babies
Pal is so nice and kind
He's so smart, he can play Mastermind!
One time, Pal read a book
Do you know how long it took?
He's so trained
sometimes I think he's a Great Dane
The good thing is he's a Golden Retriever
I'm so happy he's not a beaver
One time Pal took a trip
we all thought that he was sick
Do you know why I made this up?
I really want a pal that's a pup!

Chaitanya Vakil, Grade 3
Rutledge Hall Elementary School, IL

A New Cat

Cute
Pretty
Loud
Playful
Friendly
Soft
Scared when it storms.
She is the best cat in the world!

Megan Fike, Grade 1
James R Watson Elementary School, IN

Healthy Is...

Carrots,
vegetable soup,
salad,
watermelon,
grapes,
meat,
chicken,
I love healthy.

Schaide Maitland, Grade 1
Hamilton Community Elementary School, IN

Hershey

Hershey
Brown, large
Soft, protective, friend
He loves to run
Dog
Jacob Bergeski, Grade 3
Atwood Elementary School, MI

Ice Cream

Pecan ice cream
Buttery, delicious
Mouthwatering, crunching, freezing
It is very yummy and good tasting
Sherbet
Paige Murphy, Grade 3
Lorain Community School, OH

Football Day

Look at the kid run the ball
Look he got a touchdown
Look he caught the ball.
Brett Olsen, Grade 3
Henryville Elementary School, IN

Puppies

Puppies can please
You with ease.
Puppies scamper and bark,
And like to play in the park!
They love to chew your shoes…
PUPPIES!!!!!!
Ashley Clegg, Grade 2
Morley Elementary School, NE

Springtime

Springtime is here,
It's almost here,
When children come out to play!
They run around,
They scream and shout,
The flowers are blooming,
The animals are awake!
Tyra Harris, Grade 3
Lorain Community School, OH

Colors

Gray the color of the sidewalk
Red the color of a forest fire
Yellow the color of daffodils
Blue the color of the sparkling water
Black the color of nighttime sky
Green the color of grass
Pink the color of a flamingo

What's your favorite color?
Lindsay Cameron, Grade 3
Atwood Elementary School, MI

My Dog

My dog
sleeps and snores
every day
on his bed
because he likes it.
Cole Sawickis, Grade 1
Wethersfield Elementary School, IL

Candy

When I was little
I tried to take candy
From the bucket at home
I used to wake up early
Sneak a piece of candy
I never got caught
I am older now
So I know the consequences
Jaden Leffler, Grade 3
Woodlawn Elementary School, KS

Rainbows

Rainbows make me think of spring.
Spring makes me think of summer.
Summer makes me think of smiles.
Smiles make me think of friends.
Friends make me think of playing.
Playing makes me think of fun.
Fun makes me think of rain.
Rain makes me think of Rainbows.
Greta Kaardal, Grade 2
Cedarcrest Academy, MN

My New Cat
My new cat
black
kitten
short fur
size of a head
jumps out
from behind
a box
bites my foot!

Zane Hudson, Grade 1
South Monroe Townsite Elementary School, MI

God
He is merciful, graceful, powerful, and truthful.
Our creator, King, and Savior.
He created all of your ancestors and all of mine too.
He created all of the animals on Earth.

Brooke Bonts, Grade 3
Henryville Elementary School, IN

Swimming Lesson
Cold day, lifeguard watching.
Warm water, no diving board.
We are not going down the slide.
No goggles, not yet.
Wet swimming suits, no mask, no race till the end.
No fins or flippers, no underwater.
Really wet hair, dry towels.
We get in the lane lines. Have fun!
You get to do front crawl, and the backstroke.
What is the breaststroke?
No diving, swimming teacher helping.
Lots of chlorine, no water jets.
When you first start, you can't float.
A teacher puts down if you're a minnow.
If you are a guppy you have to go to the end.
You have to hold your breath, you have to blow bubbles out.
We don't have nose plugs. No earplugs, no dog paddle.
Big pool, the water going swish.
When you first start, you have to float on your back.
It's done at 5:40, we get to play a game.
Go to the locker room, time to get dressed, goodbye now.

Kylee Honor, Grade 3
MacArthur Elementary School, WI

Football

Football
Tackling an hard
Running tough
Hurting brave
Doing, going, kicking
Hard work
Touchdown.
Noah Hutchinson, Grade 2
Congress School, MI

Godzilla

Godzilla 2000
Cool
Blow fire
Punch
Fight
100 feet tall
I like him.
Trey Grigsby, Grade 1
Bright Elementary School, IN

My Dog Molly

Furry
Soft
White
and
Black
Funny
Messy
Friend
Aidan Brennan, Grade 2
Queen of All Saints School, IL

The Big Day

It was going to be a big day
Rain, rain, oh boy it rained
It is May
Oh did I have a fit
We got six inches of rain
What a big pain!
I will have to sit
Maybe I can learn how to spit.
Eli Hance, Grade 3
St Timothy's School, MN

Rain

Rain
It makes me
Cry like a baby
Rain
It makes
Me miss
My dad who died
Rain
It makes
Me scared
With the sound
Boom
Click
Clack
Rain
Boom
Click
CLACK
BOOM
HELP!
RAIN!
Reece Edwards, Grade 2
James R Watson Elementary School, IN

Basketball

Basketball, Basketball
Grab the ball and score,
then the crowd yells more! More! More!
They won the game and so it's true,
but now it's time to say goodbye to you,
but before you go we have to say
you have been a great audience today.
Erin Janssen, Grade 3
MacArthur Elementary School, WI

Apples

Apples are sweet, sour, and tangy,
with colors of yellowish-greenish.
They're as large as my hand or a dinosaur.
They're clean.
Smooth on the outside.
They can be crunchy, and they are good!
Breanna Sterenberg, Grade 1
Trinity Lutheran School, IA

Snow Shoes

Snow shoes
Large, flatfooted
Treading, shredding, walking
Big wooden frames keep you on the snow
Old fashioned snow boots

Matthew Piatt, Grade 3
St Michael School, OH

Space Shuttle

5
4
3
2
1

Blast off
The space shuttle
Was high in the sky
It vanished
5 days after
it took off!!

Where did it go??

Jacob Williams, Grade 2
James R Watson Elementary School, IN

A Poem

A poem is something under my bed.
A poem is something smelly in my locker.
A poem is something sour or hot.
But now you can see from me what a poem is.

Emerson VerBeek, Grade 3
Valentine Elementary School, NE

My Dad

Nice
Works
Jokes around
Snores
2nd boss
Funny
I love my dad!

Katie Eck, Grade 1
James R Watson Elementary School, IN

My Sweet Sister

My
Sweet
Sweet
Sweet
Sister
And
She is
Sweet
As a
Cupcake

NOT!!!!!!

Alec Millis, Grade 2
Pathfinder Elementary School, MI

My School

My school is so fun.
My teacher is nice.
When I have lunch,
I have some rice.
When my mom gave me some rice,
I found some dice.
I played with them,
all day and night.
I took them to show and tell,
and squeezed them very tight.

Oumima Djemaa, Grade 1
Islamic School of Greater Toledo, OH

Spring

Spring is here today
Having lots of fun
Flowers will be here

Ashley Munson, Grade 3
Suffield Elementary School, OH

My Mom

My mom
plays with me
in the afternoon
in the backyard
because it is fun.

Mackenzie Lindstrom, Grade 1
Wethersfield Elementary School, IL

My Best Friends!

My best friends are Reagan and Maddy.
They are always helping me,
They are fun, nice, tough, and
sometimes weird,
I love my friends!

Samantha Roth, Grade 3
Henryville Elementary School, IN

One Time

One time he was happy,
One time he was mad,
One time he was hopeless,
One time he was tickled,
One time he was sad,
One time he was in the hospital
and was feeling very bad!

Lindsay Roth, Grade 3
Kyle Trueblood Elementary School, KS

Beaches

swim swim
tan in the HOT sun
kids and adults see dolphins

Isaac Hummer, Grade 2
Waterloo Elementary School, IN

Mom and Dad

I love both so much.
Here is how much.
I love you more than the sun.
I love you more than the moon.
I love you more than anything.
That's how much I love you!

Thomas Coyle, Grade 3
Henryville Elementary School, IN

Snowflakes

Snowflakes are sparkly
And white
Lighter than a feather
Like white diamonds
Shattered right over the earth.

Jacob Bierle, Grade 2
Log Cabin Christian Academy, SD

Nathan

N athan is cool
A s Nathan talks he does faces
T alk about things
H angs on monkey bars
A s Nathan shoots he shoots guns and bullets
N athan has a mohawk

Cheyanne Elsner, Grade 3
Litchville-Marion Elementary School, ND

Red

Red looks like my blood when I cut myself.
Red smells like pretty roses in my grandma's field.
Red sounds like my four-wheeler when I start it up.
Red tastes like juicy grapes.
Red feels like my smooth shiny four-wheeler.

Aaron Phillips, Grade 2
Will Carleton Academy, MI

A-Z of Christmas

A pple cider
B unches of friends
C hristmas trees
D ecorations
E vents will happen
F riends together
G iving gifts
H ugs to each other
I nviting friends
J umping in the snow
K ris Kringle
L ennie gets presents and others do too
M any fun times
N obody should be sad
O ld people celebrate also
P eople get together
Q uiet times to sleep for Santa to come
R un to wake up Mom and Dad
S anta came and left presents
T rees to decorate
U ltra holiday
V ery cold during this time of year
W inter wonderland
X mas is just awesome
Y ou and me together
Z ip from house to house goes Santa

Lennie Johnson, Grade 3
South O'Brien Elementary School, IA

Spring

S unny days are here so we can play outside.
P uddles are all over the ground.
R ed roses are all around.
I nsects are crawling all over the place.
N ights are longer and warmer.
G ardens will come and grow high in the sky.

Matthew Hansen, Grade 2
Stanton Elementary School, NE

I'd Rather

I'd rather
eat cat litter
I'd rather
fly away
I'd rather
eat green beans
I'd rather
eat peas
I'd rather
do anything
than eat baked beans
I'd rather
eat cream corn
I'd rather
eat a marker
than eat
anything but chicken rings
I'd rather eat
blue jeans
than eat
salmon.

Timmy Renner, Grade 3
Henryville Elementary School, IN

Lamby

He is very old and white.
He's been my friend for forever.
He keeps me safe and warm.
Lamby knows my heart.

Brevan Mitchell, Grade 1
Woodford Elementary School, OH

Ice Cream

I ncredibly good
C hocolate flavor
E xtra caramel

C old
R eally good on a hot day
E xtremely great
A wesome tasting
M ore, I want more!!

Madison Barense, Grade 3
Woodside Elementary School, MI

Hummingbirds

sweet birds
buzzing through the air
buzz buzz buzz!
coming to get some sweet nectar
from a pretty flower
buzzing through the air
like a bee
swaying side to side
coming to get some more nectar
buzz buzz buzz!

Kaylee Crotchett, Grade 3
Henryville Elementary School, IN

When School's Over

I won't miss my homework.
I won't miss my loud bus.
I won't miss all the teachers.
I won't miss the classroom.

I will miss school.
I will miss reading.
I will miss my favorite teacher.
I will miss all of my friends.

Summer will be fun for one and all
See you at school when it turns to fall

Bradley Meyers, Grade 3
Atwood Elementary School, MI

The Squirrel

Squirrels, squirrels in a tree
Squirrels gathering nuts
And building huts.

Nitin Sagi, Grade 3
Ramalynn Montessori Academy, MN

Lions

Yellow
Growl
Mouths
Roar
Lion

Ally Nadiak, Kindergarten
Northfield Elementary School, OH

The River

A striking blue,
As it flows
A place where things are
I suppose
It runs, and runs
Sometimes they're big…
And sometimes they're small
You may fall in them
And be afraid,
But I always admire them

Kinga Hope Csikszentmihalyi, Grade 2
Madison Central Montessori School, WI

Rainbow

R ide oh ride in the car
A ll the time it's fun
I see a rainbow all the time
N ow it is gone
B ut I wish it never disappeared
O h I wish it was here
W ow that was fun!

Dailyn Shaffer, Grade 2
Jackson Center Elementary School, OH

Penguins

When penguins slip on the icy cold snow!
It gets me cold and when I come in
I get hot chocolate, it is…
    HOT!
       HOT!
          HOT!

Do you like penguins?

Logan Stein, Grade 2
Country Meadow Elementary School, IN

Astro

A stro is my puppy
S he is super smart
T rained by our other dog Turbo
R uns super fast
O ur puppy is very cute

Jurnee Silbas, Grade 3
West Broad Street Elementary School, OH

Pool
Blue
Jump
Warm
Summer
Pool
Chloe Kuenzel, Kindergarten
Northfield Elementary School, OH

Winter Walk
Sparkles in the snow
Sunny days out in the snow
Blue skies all day long
MiKayla Donohue, Grade 3
Midkota Elementary School, ND

Planets
I like Earth!
Air, people,
Animals, trees, water.
Jai Chadha, Kindergarten
Ramalynn Montessori Academy, MN

Our Earth
The Earth is white and
blue and green,
The prettiest flowers
you ever seen.

Deep blue oceans,
the tallest trees,
Birds, wild animals,
bugs and bees.

There's lots of people
with lots of cars.
We live on Earth,
instead of Mars.

So, hey everybody,
don't be mean.
It's up to us,
to keep it clean.
Alexander Rodriguez, Grade 3
Walker Elementary School, IL

Hot Wheels
These cars are fast.
They won't be last.
They can race and test
And be the best.
They can win.
The toys tracks
You can pile and stack.
With hammer and hoops
And loop-de-loops.
We race to be the
Best there's ever been.
Mark Nilson, Grade 1
Sleepy Hollow Elementary School, IL

Alex
My friend Alex
Is sweet
He is fun
He runs fast
He is polite
He has manners
Oh, how Alex is a
Good friend!
LeighAnna Passeno, Grade 1
Webster Elementary School, MI

My Cat
My cat
Is so cool
My cat
Is so rad
My cat
Is the
Coolest cat
I ever had
Egan Iwanski, Grade 2
Orchard Lane Elementary School, WI

Snakes
Snakes are so, so fast
On land, but slow in water.
Green, brown, camouflage.
Dakota Trondle, Grade 3
Atwood Elementary School, MI

Missy and Nelly

At home I have a tortoise shell cat named Missy.
Her two nicknames are Kissy and Bissy.

Missy got twisted up in some yarn.
It all happened in a smelly barn.

Nelly gobbles up just about anything such as birds and mice.
It really shocked my sister when she left a mouse on her rice.

Nelly's shade is really dark gray.
Her fur usually sparkles during the day.

Erica Everson, Grade 3
Little Red Elementary School, WI

Sacajawea

S hoshone American Indian
A dventurous
C ommunicated for Lewis and Clark
A mom to Pomp, also know as Jean Baptiste
J ourneyed to the west
A great help to the expedition
W alked to the Missouri River
E verything is important to her
A lways remembered by three mountains, two lakes,
    and 23 monuments built in her honor.

Macy Metzger, Grade 3
Dobbins Elementary School, OH

Beating My Sister in Soccer for the First Time

Burning hot humid day,
Sweating toes,
Soft ground rubbing against my feet,
I call a time out.

I get some water,
I feel the water trickling down my throat.

The game starts…
BANG! BOOM! I kicked the ball!
9 to 9!
I shoot one more! HURRAY
I WIN!!!

Jade Wang, Grade 3
MacArthur Elementary School, WI

Sierran

She sometimes feels
Happy, sad, funny.
Her favorite colors are
Red, purple, pink and green.
She is laughing, and loving.
And laughing.

She is a heart.
A loving heart.

Sierran Nutter, Grade 2
Norris Elementary School, NE

Softball

The mitt is tight,
The plates are white,
The bat is hard,
We had to guard,
The grass is green,
The team is mean,
The ball goes quick,
The timer tricks,
She caught the ball,
"Out!" the ump called.

Madeleine Martinez, Grade 2
Queen of All Saints School, IL

North Star

North Star
Beautiful, bright
Shining, twinkling
A truly wonderful sight to see
Heavenly body of light

Kara Rutkowski, Grade 3
St Michael School, OH

Spring

When the sun wakes up
and the flowers sprout,
then we wake up
and spring is here.
The snow is gone
and we have fun.

Delores Espinoza, Grade 2
Holden Elementary School, IL

My Friend Taylor

I have a friend named Taylor.
I've known Taylor ever since I was a baby.
He goes to Silver Creek Elementary,
and I go to Henryville Elementary.
We don't see each other often
but we are still best friends.

Tyler Blakley, Grade 3
Henryville Elementary School, IN

One Day the World Will Be a Better Place

One day the grass will be greener.
One day the sun will shine brighter.
One day the trees will grow taller.
One day war will be over.
One day the world will be a better place.

Taylor Evans, Grade 3
Willyard Elementary School, OH

Alex

Video game, funny
Friendly, happy
Halo 3, toy cars

My friend and I like to play video games.
Alex is my friend because he makes me laugh.

Isaac Black, Grade 3
Henryville Elementary School, IN

Stars

The stars at night
Shine so bright.
The one on the left is special
It is just right.

Maria Lopez, Grade 3
Bradie M Shrum Upper Elementary School, IN

Babies

Slobber on the floor
Throw food at the door
Cry when they are scared
Loves to pull hair
Pulls the dog's tail!

Zain Shetley, Grade 2
McKenney-Harrison Elementary School, IN

Summer

Summer is hot
With the breeze
Flowing through
My hair
It feels like
The air is
Flowing

Through
The
Sky!

Sky!

Noah Lockhart, Grade 2
James R Watson Elementary School, IN

Halloween Is Almost Here

Halloween is almost here
Ghosts and goblins are very near.
Kids are coming for their treats
They really like the taste of sweets.
The children's bags are to the top
They like to trade and like to swap.
Too much candy makes them sick
It can happen very quick.
The moon is out so shiny and bright
A lot of kids get scared at night.
Werewolves, vampires, spirits of the moor
Was that a squeak of the door?
Bats, black cats, witches, hags
I hope that curtain is supposed to sag.
Halloween is almost done
I can say that it was fun!

Gracie Majeres, Grade 3
Noonan Academy, IL

Pigs

This animal is stinky.
It lives at a farm.
It loves to roll in the mud.
It has a curly tail.
They are fat and strong.

Austin Voigt, Grade 2
McKenney-Harrison Elementary School, IN

School

S tinky buses
C ool teachers
H aving fun
O utside recess
O ne principal
L oving books
Emily Mooth, Grade 2
Arbury Hills Elementary School, IL

The Beach

The water sparkles.
Water is fun to play in.
The sunset is nice.
Samantha Grant, Grade 3
Jefferson Elementary School, MI

Silly Willy

I am silly
My name is Willy
I like money
I eat honey
I go to school
I am cool
I like swimming in the pool
Bryce Spoolstra, Grade 2
Arbury Hills Elementary School, IL

Xbox 360

I like my Xbox 360
I like playing it.
I like my STAR WARS game.
I like playing my racecar game too.
I like my Xbox 360.
Zachary McNew, Grade 1
Henryville Elementary School, IN

Pizza

Pizza
It is awesome
It can blow me away
It tastes really good and cheesy
Tasty.
Tyler Glass, Grade 3
Atwood Elementary School, MI

Rain

Rain Rain
You make me wet a lot
But I have fun anyways
I love the rain so much
I even go barefoot
Rain Rain
Don't go away
I like the rain so much
Hanna Frances, Grade 2
Patterson Elementary School, MI

I Find a Cat

I find a cat
Along the street

I take it home
And feed it milk

Meow
Meow
Meow
Emily K. Thomas, Grade 1
Bristol Elementary School, WI

The Sound of Doors

The sound of doors is
creak,
crack,
whiss,
shut,
close,
whamm!
Brody Rinehart, Grade 3
Weymouth Elementary School, MI

Spring

S inging birds
P laying
R aspberries
I ce cream
N ice outside
G rowing
Jessie Bunnell, Grade 1
Southwood Elementary School, IN

Name

A mazingly active dancer
B eautiful bright brilliant young lady
I ntelligent in reading: slow, fast, and in the middle
G racefully gleaming in the sunlight
A miable and amusing to others
I nterested in intelligent books
L ightly laughing when a joke is heard

Abigail Lester, Grade 3
Coulee Region Christian School, WI

Caring

Caring is when I care for my brother
so my mom can take a hot shower for work.
I wonder if James is going to throw a block at me.
"OUCH! James, don't throw blocks at me."
Now my nose is as red as a juicy red apple.
Taking care of babies is hard work, especially this one.
"Yeah, Mom's out of the shower"
Caring is like loving; it can't go away.

Tyler McAnally, Grade 2
Michener Elementary School, MI

Spring Is Here

S pring is here it's a very gray day with rain all day and little birds' songs.
P repare your eyes because flowers will be blooming in just a blink
    or a sip of a drink.
R eady for some ice cream and playing outside going to the park
    and having some fun.
I nside or outside spring is here so enjoy the freshness and have fun.
N o more winter clothes because spring is here so feel the breeze
    and have lots of fun.
G o outside and spare your eyes for spring is here so go outside.

Joanna Angelica Gonzalez, Grade 3
Peck Elementary School, IL

Spring

S pring is always fun.
P lay outside in the fun sun.
R ains a lot in the spring.
I love spring because you can ride your bike
N o one can play in the park after it rains.
G row flowers in your backyard.

Liliana Ruiz, Grade 3
Peck Elementary School, IL

Skyler Plays Baseball
One time I hit the ball far,
Then I hit it on a car.
Then I hit it on a fox,
Next it went into the box.
Skyler Scheid, Grade 1
Monroeville Elementary School, OH

Spring
I like to play outside
Play with a ball and a doll
All day to play in the sun
And I like to run
And take a book and cook
And run a mile to smile
And in spring I like to sing
And I see a mouse in the house
And I see a rainbow in the sky
Antonio Perez, Grade 2
Peck Elementary School, IL

Learning How to Swim
I learned how to swim
I bring both dogs in with me
They try to get out.
Brandi Zens, Grade 3
Weymouth Elementary School, MI

I Can't
I can't have candy corn for dinner?
No Scooby snacks?
No gummy bears?
No sour Skittles?
No cereal?
No popcorn?
How come?

No gum?
Or chips?

Just like in the past.
I never get the good stuff.
I just thought I'd ask.
Mitchell Tibbits, Grade 1
Northfield Elementary School, OH

What Is White?
Snow is white.
Light is bright white.
White is fluffy snow.
White is clouds.
Angel's wings are white.
I love white!
Alexander McGonegal, Grade 2
Bristol Elementary School, WI

Leaves
Yellow green and red
Leaves are different colors
Crunchy smooth and wet
Emma Hill, Grade 3
Marysville Elementary School, KS

The Chair
Back and forth
There it
Goes
The
Chair
Back and forth
There
It

Goes
Joe Robey, Grade 2
Orchard Lane Elementary School, WI

My Dog Baby
M y dog Baby rocks
Y oung dog

D ogs are awesome
O pposite of tall dog
G ood dog

B aby is a Pekingese
A mazing
B ites once in a while
Y ou know every dog rocks
Melissa Chaffin, Grade 3
Kyle Trueblood Elementary School, KS

Oh How I Love Gold
I would buy a gold house and
I would buy a gold crayon and
I would buy a gold statue of me and
I would buy a gold pool!

KeyJuan Scott, Grade 2
Holy Redeemer Christian Academy, WI

Tubing
Speeding through the water
Whipping out of the tube
Fun! Fun! Fun!
I'm scared
Pushing each other
Jerking side to side
Fun! Fun! Fun!
My life jacket is choking me!

O   C
U   H!!

Splash
Splash
Splash

I love tubing
Plop, plop, plop over the waves
Repulsive water in my mouth
Yuck!
Tubing, tubing
Splash
Splash
Splash!

Camille Holmes, Grade 2
James R Watson Elementary School, IN

Summer
Summer is fun, fun, fun.
Summer is cool, cool, cool.
I love summer.
Summer is fun, cool,
Fun, cool,
FUN!

Bridgette Wolf, Grade 2
James R Watson Elementary School, IN

Dogs

D igging holes in the mud
O utrunning mice
G rowling at predators
S triking after mice.

Hannah Nunn, Grade 3
Henryville Elementary School, IN

Little Kitty

Go to sleep little kitty
Sleep tight
I will be right here
Sleep tight
When the sun rises
You will know it's a new day
For having fun
As you may
Sleep tight

Maggie Socha, Grade 3
Hanover Elementary School, MN

Sisters

My sister's name is Sydney.
My other sister's name is Nikki.
They are not the same.
Sydney likes Barbies.
Nikki likes pigs.
Sydney is the youngest.
Nikki is the oldest.
And I'm squished in the middle!
Sydney goes to preschool
Nikki goes to college.
Sydney, Nikki and I

Jesse Schulz, Grade 3
Chaska Elementary School, MN

Paintball

I love to play paintball.
People like to play because
You get to run around.
I like paintball because I like to hide.
Paintball is my favorite sport.
I love paintball.

Jacob Lawler, Grade 3
Noonan Academy, IL

Sunrise

The sun is rising
Spreading over plants
Two people sit and
Watch the beautiful sunrise
Yellow, red, baby blue
How wonderful

Alexandra Hultman, Grade 3
Greenbriar Elementary School, IL

Race Car Driver

If I was in a race car,
I would drive it really far.
I would race it around the track,
until my tire gets popped by a tack.

Kyle Grossnickle, Grade 1
Trinity Lutheran School, IA

Softball

S oft
O h so awesome
F ly ball
T ough
B all
A mazing
L ofty
L eague.

Briana Odle, Grade 3
Henryville Elementary School, IN

Cars

Cars go fast.
They go faster and faster!!!
Like a rocket!! Faster!! Faster!!
Faster than you nanabooboo.

Michael Neu, Grade 2
Stocker Elementary School, WI

The Day!

The sun is going
The moon is up
The people go to bed
The night is beautiful

Cameron Sloan, Grade 2
Stocker Elementary School, WI

My Cat's Names
Katie, Katie, Katie
Fluffy, Fluffy
Elmer, Elmer
Markus
Sandy
Sunny
Feisty, Colorful
Sweetypie
Tiger, Leopard, Midnight
Spotty
Cloudy
Rose
I have a stranger cat and this is his name, Stormfur

Rosa Bontrager, Grade 2
Country Meadow Elementary School, IN

Jakob
Jakob
Funny, forgetful, happy.
Son of Chuck and Kim Sims.
Much loved by my dog, Floyd.
Sibling of Kali.
Wishes to head to Opening Day game.
Wants to be a baseball player.
Who is afraid of snakes.
Who feels happy, sad, mad, annoyed.
Who gives things away I don't use.
Who would like to sit in a front row seat with my dad.
Who enjoys my dad.
Resident of Wyandotte.
Sims

Jakob Sims, Grade 3
Jefferson Elementary School, MI

Snow Falls
S now is dancing down from the sky to the ground.
N ever ending little white puffs sparkle the city.
O ut come all of the children ready to have fun!
W ild wind blows and everyone shivers.
M any people have scarfs on and are running from the cold.
A large circle of dark clouds hover over the houses.
N ature is at work!

Olivia Brunning, Grade 2
Meadowbrook Elementary School, IL

Nature

Alligator swims in the water.
A bird lives in the nest.
A lion runs fast.
A rabbit jumps fast.
A butterfly flies in the sky.
Saul Perez, Grade 1
Peck Elementary School, IL

Cheerleading

I cheer
I dance
I do tumbling
I jump
I stunt
I am really good at it!
Ashley Miller, Grade 1
Bright Elementary School, IN

Brookie

Brookie
Fast, energetic
Doesn't bite, has a boyfriend
Likes to play outside
Loves me very much
Doggy
Elizabeth Sperti, Grade 2
Pope John XXIII School, IL

Ice Hockey

Ice hockey
Swift, chilly, slick
Challenging, entertaining
He hits the puck! Goal!
Face-off
Kilar Mariotti, Grade 3
St Michael School, OH

My Body

My body moves.
My body chews.
My body jumps.
It is like an ocean.
Natalie Newton, Grade 1
Bright Elementary School, IN

Cats

I had a cat and his name was Max
And he was really, really fat
It's sad to say but very true
We actually never met
Ally Duckro, Grade 2
Jackson Center Elementary School, OH

Beautiful Snow

The snow is falling
like little pearls in the sky
very beautiful
Beck Saine, Grade 2
South Suburban Montessori School, OH

Polar Bear

Polar Bear
Lying on the ice
Furry and mean
Vicious and hungry
Polar bears
Silently stalking
The seal.
Kim-Dan Doan, Grade 3
Shorewood Hills Elementary School, WI

Colors

Aqua tells me of the sea.
Yellow is the sun, hair, and a bee.

White is my pillow I sleep on at night.
Green reminds me of my buggy light.

Red is the color of my love.
Lavender is the song of my favorite dove.

Pink are the petals of a flower.
Gold is God's strength of power.

Beige is the color of my skin.
Silver reminds me of a fishie's fin.

What do colors mean to you?
Julianna DiPasquo, Grade 2
Detroit Country Day Lower School, MI

Summer

Summer is the
Time for leaves,
Flowers, ice cream,
And the hot sun.
Summer is when
The birds and
Animals come out
In the sun.
I love
Summer.

Kaitlyn Blevins, Grade 2
James R Watson Elementary School, IN

Delays

Delays, delays
How I love delays!
I get to sleep in.
I get to play
With my family.
How I love delays!

Samantha Benbow, Grade 1
James R Watson Elementary School, IN

Spring

Spring is beautiful
Spring is nice
Spring is twinkling in your eyes
So come on out and play
And we'll celebrate this beautiful day
Flowers are growing and kids are playing
And the sun is shining
Ohhhhhhhhhh spring, spring, spring
Birds are chirping
Bees are buzzing
What a beautiful day!

Hayden Winking, Grade 1
Meadowbrook Elementary School, IL

Gym

G ym is sometimes fun
Y ou will like it
M y sisters like it too

Bryden Mathis, Grade 2
Jackson Center Elementary School, OH

A Box of Crayons

C olors of the rainbow
R eady to draw or doodle
A lways keep a box or two
Y ellow, red, green and blue
O n the walls and on the mat
N ever color on your dad's old hat
S o colorful and bright

Sharyn Serbet, Grade 3
Broken Arrow Elementary School, KS

Winter

Winter is white.
It sounds like bells.
It tastes like cocoa.
It smells like steam.
It looks like a blanket.
It makes you feel cozy.

Sara Gillespie, Grade 2
Wethersfield Elementary School, IL

Zebra

Striped, fast
Drinking, eating, running
Horse

Jade Jarchow, Grade 2
Thayer Central Elementary School, NE

Ice Cream

Yummy
Sweet
With a cone
They are good
Ice cream

Katie Roberts, Kindergarten
Northfield Elementary School, OH

Little Panda

When Little Panda climbs on trees,
He playfully swings.
He eats juicy green plants.
Plants are good for Little Panda.
Yum-yum.

Jenna Gianakos, Grade 1
Stocker Elementary School, WI

Lightning Bug

Miniature moving suns
Light up sky
With your

Amazing
Glow

Sammie Lundin, Grade 2
Orchard Lane Elementary School, WI

The Hamster

Hamster
Cuddly creature
Twitching little nose
Cozy, cottony, fluffy, fuzzy
Cute

Andrew Gable, Grade 3
Atwood Elementary School, MI

Winter

Winter is cool.
You can go skating on ice,
Have a snowball fight,
Make a big fort, and
Throw snowballs at your friend.

Logan Henry, Grade 2
Patterson Elementary School, MI

I Can't Sleep

Mom!!
I can't sleep
It's too early,
Let me stay up,
I had too much candy,
I had a lot of caffeine
I can hear the train,
It's too loud
The lights are on,
The radio is on full blast,
I what?
I don't have to sleep?
In that case, I'm going to…
ZZZZZZZ

Hunter Snell, Grade 3
Smithville Elementary School, OH

The Gnarl Monster

The gnarl monster lives under my bed.
He comes out at night and messes with my head.
It puts it in knots, tangles and snarls.
That's why the monster's name is gnarls!

It makes me mad, when I wake up.
My hair is in snarls.
And it hurts when I brush my hair.

Maria McGrath, Grade 2
Cedarcrest Academy, MN

Dancing

Spinning
Plieing
Pointy feet
Finally I did it

I made
Ballet class!!!

Makenzie Brown, Grade 1
South Monroe Townsite Elementary School, MI

Summer Days!

Daisies are as colorful as the sky is blue!
The world is colorful — just like you!
The days of winter are almost gone.
"Get up and welcome the beautiful, summer days."
Because the summer is here and the winter is gone, we say,
"Good-bye slushy, frozen days!"
The sun is up and the slushy slop is gone.
So give the summer a big welcome back to the world.
Welcome, summer days!

Dianna Williams, Grade 3
Ken O Sha Park School, MI

Patton School

The school is big and nice.
I like my teacher and my friends, my principal too.
There is kindergarten — 8th grades.
I am in 3rd grade.
We have lunch tickets and we don't have to pay.
I love my school so much.

Tanisha Luther, Grade 3
Gen George Patton Elementary School, IL

Zeb

Zeb is my puppy.
I love Zeb so much.
I feed, water, walk, and play with Zeb.
I have lots of feelings for Zeb.
I have had Zeb since I was seven.
Zeb is one year old.
Zeb runs away.
Once Zeb almost got ran over
and attacked by another dog.
When Zeb almost got ran over
I screamed and kicked my sister.
Zeb is my baby.

Haley Jena, Grade 3
Henryville Elementary School, IN

Friends

Two friends together
sitting on a tree playing
games and having fun.

Joshua Kazan, Grade 2
Meadowbrook Elementary School, IL

Blanket

Blanket
So cuddly
Little blanket
With me
In
One
Little
Flash

Alyssa Nelson, Grade 2
Orchard Lane Elementary School, WI

Being an Umbrella

If I were an umbrella…
I would open my wings,
And cover the people.
I would take them all
The way home keep them
Nice and dry.
If I were an umbrella.

Brenda Raygoza, Grade 1
Strange Elementary School, WI

My Brother

All my brother does is play games.
He doesn't listen to my mom.
He gets into trouble!

Zachary M. Tracy, Grade 1
Bristol Elementary School, WI

Waterfalls

Waterfalls rush down
Blue crystal colored water
Waterfalls, misty

Ashlee Mecklenburg, Grade 3
South Prairie Elementary School, IL

Gum

Chewy
Sour, yummy
Buy it, stretch it, and eat it.
It feels like heaven in my mouth.
Taste it.

Joanna Taylor, Grade 3
Atwood Elementary School, MI

Me

Connor
Son of Kevin Burke and Sue Burke
Much loved by mom and dad
Wishes to have gold
Wants to be a dirt biker
Who feels silly
Likes flying
Enjoys movies
Resident of Wyandotte, MI
Burke

Connor Burke, Grade 3
Jefferson Elementary School, MI

Spring Wind

The wind slaps my face
Cools off the kids
Whistles a pretty little song
Makes trees move
Creates a delightful spring day

Laura Winkler, Grade 3
Coulee Region Christian School, WI

Mad

Mad is when my face gets red like a cherry.
This morning my mom sounded
like a bear when she was yelling.
I tripped over my little sister's toy
and then I was as angry as an angry alligator.
I went downstairs to get my breakfast
and my brother pushed my face in the cereal.
Then I was steaming hot
like a hot pepper with hot sauce.
I screamed like the loudest whistle ever.
I wonder what is going to happen next.
Mad is when my face gets red like a cherry.

Xavier Coon, Grade 2
Michener Elementary School, MI

Tears

Tears are little as a crumb
Tears are like rain,
They show feeling.
Like when mom moved away
It was like a ghost. It haunts you.
It feels melancholy
And scary.
I can't stop
C
R
Y
I
N
G
When will the tears go away?

Colin Becker, Grade 2
James R Watson Elementary School, IN

Cookies

I like cookies.
Cookies are great.
I like oatmeal, M&Ms,
Chocolate chip cookies
I like cookies.
Cookies are great!

Dorian Arnold, Grade 2
Shorewood Hills Elementary School, WI

Ladybugs

I love ladybugs,
So funny and cute!
They fly in the sky,
And they have
A black and red suit.
Lily Evans, Grade 1
Strange Elementary School, WI

Pizza

Pizza
Pizza
Yum
Yum
Some with cheese
Some that please
Some with pepperonis
Oh
Pizza
Makes me think
I'm in heaven
with topping!
I love pizza!
Emma Bush, Grade 2
Pathfinder Elementary School, MI

Not Just Any Horse

Gallop Mustang, gallop!
Faster than a thoroughbred
Bigger than a Clydesdale
Stronger than a Shire
Gallop Mustang gallop!
Head of the herd
Higher than a bird
More beauty than an Appaloosa
Gallop Mustang gallop!
Lila Goehring, Grade 3
Walls Elementary School, OH

Snowflake

Gently a snowflake
falls from the sky and lands
on my chin to melt.
Luke Stortenbecker, Grade 3
Chantry Elementary School, IA

I Love Cats

They are all colors,
gray, black, white
orange and some are
tiger striped and
yellow also.
Some have long
or short hair.
Their claws are long
and sharp.
Meow, meow, meow,
Purrrrrrr.
Jacob Badger, Grade 2
Waterloo Elementary School, IN

Apple

Good leaves
sweet green yellow red
sour smoothie
healthy fruit
round juicy circle
Briana Aguilar, Grade 3
Somers Elementary School, WI

Watching Fred

I sit and cook a steak.
While my back starts to ache.
I want to go to bed,
But I have to watch my son Fred.
His friend comes over to my house
While they play with their
New Mickey Mouse clubhouse.
Noah Giacomantonio, Grade 2
Hyatt Elementary School, MI

Puppy/Dog

Puppy
Soft, fun
Running, playing, sleeping
Mom, box, outside
Swimming, hunting, barking
Large, strong
Dog
Emily Tyson, Grade 1
Ladoga Elementary School, IN

Winter

Winter tastes like a hot chocolate swirl.
Winter sounds like a flute, oh, it's joyful music!
Winter smells like water from a lake.
Winter looks like a big white puffy cloud...very fluffy!
Winter feels like big lumps of sugar...delicious!
Winter is fabulous.

Lydia Williams, Grade 2
C W Neff Elementary School, MI

Spring Spring I Love You

S pring spring I love you with your beautiful
flowers and kids
P laying outside it looks so beautiful
Spring spring I love you you're dripping
R ain looks so beautiful when it hits
the window you hear the rain
I nside or outside you can hear
the rain there is
N othing better than spring then when
the rain stops you can
G o outside and play with other
kids that are playing outside too.

Diego Padilla, Grade 3
Peck Elementary School, IL

Pink

Pink looks like the sun in the summer when the sunset comes.
Pink smells like a beautiful rose.
Pink sounds like soft classical music playing at night.
Pink tastes like a cookie that just got baked.

Alivia Rebeck, Grade 2
Will Carleton Academy, MI

Golden Bull

A bull with horns
like bright Aztec gold.
Fur like very ripe oranges.

Eyes that flash topaz
like two twin suns
And a tail like a colorful
rainbow after a spring rain.

Maximilian Harold Murat Ohnesorge, Grade 3
Shorewood Hills Elementary School, WI

My Mom

My mom is pretty,
Smart and fun,
I laugh with her,
Under the sun.
We bake cupcakes,
She gives me one,
I really adore
My lovely mom.

Liz Rodriguez, Grade 2
Queen of All Saints School, IL

Summer

It is hot outside.
We like to play in the sun.
I can go swimming.

Ethan Talbott, Grade 1
Peoria Hebrew Day School, IL

Fall

The trees turn dark red
like flames in a new fireplace
warming up our body.

Justin Walters, Grade 3
St Clare Catholic School, IL

My Dad

Motorcycle
Fast
Catch me
Helmet
Race
Field
I like to race
With my dad.

Drew Rinck, Grade 1
Bright Elementary School, IN

A Rainy Day

It is a rainy day.
There is rain on the trees.
We are having a rainstorm.
I need an umbrella.

Michael Rayborn, Grade 1
Holden Elementary School, IL

Bats

Bats are black.
Bats hang upside down.

Bats are scary.

Bats are cool.
Bats are good.

I like bats!

Hanna Harvey, Grade 1
James R Watson Elementary School, IN

Horses

They let you ride.
They are not like sea horses.
The horses have four legs.
Sea horses have zero legs.

Drake Beber, Kindergarten
McKenney-Harrison Elementary School, IN

My Pet

My dog plays with mice.
I have one pet you see.
He loves me.
And I love him.
His name is Amos.
He is nice you see.
We are a perfect family.

Olivia Ruiter, Grade 2
MACCRAY West Elementary School, MN

Bugs

I really like bugs.
If I could I would give them hugs.
I like watching bees,
Go to their knees.
Searching for flowers,
To gather its powders.
There is also a fly.
But to that bug I say bye-bye.
That is why I really like bugs.
But I'd only give some bugs hugs.

William Szkwarek, Grade 3
Decatur Classical Elementary School, IL

Yellow
Candy
Books
Balls
Markers
Crayons
Scissors
Peaches
I like yellow!

Sarah Williams, Grade 1
James R Watson Elementary School, IN

Lightning, Rain, and Thunder
Lightning is so bright
I don't like it
CRASH
I don't like lightning
CRASH
BOOM
CRASH

I'm going to my room!
CRASH
I'm going to my room!
Boom!!
Mommy, I'm scared!

Josh Rowe, Grade 2
James R Watson Elementary School, IN

Summer Time
I won't miss the loud noisy bus.
I won't miss homework.
I won't miss school food.
I won't miss bloody teeth.

I will miss Mrs. Strait and the teachers.
I will miss reading books.
I will miss specials.
I will miss my friends.

Summer will be fun with cousins and friends,
See you at school when it returns fall again.

Madelyn Cooper, Grade 3
Atwood Elementary School, MI

Dog

Cute
Soft
Bark
Eat
Dog
David Sabol, Kindergarten
Northfield Elementary School, OH

Never

Never be mouthy
Never do drugs
Never smoke!!!
Never smack
your mom
for a snack
Never drive
unless you're
a grown up
Plus never be mean
Katie Butler, Grade 2
Pathfinder Elementary School, MI

Abraham Lincoln

ABRAHAM
16th president
Honest, peaceful, hard worker
Who loved his family
Who believed in freeing the slaves
Who wanted peace
Who said: "I can stop slavery"
LINCOLN
Meghan Smith, Grade 2
Our Lady of Lourdes School, WI

My School

School,
One for kids,
Only for play,
For work,
For fun,
I like my teacher.
I like my school.
Laifei Leonard, Kindergarten
Ramalynn Montessori Academy, MN

My Friend

My friend is funny
My friend is nice
My friend likes to play bowling
My friend likes to play basketball
Kayla O'Connell, Grade 2
Arbury Hills Elementary School, IL

Can You Guess?

I am short.
I eat cheese.
I live in a house.
I am gray.
I am in the wall.
I have big ears.
Can you guess what I am?
I am a mouse!
Jesus Sosa, Grade 1
Strange Elementary School, WI

Tiger

Tiger
Tan, loud
Fighting, catching, eating
Big cat
Austin Beck, Grade 2
Thayer Central Elementary School, NE

Fall Blows In

Fall blows in
With the sound of crunching leaves
And kids playing in the leaves
On a cool breezy day
With the feel of the wind
On your face
Carson Reichardt, Grade 3
Hanover Elementary School, MN

Winter

Oh the long dreary days of winter,
are nearly over
cloudy skies gloomy eyes
to the sky wave goodbye
Joey Keane, Grade 3
Noonan Academy, IL

Friends

I have fun with my friends.
I think with my friends.
I read with my friends.
Getting good grades and having your friends there to congratulate you.
But the best part about having friends is having fun.

Kylie Oleff, Grade 2
Meadowbrook Elementary School, IL

Cheer Day

Pompoms waving
pretty different colored dresses, arms in the air, shoes tapping
Jade and I were partners in dance and song!
Stage fright, hair bouncing,
different colored pompoms,
judges smiling, everybody smiling

Red and blue wall paper on the gym walls
floor getting scratched
colorful shoes, baggy pink shorts
red dress, purple skirt,
Hanna Montana song booming through the speakers!
People clapping, buzzers buzzing

BEEP, the song is over the crowd goes wild
Moms and dads cheer and hug their children!
Children are so proud of themselves…
Everyone wants to do it again!
All of the kids are running down the slippery parking lot,
Moms and dads are yelling at children not to run
People are everywhere! A wonderful evening!

Jade and I were partners in dance and song!
Now we are off to parent teacher conferences

Savannah Meier, Grade 3
MacArthur Elementary School, WI

My Job

I have a job in the summer.
It makes me want to buy a Hummer.
I have to sell lemonade to share the money.
It makes me want to eat some honey.
Then I stop selling lemonade to count up the money!

Alyssa Handspike, Grade 2
Schavey Road Elementary School, MI

Animals

Animals animals on the ground
So many animals to be found.
Animal animals in the air
Animals animals everywhere.
Animals!

Claire Demay, Grade 2
Ramalynn Montessori Academy, MN

Trees

Trees in the forest blowing
As they swerve in the air.
Then the canopy is blowing the leaves
And making music like a flute.

Jack Lee, Grade 2
Norris Elementary School, NE

Puppies

P aws are a little tapping
U sually gets in mischief
P ower to run
P ractice jumping rope
I nstead of working playing
E ats a lot of bones
S weet as a pie.

Ashley Falzarano, Grade 3
Atwood Elementary School, MI

Kevin Burping

Kevin burped up a flower,
And a rabbit too.

Really, yes, really —
All of a sudden, burp!

He burped up a treasure chest.
Another burp…
This time a chocolate bar.

Oh, my!
Now a tornado!@!*!

Isn't he weird???

Kevin Jack, Grade 2
St Robert Bellarmine School, IL

My Brother

My brother Joseph.
I love my brother.
Because he is so cute.
He makes me laugh
All the time,
And I like it!

Joanna Navarrete, Grade 1
Strange Elementary School, WI

School

Getting up so early!
Tired
Don't want to get up!
Please!
Please!
100 more minutes!?
No! But why?
I said so
2 minutes
No!
Ok
I'm going back to sleep.
GET UP!!!!!

Morgan Veenstra, Grade 2
Pathfinder Elementary School, MI

Sports/Games

sports
football
playing sports
is the best fun
games

Esme Vega, Grade 3
Phillip May Elementary School, IL

snow

snow is
a magic cloud
that you
can walk on
and a blanket
to bees

Lili Berg, Grade 2
Orchard Lane Elementary School, WI

Can I Have a Cookie?

"Can I have a cookie?"
Joey asked one day.
"I'll die without a cookie!"
He begged and begged all day.
"Have eleven or less," his mother finally said.
But Joey grabbed twelve instead.
At the first bite he glanced up and frowned.
"EEW! LEMON!!"

Ellen Gilbert, Grade 2
Greenbriar Elementary School, IL

My Shadow

My shadow creeps besides me,
While I'm walking down the hall,
I have to say my shadow,
Stands creepy, kind of tall,
It creeps while I am walking,
It copies what I do,
It seems quite shocking,
It looks like it wants to cook me in a stew.

Gabrielle Familara, Grade 3
Atwood Elementary School, MI

Pay Me Krab! — A SpongeBob Poem

Pay me money, pay me cash, pay me check!
I'm a stingy krab,
Just pay me Pay Pal or Visa,
Whatever you please
Pay me however, I don't care.
Pay me with your underwear!
Please PAY ME!!!
Come on down to Krusty Krab
Eat some patties, right off the slab
Pay me some dough
Money, money, MONEY!!!
Oh, no — a quarter on the floor?
I'll pick it up and never spend it
I need a cheer!
I like MONEY!!!
Find some and I'll never spend it,
Not there, not here.

Ben Miller, Grade 3
Matthew Duvall Elementary School, OH

Ocean

The ocean is like the sky
and the fish are like the clouds
and the waves are like birds
and the sand is like the sun.
Olivia Mangan, Grade 2
Pathfinder Elementary School, MI

Basketball

I like basketball.
Play with my dad.
We shoot hoops.
My dad always wins.
Dad shows me how to play.
Someday I will win.
Trenton France-Leaf, Grade 1
Woodford Elementary School, OH

Dogs

Food
Soft
Walk
Feed them
Dogs
Cory Huffman, Kindergarten
Northfield Elementary School, OH

Cats

Cats are really cute
Little tails very soft paws
Cats meow so loud
Sarah Ray, Grade 3
Atwood Elementary School, MI

Sunshine

When I look up
it puts sparkles in my eyes.
It smiles at me,
and I smile back.
It smiles very happily at me.
It shines everywhere
but seems as though it
is only above my head.
Cia Krall, Grade 3
Deerfield Elementary School, MI

Baseball

B aseball is a fun sport!
A wesome at hitting the ball!
S uper at catching.
E xcited about baseball.
B oom! He hits a lot of balls!
A mazing at hitting.
L ove hitting home runs.
L ove hitting.
Jason Bageanis, Grade 2
Central Elementary School, IL

Nature Walk

Walking in the woods
That is a lot of fun
You will see nature
Colton Mason, Grade 3
Mable Woolsey Elementary School, IL

Ice Cream

I like it
It is good
My mom always
Buys it for me
Cookie dough
Ice cream
Zachary Westbrooks, Kindergarten
Northfield Elementary School, OH

I Am a Monkey

I am a monkey,
You can see me at the zoo,
I swing from branch to branch.

I am a monkey,
I love bananas,
The zookeepers feed bananas to me.

I am a monkey,
I am brown
And I have a long tail.

I am a monkey
Marisha Bahney, Grade 3
Mentone Elementary School, IN

Sadness

Sadness is when nobody wants to play with me.
I feel all alone with no one around me at all.
I hope I will never be lonely again.
I dream that I will have a lot of friends and never be lonely.
I worry no one will want to play with me.
I always play alone every day.
Sadness happens to everyone.
Sometimes I feel as lonely as a cat in winter.
Sadness is a lonely cloud.

Eddie DeForest, Grade 2
Michener Elementary School, MI

My Family

Here is my sister chasing my cats in the hallway.
She runs as fast as she can trying to grab the cats.

Here is my mom in the kitchen cooking macaroni.
She pours the noodles in the pan.
Little sprinkles of water splatter out of the pan.

Here is my cat jumping on the counter.
He sees us and jumps as fast as lightning.

Carter Hrdlicka, Grade 3
North Intermediate School, MN

My Grandpa

My grandpa had a heart attack.
I hope I can see him a million more times.
What to do without Grandpa?
I won't give up in sports even if they're taller than me.
I can't wait to see my grandpa
Up in heaven.

Noah M. Coleman, Grade 1
Bristol Elementary School, WI

Blue

Sometimes blue reminds me of jeans.
Everywhere I look I see blue.
Blue can be light, dark, or just blue.
Blue and gold are my favorite colors.
It reminds me of the Earth, the sky, and a blue T-shirt.
It makes me think of the 4th of July.

Josh Leslie, Grade 2
Bristol Elementary School, WI

The Carnival

I love going
to
the carnival,
It is fun.
I love
the cotton candy,
popcorn and games,
I like,
the Ferris Wheel,
It goes
up and down,
It goes
fast and slow,
I like
the roller coaster,
It goes
high and low,
I hope I go
back soon.

Natalie Delgado, Grade 2
Queen of All Saints School, IL

Basketball

Dribble
Pass
Shoot
Score
It is 6 and 4.
Four more seconds
4, 3, 2, 1
We win!
Will that happen today?
We will have fun!

Ethen Witte, Grade 1
Bright Elementary School, IN

Dog/Boomer

Dog
Cuddle, cute
Snuggling, playing, barking
My dog is cuddly
Boomer

Kendra Harrison, Grade 2
Coy Elementary School, OH

My Pet

I want my pet to be a dog.
That would be much better than a hog.
She would be such a lady.
I would like to name her Sadie.
Sometimes we'd play in the fog.
She might even find a frog.
I hope Sadie comes today
so we can run and jump and play.

Dominick Dieken, Grade 2
MACCRAY West Elementary School, MN

Leaves

The leaves are red, and green, and yellow.
When I step on them,
they sound like paper
that rips quietly.

Elise Sanchez, Grade 1
Holden Elementary School, IL

Animals

Cats,
Dogs,
Tigers,
Lions,
Turtles,
Pigs,
Birds,
Frogs,
Bats,
Fish,
I like animals!

Eli Rohm, Grade 1
James R Watson Elementary School, IN

Summer Nights

You can see the moon.
You can taste the fresh air.
You can feel the moon dust.

I can feel the fireflies on my hands.
I can hear owls hooting in the night.
I like to play with my friends in the dark!

Gavin Krska, Grade 1
Woodford Elementary School, OH

Basketball
Run run run
Shoot
Slam dunk
I love basketball!

Andrew Hill, Grade 2
McKenney-Harrison Elementary School, IN

Careful
I see snow all over the ground.
I hear the wind blowing in my face.
I feel a soft layer of snow as I lay in it.
I taste the snow as I eat it…
But I have to be careful of yellow snow…
YUCK!
BowWow!

William Monroe, Grade 1
Woodford Elementary School, OH

Leaves, Leaves
Leaves, leaves on the tree
Leaves, leaves falling to the ground
Leaves, leaves of many colors
Leaves so we can play in

Rayonna Jones-Snow, Grade 1
Springfield Boys and Girls Club ABC Unit, IL

Me
Hannah
Nice, happy, pretty
Daughter of Karen and Mark West
Much loved by my family and friends
Sibling of Noah and Ashley
Wishes my wish is to get more Webkinz.
Wants to be a teacher
Afraid of my cat
Feels happy sometimes, sad, and mad
I try my best
Would like to go to Disney and Splash Village
Enjoys swimming
Resident of Wyandotte, MI
West

Hannah West, Grade 3
Jefferson Elementary School, MI

The Tree

There was a tree.
Who wanted to be free.
And there was a little bee
In a hole inside the tree.
Satish Uppaluri, Grade 3
Ramalynn Montessori Academy, MN

Valentines

V ases with roses
A heart by every door
L oving everyone
E verybody says it's cool
N aming Valentines
T ogether, Forever
I t's Cupid's Day
N aming Valentines
E verything filled with love
S o much happiness
Gabrielle Brakoniecki, Grade 3
Burr Elementary School, MI

Cade

C hocolate is my favorite
A pples are good
D raws pictures
E ven plays with Legos!
Cade Shipman, Kindergarten
Medford Elementary School, WI

The Panda Pet

Fur so scrunchy
Leaves crunch munchy
In the big trees
Swatting out the bees
Fur black and white
Doesn't like to fight
Eats bamboo
Lives in the zoo
Munches the leaves
And scratches at fleas
His name is Pandabeary
Too bad he's imaginary
Alex Huynh, Grade 3
Rutledge Hall Elementary School, IL

Flamingo

Flamingo, fuchsia
so delicate and puffy
graceful flamingo.
Taylor Carver, Grade 3
Chantry Elementary School, IA

Hawk

A flying
hawk soars
through the
beautiful sky.

Beware, mice!
The hawk might swoop down
and get you —
so run, hurry!
Francesca D'Orazi, Grade 3
Greenbriar Elementary School, IL

My Grandma

Grandma gives me ice cream.
It is good.

Grandma is nice.

When she cooks, it is
Good
Good
Good.
Rebecca Carol Edwards, Grade 1
Bristol Elementary School, WI

Colors

Blue is the clear sky.
Red is the good tasting cherries.
Green is the open grass.
Yellow is the hot sun.
Orange is peaceful like a butterfly.
Black is the midnight sky.
Purple is like a blooming flower.

How do these colors make you feel?
Faith Miller, Grade 3
Atwood Elementary School, MI

Christmas

I see so much snow that I can make a snowman.
I smell hot cocoa that smells so good and fresh.
I can hear Santa's bells jingle on Christmas.
I touch my presents!
I taste a delicious chicken feast on Christmas.
I feel happy and so excited about being with my family.

Alexis Hufnagle, Grade 1
Eastside Elementary School, MI

My Summer Fun

Summer is so fun 'cause you get to sit in the sun!
I think it's cool you play in the pool!
I like the summer, but it's a bummer that summer can't go on forever!
I'll remember forever.
I'll always be a member of summertime.
I love school and the pool.
On the first day of summer vacation, I'll scream…SUMMERTIME, YEA!
Summer is fun and so is the sun!
I'll tell you more after I go to the store.
Summertime YEA!

Alexa Brya, Grade 2
Schavey Road Elementary School, MI

Tape Dispenser

The tape is stretching to the shark teeth where you pull it off
It looks like a tightrope and your fingers is a little guy
And you don't even know it
    Tip Toe
    Tip Toe
    Tip Toe

Charles Koch, Grade 2
Orchard Lane Elementary School, WI

Iditarod

I ditarod means The Last Great Race.
D ogs most have eight booties.
I n the Iditarod you can start with sixteen dogs.
T he Iditarod is very icy and cold.
A musher rides in a sled.
R unning is what dogs do.
O nly five dogs are needed to end the race.
D ogs are extremely important for the Iditarod.

Radka Pribyl Pierdinock, Grade 2
Central Elementary School, IL

Paisley

P aisley is my dog
A cts like she is "Underdog"
I s very cute
S he is a medium size dog
L oves company
E ats doggy food
Y oung dog

Corey Brady, Grade 3
Woodford Elementary School, OH

Imagine Me

Imagine me, a leaf.
Falling off the tree.
Flying,
I fell into a pond.
Going up in the sky
and the clouds.
Seeing the world.
Hanging on a tree is fun.
Imagine me, a leaf.

Hiram Arreola, Grade 2
Michener Elementary School, MI

In Outer Space

One time I went to outer space
Where I joined a shooting star race
I touched 46 stars
And walked on Mars
I jumped on Saturn
And walked its cratered pattern
I encountered a falling asteroid
Which I barely managed to avoid!
If from the sun's rays I did not flee
The sun's rays would have burned me
When I neared a dark black hole
I was scared and shivery cold
Next I found the Milky Way
And saw a shiny solar ray
On the moon I saw a flag
And saw young moon kids playing tag
I met the aliens of planet Suskoot
Oh wait; did I bring my space suit?

Nicholas Ieremciuc, Grade 3
Rutledge Hall Elementary School, IL

Penguins

Penguins
Stocky, flightless
Nesting, sliding, wobbling
Find their nests in enormous rookeries
Emperor birds

Melanie Soller, Grade 3
St Michael School, OH

Monkeys

Monkeys are crazy.
Monkeys are very funny.
They like bananas too.

Kristian Simovski, Grade 3
Atwood Elementary School, MI

Mondays at Music

Music is fun
on Mondays
because we have partners
Its fun fun fun!
I love music
I never want to leave
because its fun
What's more fun?
Art…no
Media…no
Gym…no
Fridays…yes
because of music
It's best to be in music
And that's it
Music is the best!

Alexander Mason, Grade 1
Webster Elementary School, MI

Favorites

Webkinz
cozy, colorful
loving, cuddling, sleeping
I love my Webkinz very much.
cute, pretty
Linzey

Alynsia Strei, Grade 2
Stocker Elementary School, WI

Muscle Car
Fast cool red
Rrrrrrrr
I wonder if it's fast
Smells
Smells
Smells
Cool

Nathan Mahaffey, Grade 2
Country Meadow Elementary School, IN

My Dog Rosie
Licks your
face

Will be your
friend

Cute and
cuddly

My dog
Rosie!

Maggie Conley, Grade 2
Country Meadow Elementary School, IN

Your Happy Face
Your happy face,
makes my happy face,
a smiley face.
I hope my smiley face,
makes you a smiley face,
to make a smile on your face.
Make your frown turn upside down.
Your smile on your face,
is a nice piece of gold,
and brightens my day.
I hope I see a smiley face from you tomorrow,
because you made a sunny day.
So keep that smiley face,
it makes a lot of gold,
and it makes my day happy!

Saad Rashid, Grade 3
Islamic School of Greater Toledo, OH

I Am

I am a farmer
I wonder if I can go to the rodeo
I hear cows mooing
I see cattle
I want a farm with lots of cows
I am a farmer

I pretend to have my own farm
I feel good seeing cows
I touch the sandpaper tongue of a calf
I worry about the barn
I cry when cows die
I am a farmer

I understand cows need food
I say cows are nice
I dream I can own a farm
I try to help on the farm
I hope I can ride a cow
I am a farmer
Nickolas Noland, Grade 3
Kate Goodrich Elementary School, WI

Colors

Red is like the taste of strawberries.
Blue is like the bright blue sky.
Orange is my color of happiness.
Brown reminds me of my dog.
Yellow is the beautiful color of the sun.
Gold is the color of my dance medal.
Purple is the color I like.

Do you like these colors???
Alexis Wilson, Grade 3
Atwood Elementary School, MI

Fall

Fall
blow leaves
really cool
orange green
Fall
Atl Flores, Grade 3
Phillip May Elementary School, IL

Bunnies

Real soft and fluffy,
Their marble eyes shine in light,
They are very cute.
Andrea Baker, Grade 3
Jefferson Elementary School, MI

Justin

J umping
U p
S miling
T asting
I nside
N ature
Justin Jones, Grade 3
Kyle Trueblood Elementary School, KS

Spring

S wimming
P laying
R unning
I t's fun
N ice outside
G oing somewhere
Cameron Ball, Grade 1
Southwood Elementary School, IN

Mississippi Count Down

Mississippi count down
Mississippi count down
5, 4, 3, 2, 1
5, 4, 3, 2, 1
i..p..p..i..s..s..i..s..s..i..M
Mississippi count up
Mississippi count up
1, 2, 3, 4, 5
1, 2, 3, 4, 5
M..i..s..s..i..s..s..i..p..p..i
Mississippi scramble
Mississippi scramble
p..M..p..s..i..s..s..i..s..i..i
5, 1, 4, 2, 3
3, 1, 4, 2, 5
Hannah Orebaugh, Grade 3
Atwood Elementary School, MI

Sick

Sick is when I don't want to get up out of my bed.
My mom pulls me out and I scream, "No, leave me alone."
I hope it is a dream, but it isn't.
I sob to my mom and she said, "You are ok."
I whisper, "I am glad you are with me."
I'm like a sick cat because
I feel like I have a fur ball stuck in my throat.
The next day I get up and I'm not sick anymore.
I am so glad I am not sick anymore.
I yelled, "Yippee!"
To be sick is my nightmare.

Jasmine Siboni, Grade 2
Michener Elementary School, MI

Homework Excuses

I was sick.
My sister ate it.
No wait, she drew on it.

My mom made it into dinner.
I forgot I accidentally ate it.

My grandma mistook it for a bill.
Then she ripped it to bits.

It got run over by a truck.
THAT definitely was not my luck!
I dropped it in the mud out the window of my car.

My mom yelled at me so hard, it flew to Japan.

Actually, I just didn't want to.

Sophia Reece, Grade 3
Decatur Classical Elementary School, IL

Summer

S ummer is cool because we get to go to Harsens Island.
U get to go in my dollhouse and we will play in it.
M om and me will plant seeds.
M e and dad will do plants.
E xtra fun if you go swimming
R you going to walk to Seven Eleven?

Cassidy Fitts, Grade 3
Floyd Ebeling Elementary School, MI

Trunks

I dive in the pool
and splash.
I look at myself
and oh, no.
I lost my trunks.
I am naked!
How embarrassing!
Justin Smith, Grade 1
Bright Elementary School, IN

In the Night

In the night
The stars shine bright
The darkness will hold
The stories untold

The air so fresh
It tickles my flesh
When the wind whistles
It turns my skin to prickles

The trees wave
Wolves howl in their cave
As soon as I go to bed
I lay down my head

And listen to what is said:

Howl, howl
Growl, growl
Bark, bark
It is dark
Mary Kate Porath, Grade 3
St Clare Catholic School, IL

Miss Kirk

Miss Kirk
Wonderful
So much cool
Skinny and tall,
Loud and quiet
Teachers
Courtney Baker, Grade 2
Congress School, MI

Playing with My Food

I'm playing with my food
I'm making a potato for a head
I'm playing with my food
Another potato for a belly!
I'm playing with my food
Green beans for arms!
I'm playing with my food
Two forks for legs!
I'm playing with my food
I made a replica of me
I'm playing with my food
STOP
PLAYING
WITH
YOUR
FOOD!
Logan Stevens, Grade 2
James R Watson Elementary School, IN

The Magical Circus

Me and my mom went to the circus
I look at the set, it looks like a magical place
Then the lights dim and the show begins,
The spotlight goes on a funny clown
Pow! the drums go boom, tap, screech, boom!
The clown jumps on a unicycle,
Then a group of dogs jump in hoops, jump
Pow! it was amazing!
Jane Baffert, Grade 2
Meadowbrook Elementary School, IL

Too Short?

When I was five,
I was too short to dive!

When I was small,
I could not crawl!

When I tried to walk,
All I could do was talk.

It's not fun being short!
Cory Ault, Grade 3
Bradie M Shrum Upper Elementary School, IN

The Beautiful Statue

The Statue of Liberty is so beautiful
When I go inside from the top
The view is so beautiful.
The book and the torch in her hands
Welcoming freedom to this mighty land.
You came so far,
Don't go back now,
Make a house,
Get food,
And just be free in America,
The land of the free.

Kole Rosin, Grade 3
Detroit Country Day Junior School, MI

Spring

S ummer is coming with shiny light.
P retty flowers are blooming today.
R abbits are coming to hop.
I ce cream is melting in the sun.
N ew things are just waiting to come.
G ardens are getting pretty with flowers.

Allie Spence, Grade 2
Stanton Elementary School, NE

Spring Break

Going to Grandma's house
on spring break
spending the night
playing with my cousin Nick

Kendall Gilbert, Grade 2
Country Meadow Elementary School, IN

What Is Red?

Red is the color of blood.
Red is the color of shirts too.
Red is the color of apples.
Red is the color of your heart.
Red is the color of a marker.
Red is a color in our flag.

Red is my favorite color!

Riley Bowser, Grade 1
James R Watson Elementary School, IN

My Sister Knows*
My sister knows karate
I know this because
she is mean and all
but if you get on her
to try to make her
screw up on the Wii
she will kick you
in the THIGH!
Hannah Lee Metzger, Grade 2
Pathfinder Elementary School, MI
*Dedicated to my sister Maddie

Webkin Jumper
I love my Webkin Thumper Jumper,
He loves to race.
He's really fast,
He never comes in last.
Kyle Bushbaker, Grade 3
Atwood Elementary School, MI

Holiday Senses
I see the tree of Christmas.
I hear cookies crunching so well.
I taste chocolate cookies at Christmas.
I sniff the chocolate cake.
I touch the Christmas tree.
I smell the chocolate cookies.
I see the Christmas tree.
I love Christmas!
All my senses are alive.
Dylan Schueder, Grade 3
South O'Brien Elementary School, IA

Spring
When spring comes out
I come out to plant some flowers
My sister comes out
The sun comes out too
My mom is a cloud
And my dad is a bee
From flower to flower
We saw a whole day
Jennifer Aviles, Grade 1
Peck Elementary School, IL

Summer
Blasting hot
drinking water
playing with friends
neighbors
swimming
frisbee
jumping on trampoline
staying up late
chasing my dogs
swinging
sliding
flip flops
tank tops
sweaty
going out to eat
playdoh
phone
I love summer so much!
Megan Berens, Grade 2
Pathfinder Elementary School, MI

Cub/Tiger
Cub
Cute, cuddly
Sleeping, playing, jumping
Forest, creeping, jungle, hunting
Swimming, running, outside
Wild, fast
Tiger
Dominyc Emerson, Grade 1
Ladoga Elementary School, IN

Puppies
Puppies are cute and playful
Puppies bite
They are a mammal
My friend's puppy scratches,
Sometimes my puppy kisses me
My puppy's name is Arnold
My puppy is one
Puppies are nice
I love my puppy
Lilly Ramalingam, Kindergarten
Ramalynn Montessori Academy, MN

When the Clock Struck Ten

When the clock stuck ten it startled the zoo,
Which made the monkey run all over the zoo,
Which upset the lion, that made a fearsome roar,
Which made the giraffe jump over the fence
And get its neck stuck in a tangled up branch,
Which startled the zookeeper and made him run home.
That's what happened when the clock struck ten at the zoo.

Joshua Elkhawand, Grade 3
Atwood Elementary School, MI

As the Sun Shines Over Me

As the sun shines over me I feel bright, for the sun is bright yellow, as it sparkles
and shines all over me.
I feel imaginative.
I feel like the sun is going to burst out the daisies right at my eyes.
As the sun shines no one is looking but everyone is seeking.
They are seeking the trees and the butterflies ahead, for the creatures they see
come head to head.
As the sun shines over me, I am listening, listening to the birds chirping and
listening to the breeze laughing.
As the sun shines over me I am gazing at the light, smiling in the bright.
Everyone might see me but they won't appear.
Instead I can hear them right in my ear.
As the sun shines over me I imagine everything is happening.
As the sun stops shining and the moon comes above,
I start to fall asleep listening to a dove.

Shreya Shaw, Grade 3
Cline Elementary School, OH

Alexis

Alexis
Nice helpful, smart, thoughtful.
Lover of Lake Michigan and Detroit Lions.
Who feels sad when my mom yells at me,
glad when I get to go outside,
mad when my brother hits me.
Who gives help when old people fall.
Who gives hugs and kisses to Mom and Dad.
Who fears something is going to fall like the Twin Towers.
Who would like to see the sharks and other animals.
Resident of Michigan
Johnson

Alexis Johnson, Grade 2
Michener Elementary School, MI

Spring

S un's heat is warm.
P retty flowers burst out of the ground.
R oots are growing bigger.
I will plant flowers in the ground.
N ever stay inside.
G rows beautiful flowers.

Isabelle Caldwell, Grade 3
Bentley Primary School, KS

Reading

R eading is fun
E ven a chapter book
A chapter book is easy to read
D inosaur books are the best
I think dinosaur books are easy to read
N ever stop reading
G rouch people sometimes quit.

Ronald Hudson, Grade 2
Stocker Elementary School, WI

The Pumpkin

The pumpkin glows.
At midnight the cars drive by
With an oooh and an aaah.
The candles glow in the dark.
It is a sparkle of the light.
At night the candle slowly melts.
It is Halloween.
At night I see about
20 jack-o'-lanterns.
I got a little bit of candy.

Colton Clifford, Grade 2
Country Meadow Elementary School, IN

Chicago Aquarium

I see a dolphin show at the aquarium.
In a big city called Chicago.
I hear it splash, splash in the salty sea.
I smell the fishy area
And I taste the nasty ocean water.
I feel so happy here at the Chicago Aquarium.

LeeAnn Hurst, Grade 1
Eastside Elementary School, MI

Page 172

Rose Petals

Rose petals fall like years passing by.
My great grandma, ninety, when will she die?
I'm at my mom's house when it happened
My mom grows roses in her garden.
A rose used to say, "I love you,"
Now they fall by ones or twos.
They weigh less than an ounce
when they fall they never bounce.
My great grandpa died and
rose petals still go by.

Auni Williams, Grade 3
Kyle Trueblood Elementary School, KS

Tracking

Running fast, running slow, running here we go
5, 4, 3, 2, 1
running until we are done
until we are done let's have some fun
Run, Run, Run!

Molly Bohrer, Grade 3
MacArthur Elementary School, WI

Michael Jordan

Michael Jordan
Flew, floated, soared,
Played basketball for the Bulls
From 1984 to 1993
In Chicago
So he could become a great basketball player.

Francisco Campos, Grade 1
Charles Hammond Elementary School, IL

Ronald Reagan

RONALD
40th President
Witty, actor, governor
Who loved his country
Who believed in the greatness of America
Who wanted peace through strength
Who said we need to see a confident America
REAGAN

Cal Konshak, Grade 2
Our Lady of Lourdes School, WI

April

April is here
let's give a big cheer,
flowers are blooming
birds are zooming,
the sun is out
let's give a big shout.
Emily Mayoras, Grade 3
Deerfield Elementary School, MI

Puppies

Bark
Play ball
Fast
Play outside
Chase cats
Little
Fun
Brown
Black
White
Yellow
Puppies
Madison Knight, Kindergarten
Northfield Elementary School, OH

Libraries

Where you read books,
Other things too,
Books you read!
Niklas Olson, Kindergarten
Ramalynn Montessori Academy, MN

Water Slide

Lots of water
Whoosh!
It's slippery.
Woo!
Spinning,
Splash!
Again
Fun
Let me stay!
Tatum Hemmingsen, Grade 1
Carriage Hill Elementary School, NE

My Kitty

Playing with some yarn,
Sleeps like a baby angel
Kissing her goodnight.
Emme Triplett, Grade 2
J C Hoglan Elementary School, IA

Sun

A sun is cool
A sun is yellow
A sun is shining
Sun I love you
Josh Blaine, Grade 2
Orchard Lane Elementary School, WI

My Dog

My dog is fun.
My dog is cute.
He likes people.
Shelby Fluhr, Grade 1
Henryville Elementary School, IN

Sharks

I love sharks
I can see the teeth
I can see black eyes
You can see its jaws
I love sharks
Bryson Smith, Grade 1
Henryville Elementary School, IN

Cherry Tree

C herries are yummy.
H ow many cherries are in a pie?
E normous cherries.
R ound cherries.
R ipe cherries.
Y ummy.

T aste good on your tongue.
R eally ripe.
E xtra cherries are awesome.
E veryone likes cherries.
Kade Nelsen, Grade 2
Anita Elementary School, IA

Colors

Yellow — the sun that brightens up our day.
Red is the sunset, that's what we say!

Gold, for the rich that own the big.
Silver shovel — you need to dig.

Aqua for the sea so bright.
Brown for the tree trunk with lots of might.

Blue, the sky with birds that soar.
Green, the parrot that likes to snore.

Black reminds me of shoes that shine.
Purple, of streaks in hair that's fine.

What do colors mean to you?

Anna Mascarenas, Grade 2
Detroit Country Day Lower School, MI

Frogs and Toads

Little   and   green.
Slimy   not   clean.
Hides   in   a   tree   stump
   with   warts   on
          his   knees!
You   find   them
swimming   in   the   swamp.

Kabe Christian, Grade 2
McKenney-Harrison Elementary School, IN

Blue

Colts,
Blueberries,
Cupcakes,
Shirts,
Folders,
Blocks,
Water,
Pens,
Books,
I love Blue!

Jonathon Bell, Grade 1
James R Watson Elementary School, IN

Ice Cream

It's so tasty.
You can eat it on a hot day,
so many different colors,
my favorite treat.
ShirleyAnna Twarowski, Grade 3
Atwood Elementary School, MI

I See

I see a bat that is fat.
In spring birds sing.
I see a fly in the sky,
But no butterfly.
Tino Taylor, Kindergarten
Bristol Elementary School, WI

Buffalo

Furry, big
Roaming, eating, running
Cow
Max Madsen, Grade 2
Thayer Central Elementary School, NE

Spring

Everybody cheers
Spring is here in the world
I smell red roses
And I hope that you do too
Everybody smells roses
In the outside world
Yay Yay spring is here
Mohammad Abdelkarim, Grade 2
Peck Elementary School, IL

Harry Ape

Brown
all over
but
no hair
on his
head.
Who?
My dad!
Emily Dahlgren, Grade 1
Carriage Hill Elementary School, NE

Squirrel

Squirrel on the grass,
he has holes to dig today
for nuts for winter.
Ginnie White, Grade 3
Greenbriar Elementary School, IL

If I Were Spring...

I would hear birds humming.
I would see people running around.
I would smell the flowers.
I would taste the smoke from fires.
I would feel the clouds.
I would make it feel like summer.
Katelyn Hannaman, Grade 2
Stocker Elementary School, WI

Grandma

Funny, nice
Baking, loving, walking
We go swimming sometimes
Mary
Taylor Lay, Grade 1
Wethersfield Elementary School, IL

Spring

Warm wind blows, daffodils grow
Sun shines bright, what a sight
Cool fresh grass between my toes
No more snow, buds grow
Picnic once, picnic twice
The warm weather is so nice.
Katherine Larsen, Grade 2
Greenbriar Elementary School, IL

Black

Black is the night sky.
Black is a high mountain in the sky.
Black is a very dark cave.
Black is a train zooming by.
Black is a big storm in the sky.
Black is a big rock.
Black is a piece of chocolate.
Brady Dhom, Grade 3
Southern View Elementary School, IL

I Am

I am a child
I wonder why holidays come once a year
I hear children playing outside
I see clouds flowing in the air
I want to see a real shark
I am a child

I pretend to be the President's daughter
I feel the air in my hair
I touch the playground at recess
I worry that I won't get the things I need done
I cry when I think about sad things
I am a child

I understand how to play checkers
I say to my friends, "Let's play in the mud"
I dream to be a professional athlete
I try to do my best in school
I hope people can find a way to end world hunger
I am a child

Gretta Fermanich, Grade 3
Kate Goodrich Elementary School, WI

When I Fell in the Store

When I fell in the store it really hurt.
When I fell in the store my eyebrow was all bloody.
When I fell in the store I ran and tripped.
When I fell in the store there was no cushion to help me fall.
I didn't have to get stitches.
Doctors had to glue my eyebrow together.
I didn't like it!

Samantha Koch, Grade 3
Kyle Trueblood Elementary School, KS

Brookfield Zoo

When it's warm and hot,
I like to be there at noon,
To hear the people yelling and the dolphins splashing,
To see anteaters sleeping and seals swimming.
While I look at the monkeys and elephants.
I'll go there next summer,
And that makes me happy inside!

Orion Heinosch, Grade 3
St Robert Bellarmine School, IL

Moon

I walk in the moon
The moon is light
The moon is beautiful
Lesly Martinez, Grade 1
Peck Elementary School, IL

Pools

Pools
Splashing,
Swimming,
Under water,
Playing,
Fun.
Anthony Jarta, Grade 2
Queen of All Saints School, IL

Tiger

The name of a WW 2 tank.
The name of an animal.
Both take lives.
Quiet, stunning.
Jungle, water, nowhere
is safe from the tiger.
Dalton McAlkich, Grade 3
Levan Scott Academy, IN

Hail

Hail
Small, big
Falling, damaging
Stay inside during a hail storm
Ice balls
Christopher Aman, Grade 3
St Michael School, OH

Snow Leopard

Snow leopard
Alert, graceful, cunning
Hunting, pouncing, devouring
Their mountainous home
Is 13,000 feet in the air
Asian cat
Abby Mogan, Grade 3
St Michael School, OH

Spring

S mells like spring is here.
P retty butterflies will now be seen.
R oses and violets will grow.
I will play all day long.
N o people will waste this beautiful spring.
G oing to have a sunny and playful spring.
Jocelyn Perez, Grade 3
Peck Elementary School, IL

The Wonderful Basketball Game

Hot July day,
Daniel dribbling, bump bump
Dad blocking.
Rachel open, Daniel passes
She caught the ball!
I try to block her
She goes past me…
She shoots, she scores!
Daniel so happy!
I get the ball, I pass to Dad
I run to the hoop.
Dad passes the ball
I shoot, but I miss, I get the ball
I shoot…Daniel blocks the hoop
The ball flies right past him
"Yea we did it!" My first score of the game!
Daniel gets the ball, he shoots
The ball goes flying into the hoop, he scores!
The game has to end.
Daniel and Rachel win!
But we all had fun!
Elizabeth Desautels, Grade 3
MacArthur Elementary School, WI

Andy and His Candy

There is a boy named Andy,
Who really loves his candy.
He loves trips to the beach,
Especially with his favorite flavor peach.
But he hates it when his candy gets all sandy,
So he puts it in a pocket, which is very handy.
Andy really loves his candy.
Catherine LaRosa, Grade 3
St Eugene School, WI

Rain
Rain.
Pours.
Drip, Drop.
Drip, Drop.
Thunder,
Lightning
BOOM!
BANG!

Gavin Scranage, Grade 2
Country Meadow Elementary School, IN

Outside My Window
There is green grass blowing,
Bald trees in the woods,
Blue water in the pool,
Big gray barn,
Big, black car sitting,
I like the sights I see.

Tori Creager, Grade 1
Hamilton Community Elementary School, IN

Frogs
hop
sit
splash
green
tadpoles
frogs eat flies
hop away

Kaleb Martindale, Grade 1
James R Watson Elementary School, IN

Save the Earth
Help save the Earth,
Make it a nice place for you and me,
So everything can be free,
Even you and me,
So pick up trash or anything you see,
We can be free,
Help save the Earth,
Be the best you can be.

Keyshawn Amos, Grade 2
Gen George Patton Elementary School, IL

Ribsy

R uns a lot
I s a good dog
B een lost for over a month
S hakes with left paw
Y elped for help

Nancy Torres, Grade 3
Phillip May Elementary School, IL

The Cat

Once I saw a little cat,
She was cute but very fat.
I walked up to her,
Oh, what nice fluffy fur.
And then she walked away.
Then she seemed to say,
I hope I see you again someday.

Anna Grashel, Grade 2
Pike Christian Academy, OH

Snowflakes

Snowflakes snowflakes in the air.
Snowflakes snowflakes you are fair.
Snowflakes snowflakes on the ground.
Snowflakes snowflakes all around.

Melanie Miller, Grade 2
Ramalynn Montessori Academy, MN

Friendship and Nature

Friendship goes by the hour.
Way up high like a tower.
Nature has lots of power.
Apples in the trees are very sour.
There are pretty things like flowers.

Nikita Bantey, Grade 2
Ramalynn Montessori Academy, MN

Jelly

Jelly is healthy for your belly.
Yummy, yummy in my tummy.
It's slippery on my bread.
It does not hurt my head.

Sean Sostaric, Grade 1
Montgomery Elementary School, OH

Banana Smoothies

Don't you just love banana smoothies?
I like banana smoothies
They're made with real fruit,
They're smooth and creamy.
Banana smoothies melt in your mouth
Like an ice cube in the sun.
Banana smoothies are awesome.

Courtney Hengy, Grade 3
Atwood Elementary School, MI

Spring

I see the sun when it is spring.
When it is spring the flowers grow
with nice leaves.
The birds sing and sing
when it's time for spring.

Ariana Vargas, Grade 2
Peck Elementary School, IL

School

There is work
Ahead of us
When we get there
We start working
Barely
Anytime
For play
There is work
Ahead of us

Kayla Olstinske, Grade 2
Orchard Lane Elementary School, WI

Walking

I went on a walk
and I started to talk.

I walked to the park
and I heard a dog bark.

I walked in the sun
I am sad it is done.

Michael Parsons, Grade 3
Atwood Elementary School, MI

Winter

Winter tastes like yummy hot chocolate burning my tongue.
Winter sounds like the wind whistling through the air.
Winter smells like hot chocolate floating in the air up into my nose.
Winter looks like snow falling from the sky like little angels.
Winter feels like freezing snow.

Connor Merryfield, Grade 2
C W Neff Elementary School, MI

Her Words to Us

People from far and wide
Came in my need, just to be free.
For I am the great Statue of Liberty.
America's children's ancestors were once immigrants
Who came to this great land.
I stand alone, but never lonely
Because I always see a new face, a new person, a new soul.
Immigrants of hundreds, thousands, and millions
Came to see this mighty land,
Breathe the fresh air,
Feel the breeze of America, sink your feet into the soil.
Be brave, have courage, and be an American.
How you ask?
Just believe my child, just believe.

Alexandra Hardin, Grade 3
Detroit Country Day Junior School, MI

Gray

Gray looks like big, round stones on the side of the school.
Gray smells like the exhaust from my grandpa's truck.
Gray tastes like my metal braces when I drink cold water.
Gray sounds like a snowplow going down my street.
Gray feels like cold tiles on my bathroom floor.

Daniel Hassenzahl, Grade 2
Will Carleton Academy, MI

Spring

S unny days are so relaxing.
P icnics are so peaceful you can be talking.
R ainy days can help us but we can't be walking.
I ce cream shout kids tasty ice cream.
N ice wonderful weather and hear the birds singing.
G reen green grass huge leaves on trees what a beautiful spring it is.

Angelica Diego, Grade 3
Peck Elementary School, IL

Flowing of the River
As the river flows my heart beats,
As the river pounds against my wounds
All I think I hear is freedom calling me,
Freedom is coming.
As I struggle to stay above water,
As I try not to scream,
I know freedom is calling me.
Brianna Eittreim, Grade 3
Liberty Elementary School, MN

Swimming
Wade
Swim
Pool
Dive
Outside
Sun
Swimming
Olivia Paull, Kindergarten
Northfield Elementary School, OH

Puppies
Puppy
Small, tiny
Running, wiggling, squirming
Fast, playful, sharp teeth, long
Chewing, tackling, tricking
Big, tall
Dog
Benito Romero, Grade 3
Atwood Elementary School, MI

Mommy
My mom is so nice.
She makes really good rice.
My mom is so funny.
She spends a lot of money.
My mom is so cute.
She can really scoot.
My mom's hug is big.
I eat her food like a pig.
Esmeralda Ramos-Perez, Grade 1
Strange Elementary School, WI

Powwow Dancers
Everybody dancing in dresses
Men's final championship
Jingle bells on the outfits
Every year we celebrate
The old religion of people of long ago
We make special gifts
To worship our kind ancestors
We respect our elders
On a special secret
Only our elders know
Everybody dances to be happy
To show emotions for our tribe
Aziza Smith, Grade 2
Broken Arrow Elementary School, KS

Long Neck
Hi long neck
Your neck
Is very
Long
It looks
Like
A
Rain cloud
When
You
Tower
Over
Me
Kaitlin Tadlock, Grade 2
Orchard Lane Elementary School, WI

April Fools You
Now it is April
the sun is out
but when I open the curtains,
I just want to shout.
Another droopy, moopy day
with no fun or no sun
and now the day is over
with no pranks, have I done.
Nayan Makim, Grade 3
Deerfield Elementary School, MI

Sad

Sad is when you cry.
I am very sad because my dog died.
I cry all night like a baby.
I hear from my mom's friend because
she was behind the person who ran over her.
I am too sad because my brother let her out.
I searched all night at my old house.
I worry about her all of the time.
I had her all my life since I was a baby.
I will never like my brother.
I hope she is ok and I miss her a lot.
My dog's name was Jackie.
She was almost like a lion.
I am sad, very sad.

Zeke Frederick, Grade 2
Michener Elementary School, MI

Spider Man 3

Spider Man can climb walls.
Spider Man can beat up bad guys.
Spider Man can shoot out webs.
Spider Man can do web swinging.
Venom killed Harry.
He was Peter Parker's friend.
Spider Man can do anything!

Joe Maddalone, Grade 2
James R Watson Elementary School, IN

Kittens

Cute
    Cuddly,
        Funny,
            Sassy, very sassy!
                Always hungry, hungry, hungry
                Jumping, jumping, jumping
                Meeeooowwww
                Meeoowww
                Meoww
Kittens are sweet, sweet, sweet
I love, love, love, kittens
I still want a kitten, kitten, kitten!

Emily Klawiter, Grade 1
Rock Ledge Elementary School, WI

Squirrel Hunting

Squirrel hunting
is so fun,
but when you miss
it means a ton.
Mason Cordell, Grade 3
Weymouth Elementary School, MI

Elephant

A big animal
moves through the jungle
slowly eating leaves
as it slowly goes by
The jungle is filled
with animals
of all kinds
Monkeys and snakes
of all kinds
And don't forget
the biggest animal
of them all
the elephant!
Charley MacIsaac, Grade 1
Webster Elementary School, MI

Old

I am old.
I am tall.
I have leaves.
I have roots.
Can you guess what I am?
I am an oak tree.
Gilberto Gonzalez, Grade 1
Strange Elementary School, WI

The Fun Birthday Party

The fun birthday party
Fun pool,
Fun movies,
Fun hotels,
Fun jokes
Fun party.
Kamile Yocum, Grade 1
Mentone Elementary School, IN

Spring

S unflowers are pretty.
P uddles are on the ground.
R ainbows are in the air.
I ce is melting away.
N ice little rabbits come to me.
G rass is growing in the garden.
Ashlin Rang, Grade 2
Stanton Elementary School, NE

Cough Cough

I'm sick, sick, sick.
I don't feel good at all
I am coughing really bad
I don't know why I feel
So sick, sick, sick
I can't feel my
Legs even my arms
My boogers are bad
I have a sore nose
My coughs are bringing
Boogers up my throat
I'm sick, sick, sick.
Farrah Bologna, Grade 2
Patterson Elementary School, MI

Fire Breathing Dragon

D eadly!
R arely seen!
A mazing!
G iant eyes!
O h so big!
N ow he's a fire breathing dragon!
Mackenzie Koning, Grade 3
Woodside Elementary School, MI

Families

Once I had a families
I loved my family
Bruce, Paige, Eidan
They read me stories
They gave me treats!
Maya Silver, Kindergarten
Ramalynn Montessori Academy, MN

Winter

Winter tastes like hot chocolate.
Winter looks like a polar bear watching me.
Winter feels like fluffy snow.
Winter sounds like blue jays whistling in my ear.

Ayla Adams, Grade 2
C W Neff Elementary School, MI

The Statue of Dreams

Mrs. Liberty you are so nice.
You try to give immigrants a chance for a better life.
Every day and all night.
You will be there to protect and help us all the time.
Oh, Mrs. Liberty, it is you,
Who makes our country different from all the others.
Most of all you give us the privilege and the honor
To be called the United States of America.

Rahul Khambete, Grade 3
Detroit Country Day Junior School, MI

Summer

Summer is really cool, there's not even any school!
It's also very fun, especially when you get to play in the sun!
When you jump in a pool, you'll say, "Ahhh, now I feel very cool!"
Sometimes you'll go down a water slide, then you'll say,
"Wow, that was a ton of fun!"
It seems like only a few more days of summer, but we still have a ways to go.
I hope it lasts longer because then school starts all over again!
A few more days in the pool, then there you are back to school.
Back to reading, math, writing too, and it all comes back to you!
Yoo Hoo!

Elliana Simon, Grade 2
Schavey Road Elementary School, MI

John Kennedy

JOHN
35th President
Swimmer, sailor, athlete
Who loved serving in the Navy
Who believed in peace
Who wanted equal rights for everyone
Who said: "Ask not what your country can do for you"
KENNEDY

Molly Mapes, Grade 2
Our Lady of Lourdes School, WI

Clover

Rover Rover I roll over
I find a four leaf clover
Look at me
I am free
I have green eyes
I smile wide
And I make the most of life
Mariah Taylor, Grade 3
Hyatt Elementary School, MI

Happy Flowers

Dandelions bloom,
Lilies dance in the sun,
While the others join.
Alex Christensen, Grade 3
St Clare Catholic School, IL

Ice

Ice
Slippery, wet
Freezing, expanding, cooling
Can be hail, ice, or frost
Frozen water
Nicholas Wehrle, Grade 3
St Michael School, OH

Blizzard

There was a blizzard today.
The blizzard felt like
The moon in the sky.
I felt cold.
You can feel the snow
On your hand.
Hayden Moss, Grade 2
Norris Elementary School, NE

Arctic Fox

Arctic fox
Hunter, camouflaged
Growing, howling, snapping
Hunting in the arctic snow
Snow stalker
Josey Waltman, Grade 3
St Michael School, OH

Boxers

Light brown,
Sloppy face,
Run fast,
Sharp teeth!
I love
BOXERS!!!!!
Alyssa Land, Grade 2
McKenney-Harrison Elementary School, IN

Joy

Joy is a nice mom
Who feels happy
Who likes to feed me
Who loves us
Who likes work
Who likes people
Needs love
Who fears bad things
Dylan Karlgaard, Grade 3
Litchville-Marion Elementary School, ND

John Quincy Adams

JOHN QUINCY
2nd President
Honest, trustworthy, brave
Who loved his children
Who believed in his new country
Who wanted peace for all people
Who said he really did not want to be president
ADAMS
Morgan Baeten, Grade 2
Our Lady of Lourdes School, WI

My Grandma

My mom likes to take me
To my grandma's
And to my grandpa's car lot.
My grandma comes
To pick me up.
I go to her house
And play with her dogs.
My grandma.
Ethan Slone, Kindergarten
McKenney-Harrison Elementary School, IN

Dead Dog
Sad
Scared
Tears in my eyes

Life is lonely without my dog,
Chipper.

Layton Miller, Grade 1
James R Watson Elementary School, IN

I Love Soccer
I love soccer.
When I run
The wind feels good.
The wind hits your face.
It cools you off.
It gives you a boost.
I pass to a teammate.
He shoots.
He scores!
WE WIN!
I love soccer.

Ethan Wilson, Grade 2
James R Watson Elementary School, IN

Otter
Swimming, swimming in the water.
It looks like a type of otter.
An otter has webbed feet.
It looks like that otter and I are about to meet.
It looks like it swam down to eat.
It ate a fish made out of meat.

Ben Daugherty, Grade 3
Henryville Elementary School, IN

Me?
Long hair
Blonde hair
Brown eyes too
Hangs upside down
And looks
At you

Amber Lawhorn, Grade 3
Highland County Christian School, OH

My Sister

Here I talk on the phone.
OH NO!
Here comes my sister

interruption
interruption
Blah
Blah
Blah.

I am playing all alone
OH NO!
Here comes my sister

interruption
interruption
Blah
Blah
Blah

My friend and I are playing
OH NO
Here comes my sister
We let her play.

Nathan Patrick Garris, Grade 2
Orchard Lane Elementary School, WI

Jellyfish

Jellyfish sting, zap
underwater talks to friends
ziggaly, zap, zig.

Lyndon Bright, Grade 3
Chantry Elementary School, IA

Spring

S pring is the best season
P eople feel happy
R ain is good for my mom's plants
I ce cream is good in spring
N ice people come out in spring
G reat things happen in the spring.

Anthony Wathen, Grade 2
Stocker Elementary School, WI

Skunk

Very disgusting
They really have a bad smell
Skunks will spray you too!

Kelsey Reschar, Grade 3
Henryville Elementary School, IN

Spring Is Here!

If you are in the spring you can sing.
It's so much fun
and the sun is bright as a light.
The trees are free
with the water in the grass.

Anthony Martinez, Grade 2
Peck Elementary School, IL

If...

If I were a cat,
I would lick myself
All day in the sun.
And sometimes,
I would sleep by my owner.
If I were a cat...

Kylie Rollins, Grade 1
Strange Elementary School, WI

Cats

I have four cats.
My cats like eating rats.
Morris is so beautiful.
I pull Morris back to her bowl.
Because she budges the other cat.
I think she's going to be fat.

Alex Kocian, Grade 2
Zion Lutheran School of Wayside, WI

Fat Pat

There was a girl named Pat
Who came from the city Rabat
Having a bad sensation
She took the wrong medication
And now she is terribly fat

Roman Lipinski, Grade 3
St Clare Catholic School, IL

My Grandpa
My Grandpa
Was feeling
Sick
For
5 days
He died
I love him
I wish
He would come back

Alec Johnson, Grade 1
South Monroe Townsite Elementary School, MI

Halloween
H alloween is a real scream
A lot of scary costumes
L ots and lots of screams
L ots of scary houses
O ur house is a real scream
W hy don't people make an extreme scream
E verybody should get scared
E verybody gets spooked by a scream
N ow that's a real scream

Brandon Deem, Grade 3
Woodford Elementary School, OH

Spring
S ounds of wind chimes our charms.
P eople walking their pets on a glorious sunny day.
R ainbows are coming after the rain.
I nsects are on the green leaves.
N o winter clothes is an excitement for the town.
G rass is growing so you need to be ready to cut the lawn.

Abraham Alonso, Grade 3
Peck Elementary School, IL

Red
Red looks like my brother's hair.
Red looks like a big heart that is in a gift.
Red smells like a big red flower in the garden on my farm.
Red sounds like a crackling campfire in our backyard.
Red tastes like a big juicy apple in an apple tree.
Red feels like the soft cuddly blanket that I use in the winter.

Allison Marshall, Grade 2
Will Carleton Academy, MI

Football Season for Santa

It was a cold day in November.
It was a sunny, but cold as it could be.
Santa was looking at his clock
and put down his toast and warm tea.
He got all the elves outside,
And all of his team, too.
He went out on the field
and said something new.
"We are playing football!
Blitzen, pick your team
I will pick mine!"
He said with thoughtful gleam.
So they all played football,
And Santa's team did very good.
It started to rain,
But Santa just pulled down his hood.
"Keep on playing!"
Was all he said.
So they kept playing
and soon went to bed.

Brooke Rogers, Grade 3
John H Castle Elementary School, IN

Dirt Bikes

I love dirt bikes
You can ride them
You can love them.

Aden Dennison, Grade 1
Henryville Elementary School, IN

Dreams

Roll, Roll, Roll
Rolling in my sleep.
Step, step, step
Walking in my sleep.
Fall,
  Fall,
    Fall
Waking from my sleep.

Good Morning!

Jake Reas, Grade 3
Henryville Elementary School, IN

Friends

friends are cool
friends are great
friends are there
when they're needed
sometimes they're not
but that's OK
just remember that
you need friends
to behave!

Preston Allen-Hernández, Grade 2
Hillcrest Elementary School, KS

All About Hockey

Hockey stick,
Hockey puck,
And hockey pads.

Stick handle,
And goal blocks.

Skate fast,
You got to move,
Around people.
HAVE FUN!

Nathan Beaudry, Grade 1
Strange Elementary School, WI

Flowers

Flowers are graceful beautiful plants.
They blow in the wind.
They flow as if they were bird's wings.
I love flowers.

Logan Wallace, Grade 3
Noonan Academy, IL

Cats

Purring
Scratching
Biting
Pouncing
Happy

Isabel Hasselman, Grade 2
Pathfinder Elementary School, MI

Happiness Is...

Swinging on the swings,
Climbing on trees,
Going around and around
On the merry-go-round,
Running around on the grass,
I like everything.

Hannah Wade, Grade 1
Hamilton Community Elementary School, IN

When It Snows

When it snows,
it is most likely to get higher than our toes.
When it snows,
my dog moans and groans.
When it snows,
we all have to blow our nose.
When it snows,
it sometimes blows and blows.
When it will snow, only God knows.

Perry Winer, Grade 3
Ridgeway Public School, NE

Earth

Earth is so nice
Earth is so fun
The planet Earth is my favorite one of all.
Earth is very colorful
Which makes it very beautiful
And this is why I like the Earth.

Josh Lambert, Grade 3
Noonan Academy, IL

Centaurs

Big
   Hairy
      Monstrous
         Scaly
           Dwellers of the night
Taking children, robbing banks,
all through the night
Horrible CENTAURS

Addy Hall, Grade 2
Country Meadow Elementary School, IN

Flowers

What a lovely sight,
Pretty pink, purple, and blue
Daisies growing tall.
Angela Dunbar, Grade 2
J C Hoglan Elementary School, IA

Tropical Island

A tropical island
fun and beauty
tall palm trees are swaying
in the wind
relaxation is here
ocean of blue, turquoise and green
a fantastic sight you don't want to miss

You want shade?
Find a hut
along the warm sand
squishing between your feet
yes it is a tropical paradise.
Ellie Jordan, Grade 3
Greenbriar Elementary School, IL

Dawn

The light
Brings out
Beauty
The air feels
So fresh
When you
Wake up
In dawn
Srishti Rathore, Grade 2
Orchard Lane Elementary School, WI

Billy Bob Joe

Billy Bob Joe likes to learn…
about science, math, gym,
and a whole lot more as he learns.
When recess comes it's time to play.
But sometimes kids don't get their way.
Treyton Sleight, Grade 2
Schavey Road Elementary School, MI

Winter

As winter rushes in
It gets colder and colder
You just might get frostbite
It starts to snow
Then you know Christmas is near
It is almost the new year!
Landon Tourville, Grade 3
Montrose Elementary School, MN

The Sea

Turtles
eels
sea urchins
at the bottom of the sea

coral mountains
with jagged peaks
sea stars lay on the bottom
not very lively
at all
Jeffrey Van Spankeren, Grade 3
Greenbriar Elementary School, IL

A Friend

A friend that has a fin
will put on her cool chin
and swim. That's my friend
that has a fin
Decator Simpson, Grade 3
Weymouth Elementary School, MI

You Might Win!

Shush, boy,
You tried your best.
I lost too,
You tried your best.
When you come back,
You may win.
And beat the others,
I'll cheer for you then.
You tried your best.
Ty Heckenlaible, Grade 3
Montrose Elementary School, MN

The Lonely Ice Cream Cone
There once was an ice cream cone,
When people took a bite of his cone, he always moaned.
On a very gray day in May
He ran away.
Then he found a friend
His friend's name was Brend
They became friends until the end.

Emily Leffler, Grade 3
Florence Elementary School, WI

Sounds of Spring
I step outside, sniff the misty air. I hear the birds chirping, the crickets rubbing their legs together, all the bugs crawl out where they were hiding. The ducks are swimming in the pond, the flowers are starting to bloom and the sky is so blue, so peaceful sounds of spring.

Laine Ridenour, Grade 3
Hyatt Elementary School, MI

Humor and Riddles
When all bananas are lost by a monkey?
What do you call a teeter-totter built by a donkey?
Which way is north if the sun is over head?
Is funny in my heart, or in my head?

Furious George!
A hee-haw!
Just wait a few moments…
Both!

Without riddles could we think?
What can't float, but can't sink?
Where does a baby cow go for lunch?
Why is a funny joke line called the punch?

Not likely!
Water!
Calf-ateria!
Oh, my belly!

For music, you hear horns and fiddles,
for humor, you use jokes and riddles!

Anthony LaFond, Grade 2
Cedarcrest Academy, MN

Monkey

Monkey
Brown, funny
Swinging, jumping
Likes to eat bananas
Animal
Willis Goodwin, Grade 2
Pope John XXIII School, IL

Cold

It is cold outside.
It is cold today.
Brrr, I'm cold.

It is a snowy day today.
I don't like the snow.
I'll stay in the house to play.
Antonio Bardeau, Grade 1
Holden Elementary School, IL

Snowflake

Snowflake
Delicate, graceful
Falling, landing, drifting
Coming faintly to the ground
Winter design
Emma George, Grade 3
St Michael School, OH

Me

Dani
Adventurous, playful
Drawing, playing, molding
Loves to draw animals
Friend
Dani Palmer, Grade 2
Pope John XXIII School, IL

Plants

Plants grow
Plants grow in May
Plants need water
Plants need sun
Natalie Cahue, Grade 1
Peck Elementary School, IL

The Day I Didn't Get My Homework In

I was walking out the door one day,
When my shoes turned to hay!
I screamed to my house,
But my mom turned into a mouse!

The trees were rocking,
And everything was completely shocking!
I couldn't find my way to school,
And the bush called me a fool!

When I sat down, my homework wasn't there,
Because of a grizzly bear!
I tried to find him,
But then I ran into Jim!

He asked what was wrong,
And he said to be strong.
We ran into the city,
But we saw a lost kitty!

We started to weep,
But then we saw a huge sheep!
So I'm sorry to say,
That's why my homework isn't here today.
Josey Miller, Grade 3
Coulee Region Christian School, WI

Dogs

Dogs are so very sweet and neat.
They are playful with each other.
And respecting one another.
You're able to dress them up and train them.
They are very very lovable and cute.
They are smart and funny.
They love to play with people and kiss people.
Natalie Nafoosi, Grade 3
Noonan Academy, IL

Video Games

Some easy, some hard
Some fun and some boring
Cool and lame
Donavan Costa, Grade 2
McKenney-Harrison Elementary School, IN

Snow

I like snow.
It is chilly.
I like to jump in it.
It is fun to play in it.
I like snow.
I like to play with my friends
In the snow.
Snow,
It is white,
It is sparkly,
I love snow,
I love snow!

Brooke-destinee Lockwood, Grade 1
James R Watson Elementary School, IN

Spooky, Snoopy, Loopy

Spooky, Snoopy, Loopy
you look woopy!
Do you know
What's going on
with Spooky, Snoopy, Loopy?
Is it a disease?
Or is it a cazease?
What is it? What is it?
Tell me what it is!

Abigail Lynch, Grade 2
McKenney-Harrison Elementary School, IN

Sharks

Sharks are
Dangerous,
Big,
And small.
Sharks have great senses.
There are
Whitetips, Blacktips,
Nurses, Great Whites,
Tigers, Reefs,
Bulls, Lemons, Whales,
Basking, Makos, and Blues.
Do you like sharks?

Colin Goebel, Grade 2
James R Watson Elementary School, IN

Freaking Out

In the third grade classroom
Daniel is freaking out
At 9:59 AM

Daniel Boyes, Grade 3
Smithville Elementary School, OH

King Cobra

Slithering in grass,
Big, long, strong, hissing my way
Very scared of him.

Martin Cervantes, Grade 2
J C Hoglan Elementary School, IA

I See Spring in My Eyes

I see grass
I see trees
I see flowers
I see leaves
I hear birds
I hear wind
I hear wind chimes
I hear bees
I smell BBQ
I smell soil
I smell grass
I smell dew
I feel cozy
I feel hot
I feel great
I feel cool

Darius Cecil, Grade 3
H. R. McCall Elementary School, IL

I'd Rather

I'd rather clean the whole house.
I'd rather drink out of the toilet.
I'd rather jump into a lake.
I'd rather eat a piece of raw fish.
I'd rather feed our piranha.
I'd rather be blind and not see
Than eat one piece of a pea!!

Breanna Hawkins, Grade 3
Henryville Elementary School, IN

Puzzle Piece

A puzzle piece
Is a mystery
Waiting
To be solved
Waiting
To be corrected
Waiting
To be seen.

Jenelle Elise Rolli, Grade 2
Orchard Lane Elementary School, WI

Zebra

Zoom!
goes the Zebra
the Zebra ran.
from the lion
Growl!
the lion tags
the Zebra
Man!
I'm out!

Bailey Lewis, Grade 3
Henryville Elementary School, IN

Spring Is Everywhere

I see birds in the air.
I see puddles everywhere.
I hear children playing.
I hear children laughing.
I feel warm.
I feel relaxed.
I love spring.

Shanetra Daniels, Grade 3
H. R. McCall Elementary School, IL

Sad Joe

There once was an elf named Joe
Who had a big cut on his toe.
He ran to his dad
Because he was sad
"Fix it Dad, I've got to go!"

Tyler Moomaw, Grade 3
Smithville Elementary School, OH

Science Fiction

S uper
C reepy creatures
I ncredible
E nables you to be scared out of your socks
N o happy endings
C urses
E rases your bravery

F un for Halloween
I nvincible
C ourses through your mind
T all tales
I mpossible
O gres
N othing can beat Science Fiction!

Johnny Dietrich, Grade 3
Henryville Elementary School, IN

A Great April

It's a rainy April.
Every day you see more and more flowers and showers.
You see the bright yellow sun and green grass.
Clouds are moving away and so are we.

Jason Katz, Grade 2
St Robert Bellarmine School, IL

How Dinosaurs Roamed the Earth

A long time ago, dinosaurs roamed the Earth…65 million years.
Flying reptiles ruled the skies, squawking and cawing.
If you could imagine a bat's wings that's how a Pteranodon's wings are.
Now, Allosaur's teeth were like daggers…same as Tyrannosaurus Rex's teeth!
So after that long, they died.

Takoda Spears, Grade 3
Emerald Elementary School, MI

Blue

Blue looks like the sky in the morning.
Blue smells like the sea when the waves are flowing by.
Blue tastes like tears that fall from your face.
Blue feels like a wedding ring made of diamonds.
Blue sounds like boots stomping in puddles.

Vanse Harris, Grade 2
Will Carleton Academy, MI

My Shoe Is In The Stew

My shoe fell in the stew
It turned to goo
Oh, what should I do?
I looked in the pot
I saw a little blue dot
Yes, it is true I kicked off my shoe
It fell in the stew
I was sent to bed
Without being fed
Mom was sad
Dad was mad
They thought I was bad
I was not glad

Hayden Ourada, Grade 3
St Clare Catholic School, IL

Sun

I was sleeping,
The sun shown
In my eyes,
I opened
One eye
Then the other,
I awakened.

Zach Scott Wojcik, Grade 2
Orchard Lane Elementary School, WI

Why Do They Go?

I never got to
see them again!
good bye 1999
good bye 2000
good bye 2001
good bye 2002
good bye 2003
good bye 2004
good bye 2005
good bye 2006
good bye 2007
and hello 2008
but you will leave too!

Danny McCombs, Grade 2
Pathfinder Elementary School, MI

Summer

S ummer
U mbrella
M ouse
M emories
E leven
R un

Alyssa McCurrie, Grade 2
Arbury Hills Elementary School, IL

Summer

Summer is really hot
It feels like I'm in a steaming pot.

Summer is very fun
I think I'm going to go on a run.

Summer sun is very bright
And gives us a lot of light.

Randy Golasinski, Grade 3
Atwood Elementary School, MI

Rory

Rory
was my
best
friend ever
and
now he's moved
and I am
shocked
that he moved
and I am
sad.

Kenneth Fleming, Grade 2
Pathfinder Elementary School, MI

School

Fun
Write
Gym
School

Jackie Kopniske, Kindergarten
Northfield Elementary School, OH

I Am a Big Car

I am a big car.
I drive fast, rum, rum.
We go left and right, rum, rum.

I am a big car.
We need more gas, rum, rum.
After that, we drive away real fast, rum, rum.

I am a big car.

Donald Bradley, Grade 2
Mentone Elementary School, IN

Talking to My Teddy Bear

Teddy Bear, Teddy Bear
Are you cold?

Put on my T-shirt
It will be warm

And then some socks
(That'll be a bit big)

How about some underwear
(They will be very big!)

Teddy Bear, Teddy Bear
Don't be cold!

Kendra Nealey, Grade 3
Shorewood Hills Elementary School, WI

Winter

Winter, winter, the air is cold.
The grounds are white with sparkling flakes.
Mittens and jackets come into your house.
Tracks are in the snow, like deer tracks.
Bunnies with black on the tips of their ears.
They're called hares.
They're bunnies that love the snow.
Crows, foxes and some deer come out too.
Winter's so much fun,
I don't know what to play in it!

Hazel Swain, Grade 1
Woodland Elementary School West, IL

We Went to Chuck E. Cheese's

I liked playing video games
Rock liked eating
Mom liked spending time with us
Dad liked winning
Savannah liked her ball
We had fun!

Anthony Kincaid, Grade 1
Webster Elementary School, MI

Penguin

Penguin
Black, white
Fishing, eating, swimming
Bird

Scylar Roop, Grade 2
Thayer Central Elementary School, NE

Kittens

My kittens are special to me
because they are cute and cuddly.
I don't want to get rid of them
but my mom and dad do.

Kaitlin Dood, Grade 2
Pathfinder Elementary School, MI

Makes Me Think of Spring

Spring makes me think of rain
Rain makes me think of water
Water makes me think of a waterfall
A waterfall makes me think of spring

Adam Swartz, Grade 3
Suffield Elementary School, OH

Me

I like the colors
black, red and white.
I'd love a flight
to Los Angeles,
I like my fishing game,
and I love my frame
with the picture of my dad and me.

Lizzie Ramirez, Grade 2
Queen of All Saints School, IL

My Silly Dog

My silly dog
Silly jumping,
Silly tackling,
Silly chasing,
Silly digging,
Silly ramming.

Wyatt Hall, Grade 1
Mentone Elementary School, IN

The Sun

The sun is out in the day,
So come out and play
The sun says hi, and then says bye.

The sun comes out in the summer
Until winter ends, it's a bummer,

The summer is a lot funner,
And on a hot day,
We can go outside…and play.

Deztini Johnson, Grade 3
Lorain Community School, OH

Kitties

Kitty, kitty, kitty
Kitty is my favorite cat.
Black, white and orange
Kitty is a naughty cat.
Romo, Romo is a cat.
I love her
But Kitty does not love Romo.
Fight, fight
All night.
They hate each other so much.

Marissa Hernandez, Grade 1
Strange Elementary School, WI

Raindrops

One raindrop falling
out of the darkened black sky
making a puddle.

Kameron Wederquist, Grade 3
Chantry Elementary School, IA

Love

Love is when my family is around.
Love is when my mom is with me.
Love is when my mom says, "Time for school honey."
Love is when my mom helps me cook chicken.
Love is when my mom makes a good dinner.
Love is when my mom is helpful.
Love is when my mom makes peanut butter cookies.
Love is when my dad is there.
Love is when my dad helps me ride my bike.
Love is when my family is as sweet as a rose.
Love is God, Jesus and Heaven.

Sky Mason, Grade 2
Michener Elementary School, MI

Soldiers

When I am in my nice warm bed.
He's on the ground with his helmet on his head.
When I gasp he is in Iraq under attack.
When I am sick.
He sticks to his plan and goes for it.
When I throw a stick at the wall.
He gets a picture of his daughter in his stall.
When I am in the store.
He is in war.
When I am Christmas shopping.
He is screaming in pain and sobbing.
When people are on the wall.
Soldiers are thinking why they came to war at all.

Mackenzi Matthews, Grade 3
Southern View Elementary School, IL

Blue

Blue looks like the sky and some storybooks
Blue sounds like the water when it rushes
Blue smells like a cotton candy at the fair.
Blue makes me feel like I'm in a meadow with blue flowers.
I see the color blue when I look in the clear sky.
Blue tastes like blueberries that are fresh.
Blue looks like bluebirds flying.
Blue looks like the construction papers we use for art projects.
Blue makes me feel like sitting on my very comfortable blue beanbag.

Lily Shane, Grade 1
JFH Educational Academy West, IL

Spring

When spring begins,
The hibernating is over.
The flowers grow
And the ones that survive
Bloom.

Jason Hogan, Grade 1
Holden Elementary School, IL

Wool Hat

Wool hat
Cozy, comfy
Stretching, warming, hugging
Fits your head snugly
Warm cap

Samantha Morse, Grade 3
St Michael School, OH

The Colorful Dog

There once was a dog
he was red, white and blue.
He liked to have fun
and play catch too.
Whenever he played catch
he would always fall down.

Brandon Kaluza, Grade 2
Hyatt Elementary School, MI

Bisou

Bisou
Fat, heavy
Meowing, sleeping, lazy
Lives at my house
Cat

Cameron MacEwen, Grade 2
Pope John XXIII School, IL

Winter

Winter
Snowy, cold
Slipping, sledding, snowing
I like sledding.
Excited

Alejandro Newberry, Grade 2
Peach Plains School, MI

My Rock

My rock is blazing silver
With innumerable
Knife-edged sides.
Gleaming with reflecting
Light!
Two centimeters long.
It can fit in my palm.

William Jarrard, Grade 3
Shorewood Hills Elementary School, WI

Sea Life

Indigo is the watery sea,
Orange is a small fish, spying on me!

Apricot is a sting ray,
Bronze is a murky day.

Aqua is a dolphin shimmering,
Ebony is a shark slithering.

Pearl is a humongous whale,
Walnut is a rusty, old nail.

Moss is the color of a squid,
Mustard is a sea creature called a "Nid."

Lime is the color of seaweed,
Olive is the color of an old reed.

My colors, your colors,
My sea, your sea.
Every day the colors lurk.

Lauren Smith, Grade 3
Emerald Elementary School, MI

My Teacher Is Fun!!

0+0 my teacher is my hero
1+1 my teacher is fun
2+2 she shows me what to do
3+3 I like her and she likes me
4+4 she is always in and out the door
5+5=10 now I am starting all over again!!

Caroline Igo, Grade 3
St Columbkille School, IA

What if I Am

What if I am a girl who goes to church,
and learns how to praise God.
What if I was born in a different state?
What if I am a girl that don't have a mom,
or dad, or a brother or sister or a family?
I still have God.
What if I am bald headed?
I am still beautiful.
What if I have no friends?
I am me in my own way.

Anana Givens, Grade 3
Cityview Performing Arts Magnet School, MN

Spring

S unshine is shining away.
P ink flowers are blooming.
R ainbows are looking pretty.
I ce cream is tasting good.
N ice birds are singing.
G ardens with vegetables are healthy.

Amara Frisch, Grade 2
Stanton Elementary School, NE

Guitar Hero III

G uys with mohawks
U nbelievable
I t has over 65 songs
T hrough the fire and the flames
A wesome!
R ock and roll all night.

H ard is a level
E very character is sweet
R OCK!
O ne guy is a robot

T hey make it for Wii
H undreds of people have bought it
R ated T
E asy is also a level
E xpert is a really hard level

Andrew Deeter, Grade 3
Floyd Ebeling Elementary School, MI

What Is Purple?
Purple is shirts
And pants, too.
It is plump grapes hanging on vines
waiting to be picked and eaten.
Purple is flowers in my backyard.
It is a bruise from falling down.
It is jelly on a peanut butter
and jelly sandwich for lunch
And Easter eggs lying in a basket.
Purple is my sister's favorite color.

Carlee Schramm, Grade 2
Morgan South Elementary School, OH

Alpine
Alpine
Always biting
Always chasing
Always barking
Always
Always
Always
On the go

Kyle Pell, Grade 2
Pathfinder Elementary School, MI

Potatoes
Potatoes are delicious,
They are cut in half,
They are very HOT,
Potatoes are like ovals,
There are many types,
There are few instructions.

Daniel Miller, Grade 3
Mentone Elementary School, IN

Teen the Toad
Teeny puffs up his little neck.
He is cute.
He is brave because he wasn't scared
When my brother grabbed him.
Joey, please don't touch Teen the toad!

Emily Zuleger, Grade 1
Stocker Elementary School, WI

Stars
Stars in the night
Sparkling
Bright in the sky
With the moon
Bright in the sky
Like the sun when
It shines
Little star
In the night

Menna Ibrahim, Grade 2
Hillcrest Elementary School, KS

Lambeau the Doggy
When he climbs up on my bed
He is very cuddly.
He is black and white.
Big and cute!
He gets excited!
But, he is very nice.
I love Lambeau the dog!

Ella Kaebisch, Grade 1
Stocker Elementary School, WI

Friends
friends are special
because we would
have no one
to play with
that would be boring
you would just sit there
doing nothing
that is why
I like friends
like my friends!

Nakita Westenfelder, Grade 2
Pathfinder Elementary School, MI

Trees
Stands tall to my town
Looks different each season
A home for cute squirrels

Tyson Brock, Grade 3
Mable Woolsey Elementary School, IL

Brave Rocks

The rocky edge
Bravely standing up against
Terrifying waves
Sea green waves
Fiercely making their way
Toward brave rocks
The still sky
Watches the commotion
Clouds
Quickly dash through
Rocks in back
Try not to get into anything
The brave rocks
Crispy brown
With lots of reddish black dents
Water splashing up on them
Making the rocks damp like the underneaths of logs
It's like there's been an earthquake
Under the sand
Made the waves all jumpy
They're just brave rocks!

Kelsey MacDonald, Grade 3
Greenbriar Elementary School, IL

The Statue Gives Dreams

Lady Liberty stands proud and tall,
She unites Americans all,
She will be faced by those who survive,
By the ones of the Islands of Hope and Islands of Tears
And by those who passed here through all the years
She stands here to welcome people into this country
To make dreams come true,
In a free country, with lots of hopes to come true!

Sydney Wodika, Grade 3
Detroit Country Day Junior School, MI

Sledding

Sledding tastes like snow melting.
Sledding looks like snow flakes shattering.
Sledding feels like the breeze.
Sledding sounds like the sled whistling over the snow.

Ashlyn Pretzel, Grade 2
C W Neff Elementary School, MI

Brieann

Friendly, funny
Nice, sweet
Movies, fun
She is pretty all the time.
Brieann is nice and likes playing
video games.
She stays all night with me.

Bailey Eichenberger, Grade 3
Henryville Elementary School, IN

A Little Lizard

A little lizard
With a big tail
Silently in the quiet night

Miguel Cedeno, Grade 3
Lorain Community School, OH

The Nut

It looks like an acorn
So big and wide
Falling from the evening
Sky

Tracey Joswick, Grade 2
Orchard Lane Elementary School, WI

Oranges

Healthy
Vitamin C
Yummy
Oranges

Hritik Gupta, Kindergarten
Northfield Elementary School, OH

fat or skinny

fat
eat, sit
sitting, eating, sleeping
mcdonalds, chips, carrots, salad
run, play
running, playing
skinny

Austin Lawens, Grade 3
Weymouth Elementary School, MI

Imagine Me

Imagine me, a scarecrow.
Staring at the blackbird.
Scaring the people passing by.
Birds are singing, first one bird
and now two birds come.
I do not want to be alone.
Imagine me, a scarecrow.

Evelyn Hernandez, Grade 2
Michener Elementary School, MI

Reflect

Setting sun
water in between
wave after
wave
crash after
crash
no beach
or so it seems…

Brennan Hughes, Grade 3
Greenbriar Elementary School, IL

About the Sun

The sun is bright,
The sun is my light
The sun is for me.
We need the sun for plants,
Animals and people.
The sun is bright.
The sun is my light.
The sun is for me.

Tatiana Gillis, Grade 2
Hosford Park Elementary School, IN

Spring

Some people think spring is one mile.
But when it is here I want to smile!
Some flowers are pink
some flowers are red.
Some birds chirp for
a little piece of bread.

Esmeralda Orozco, Grade 2
Peck Elementary School, IL

My Brother

My brother
Warms my heart
Every day.

When I wake up
He is always smiling.
When he walks
Down the stairs,

His eyes
Deep blue
In color.

Seamus M. Doyle, Grade 3
Shorewood Hills Elementary School, WI

Colors

Our national flag is red, white, and blue.
Our flag reminds me that we are true.

Gold is a trophy that will always glow.
You'll have it while your skills grow.

Silver is a shining quarter.
Go to the bank, put it in, you'll get more.

Green meadows down far below.
Watch as grass blades grow.

Bronze, brown — a little the same.
If you ask me, they're both in the hall of fame.

What do colors mean to you?

Peter Gallette, Grade 2
Detroit Country Day Lower School, MI

Marshmallows

White or colorful,
Golden brown.
Makes s'mores.
Eat some more!
They melt in my mouth.

Natalie Davis, Grade 2
McKenney-Harrison Elementary School, IN

Summer

Summer
Fun, warm
Swimming, playing, running
Shining, blazing, darkening, freezing
Sledding, skating, playing
Cold, white
Winter
Mia Bryant, Grade 3
St Clare Catholic School, IL

Boys

Boys are cute.
Boys act tough.
And some are crazy.
Boys are weird.
They act like such men.
Taylor Stinnett, Grade 2
Woodford Elementary School, OH

Animals

Animals, animals, animals.
I love animals.
I have all of them.
And they are cute and furry.
They are sweet and stuffed.
Animals, animals, animals.
Dasia Hairston, Grade 2
Woodford Elementary School, OH

I Am a Teddy Bear

I am a teddy bear,
Soft and warm,
Stuffed with a lot of love.

I am a teddy bear,
To be hugged,
With a purple bow tie.

I am a teddy bear,
Ready to go to bed,
I am a teddy bear.
Devyn Masterson, Grade 3
Mentone Elementary School, IN

Little Mocha

Little Mocha is so cute.
I love him and he loves me.
I want to have him as my pet.
Little Mocha is my grandma's cat.
Nicole Knoerr, Grade 1
Stocker Elementary School, WI

My Mom

I love my mom
I give her hugs
I give her kisses
Kiss, kiss, kiss
Hugs, hugs, hugs
I love my mom!
Dalaya Hawkins, Grade 1
Webster Elementary School, MI

Skateboard

Skateboard
good air
bad air
fun
cool
awesome
rad
slow
big
small
Max McDonald, Grade 3
Somers Elementary School, WI

I Love Spring

I love spring.
Spring is here.
Kids are playing.
Wind is blowing.
Birds are chirping.
My body is relaxed.
I feel really happy.
I love spring.
I love spring.
Monique Martinez, Grade 3
H. R. McCall Elementary School, IL

William Spaulding

William
Boy, funny, helpful
Son of Ronald and Mandy
Lover of race cars, remote control cars, car toys
Who feels sad when my brother doesn't let me play,
happy at school
Who fears boogie man, bombs, pumpkins
Who would like to see McDonalds
Resident of Indiana, USA
Spaulding

William Spaulding, Grade 2
Country Meadow Elementary School, IN

Book Club

B ecoming a good reader,
O ver to school an extra hour every Tuesday.
O ut at 4:30!
K odi barely brings her book.

C aring for my book.
L aying my book on a desk.
U se my book every Tuesday.
B ooks for twelve children.

Jeffery Blackwell, Grade 2
Hosford Park Elementary School, IN

Writing Hides

Writing hides in my yellow, chocolate smelling, blanket.
Writing hides in my lost green sand dollar.
Writing hides in the number two.
Writing hides in my messy attic.
Writing hides in my busy, strong and smart dad.
Writing hides in the sports I play every spring, summer, fall and winter.
Writing hides in my dreams of becoming an author.
Writing hides in the sounds that tables make as they scratch the floor.
Writing hides in the cover of the book that I never finished.
Writing hides in my cute little sister.
Writing hides in my family's laughter and tears.
Writing hides in the tight hugs I give my mom.
Writing hides in my hands with love.
Writing hides in me.

Cindy Ji, Grade 2
Mason Heights Elementary School, OH

Basketball

Basketball players use their hands to block the ball.
Basketball players fall.
Basketball players put it in the net.
Basketball players sweat.
Basketball players play the game.
Basketball players have fame.

Zack Roa, Grade 3
Atwood Elementary School, MI

Butterfly

B eautiful butterflies blooming on flowers.
U nbelievable beautiful colors just coming in hours.
T raining his own to fly.
T ry young butterfly, try.
E verything he does is up in the sky.
R ain gets on them and they get wet, wet, wet.
F lying high up in the sky.
L oving the butterflies is the best thing to do.
Y et the butterflies have to go, they are still with you.

Gabriella Stratton, Grade 2
Stocker Elementary School, WI

Gymnastics

Gymnastics is a hobby but most of all it's mine.
If you just watch gymnastics your eyes will surely shine.
If you go on a bar, it's twice as fun
So just get over here and get it done.
Also try a beam it's one thing you'll want to do,
Come over here try this, too!

Allison Caroline Childs, Grade 3
MacArthur Elementary School, WI

Friendship

Friendship is very fragile.
You have to treat it like a cherry tree.
You have to water it like you help your friends in need.
You have to pull weeds
like you stop bullies from picking on your friends.
And the most important thing of all is
you have to watch your cherry tree grow
like you watch your friends have fun with you.

Samantha Pfleger, Grade 3
Somers Elementary School, WI

A Cow
If I were a cow,
I would have three empty stomachs
If I were a cow,
I would run away when people tried to milk me
If I were a cow,
I would say moo, moo
If I were a cow,
I would eat hay
If I were a cow,
I would be black with white spots
Or white with black spots I wouldn't know.

Destiny Stebleton, Grade 3
Weymouth Elementary School, MI

Rain
Rain
Is like when I'm with
My dad. I miss my
Mom and I cry
Rain
It feels like tears rolling
Down my cheeks
Rain
It
Feels
Like
Rain
Is
Pouring
In God's
World too.
And it all happens
in the *RAIN*!

Emary Koehl, Grade 2
James R Watson Elementary School, IN

Computers
Computer do thinking
Computers tell you stuff
Computers take lots of
MONEY!

Michael Krehl, Grade 2
Country Meadow Elementary School, IN

Bee Sting

I saw a striped bee,
it stung me.
It hurt real bad,
I was really mad.
Then it buzzed away,
and didn't stay.
Mason Bryant, Grade 1
Trinity Lutheran School, IA

Northern Fur Seal

Northern Fur Seal
Sleek, silky
Swimming, flipping, migrating
Flippers make them
Powerful swimmers
Sea torpedo
Kasey Kelly, Grade 3
St Michael School, OH

Spring

Spring is here
Time to cheer
I cry and shine when spring
is here
I listen and talk
on a clock I go tick-tock
when spring is here
Britney Almanza, Grade 2
Peck Elementary School, IL

Rabbits

Eat carrots
Bite
Make sounds
Run away
Hop fast
Scratch
Eat, eat, eat
Hop, hop, hop
Run, run, run
Chase, chase, chase
Now we can catch it!
Sarah Tabaja, Grade 1
Bright Elementary School, IN

Leprechaun

I once met a leprechaun from Mississippi.
Every day he met a hippy.
But whenever he slapped him,
The hippy kicked Jim,
That strange leprechaun from Mississippi.
Chris Brandt, Grade 3
Somers Elementary School, WI

My Hamster

My hamster exercises on his wheel
My hamster eats carrots
My hamster sleeps on wood chips
I love my hamster
Brittany Walker, Grade 1
Holy Redeemer Christian Academy, WI

Bears

Bears are so big I'm so little
They are really dangerous
I try to shut my mouth and run away from
Bears
  Bears
    Bears
Bears they're really furry they try to steal my
Fish
  Fish
    Fish
I try to shoot them but I
Miss
  Miss
    Miss
Though bears are scary,
They scare me out of my skin.
Derek Hamman, Grade 2
Country Meadow Elementary School, IN

Legos

Legos there's so many things to build.
I put all my inventions up on the windowsill
houses and cars, trains, and planes
all the things I will ever need
are right here in my box you see.
David Garbarino, Grade 3
Floyd Ebeling Elementary School, MI

Spring

S unflowers bloom on a nice sunny day.
P urple and pink tulips bloom.
R ainbows come when it rains.
I ce is in my Kool-aid glass.
N ice enough to go and play.
G reen grass is growing very healthy.

BreAnna McNutt, Grade 2
Stanton Elementary School, NE

Comanche

Comanche, Comanche
My wonderful pony
He's cute and he's spotted
And knows how to rope.
I took him to break away and he reared up.
But, I caught the cow anyway.
I love my little Mexican pony.
Comanche.

Anastacia Greene, Grade 3
Henryville Elementary School, IN

We Help the Earth

We help the Earth by keeping
the flowers watered,
The Earth helps us by giving
us rain on dry days,
We help the Earth by
planting flowers,
The Earth helps us by
making those flowers grow.

Alecia Polk, Grade 2
Gen George Patton Elementary School, IL

Lions and Tigers

They fight
Like wild cats.
They growl
At each other.
So if you are scared,
Go home!
Go lions and tigers!

Spencer Mohre, Grade 2
James R Watson Elementary School, IN

Jaguars

Jaguars run
Jaguars eat
Jaguars love to eat
Jaguars live in jungles
Jaguars

Justin McConnell, Kindergarten
Northfield Elementary School, OH

Kids

kids
kids
kids
screaming
yelling
jumping
crazy
kids
kids
kids

Rachal Overla, Grade 2
Pathfinder Elementary School, MI

Meatballs

M y favorite
E at them up
A treat from Mom
T op with sauce
B ig
A nd
L ittle
L ots of noodles
S o good

De'Andre Henley, Grade 1
Strange Elementary School, WI

Grandma

Grandma
Special, nice
Baking, loving, helping,
Playing games with me
Shirley

Rachel Gomez, Grade 1
Wethersfield Elementary School, IL

Soccer

I like soccer
White black
I like soccer
I am the goalie
Soccer

Hunter Knox, Grade 1
Henryville Elementary School, IN

Baseball

You run to first base,
see dirt flying
off the cleats,
see the ball fly
so high in the sky.
Home run
I love my sport.

Isaac Middleton, Grade 3
Henryville Elementary School, IN

Bees

I don't love bees
Bees hurt you.
Scary bees buzz...
I run inside
I don't like bees!
Bees!

Daisy Myers, Grade 2
Webster Elementary School, MI

Encouragement

When you try very hard,
On your very first try,
On your very first day,
Don't count on succeeding,
Work as hard as you can,
Obey the rules, and you'll do fine
Really try hard and be very
Kind,
In the possibilities,
NEVER
GIVE UP!

John Rechner, Grade 3
Houdini Elementary School, WI

Cookie Monster

"Oh, Cookie Monster, why did you eat those chocolate chip cookies?"
"Oh, Cookie Monster, why did you eat those vanilla chip cookies?"
"Oh, Cookie Monster, why did you eat those cinnamon cookies?"
"Oh, Cookie Monster, why did you eat those oatmeal cookies?"
"Oh, Cookie Monster, why did you eat those raisin cookies?"
"Oh, Cookie Monster, why did you eat those apricot cookies?"
"Oh, Cookie Monster, why did you eat those peanut butter cookies?"
"Oh, Cookie Monster, why did you eat those almond cookies?"
Cookie Monster replied, "I ate them because they were yummy!"

Larry Li, Grade 2
Onaway Elementary School, OH

The Sun and the Moon

The sun is bright.
The sun is shining.
After the sun the moon is next.
When I get tired, I go to sleep.
When I wake up, I get up and go outside to play.
It's five o'clock.
I go in and the sun is still out.
Then I eat my hot dog on a bun.
It's night time — shut the lights out.
I say good night.
I go to sleep and dream.
How fun the next day will be.

Zak Yanders, Grade 2
Woodford Elementary School, OH

Spring Is Beautiful

Spring is like the breeze whooshing through my hair.
Bunches of flowers are everywhere.
The sun is shining oh so brightly and the trees are oh so green.
Apples and pears are gliding on the great big brown branches.
To introduce the pretty birds they do a little song chirp chirp chirp.
With laughter and songs and little tricycles riding through the parks.
I must say that spring is beautiful.
With blue ponds shining like the stars.
And beautiful clear skies and white fluffy clouds.
And as they say spring showers bring May flowers.
I say, spring is beautiful.

Ahlam H. Khatib, Grade 3
Aqsa School, IL

Summer Day
Summer
Warm, rocks
Jogging, biking, playing
Summer is sooooooo cool.
Vacation day.
Alex Gold, Grade 2
Stocker Elementary School, WI

Puppy
Puppy
Sleeping mostly
Loving, cozy, caring, friendly
Sweet
Marissa Garbe, Grade 3
Atwood Elementary School, MI

My Dog
My dog is cute,
My dog is kind,
My dog is big now,
but she still is cute!
My dog loves me,
I love her so much!
I wish she could stay inside,
My dog is my little baby.
If I tell her to come,
she will do it.
If you have a dog,
you are really lucky!
Rachel Echelberry, Grade 3
Kyle Trueblood Elementary School, KS

My Dirt Bike
I have a dirt bike
that I really like.
I like to race
when I don't get mud on my face.
It doesn't have a scratch.
If it falls I try to catch.
It is very good.
When riding I don't wear a hood.
Jayton Hull, Grade 2
Trinity Lutheran School, IA

Andrea
Nice and very sweet,
Loves people and loves her friends,
Is an awesome friend.
Rylee Trombley, Grade 3
Jefferson Elementary School, MI

Spring
S unny days
P laying outside
R unning in the wind
I nsanely beautiful
N othing but sunshine
G ardens starting to grow
Shelby Noveske, Grade 3
Suffield Elementary School, OH

My Hamster
It was a cold and white night
Everyone was snuggled up tight.
The wind howled
My dog growled.
I wanted to go back to my room
But it would be morning soon.
I went into the kitchen and there it was
My little hamster named Fuzz.
Kendra Larwin, Grade 3
Walls Elementary School, OH

Daniel
Daniel
crazy, athletic
talking, hyper, playing
always saying something strange
Dan
Justin Fath, Grade 3
Smithville Elementary School, OH

Oak Tree
Lively, summer oak
Swinging her wild branches
Dropping leaves later
Dylan Kemp, Grade 3
Mable Woolsey Elementary School, IL

I Love Lakes
Swimming
Diving
Sleeping
Eating
Playing

Mommy days at the lake are happy!

Owen Walter, Grade 1
James R Watson Elementary School, IN

Rainbows in the Sky
Rainbows shining in the pretty sky.
You can see all the pretty colors
In the sky
Do you like the pretty rainbows
In the sky?
I like the pretty rainbows
In the sky.
I
Like
Rainbows!

Angelica Alvarez, Grade 2
James R Watson Elementary School, IN

Spring
Spring spreads joy
When the singing birds appear
When the days start getting longer
On a rainy cloudy day
With flowers blooming and sun shining.

Megan Ryan, Grade 3
Northfield Elementary School, OH

The Greatest Friend
I like my friend Dakota
She is special because she was a good friend.
I liked her but now she is gone
It does not feel good.
I feel really blue when she is gone far away
All around me is blue because
she made my life full of surprises.

Ya'Rya Edelen, Grade 3
Henryville Elementary School, IN

Lightbulbs

Do lightbulbs need x-rays?
Do lightbulbs ever want to go and play?
Do lightbulbs get tired
of hanging above chairs?
Do they have teddy bears?
Benjamin Smith, Grade 3
St Paul's Lutheran School, MN

Tristin

Funny, helpful
video games
Nice,
My friend and
I like to
play games and
have fun.
Stephen Rogge, Grade 3
Henryville Elementary School, IN

My Teacher

My teacher likes books
My teacher is nice
My teacher likes children
My smart teacher
Emma Freimark, Grade 2
Orchard Lane Elementary School, WI

Diamond

If I were a diamond…
I would be on a finger.
I would be shiny.
I would be rich.
If I were a diamond.
Jesse Woodward, Grade 2
Woodford Elementary School, OH

Webkinz

Webkinz World is tons of fun,
At the "W" Shop you buy a bun.
Designing a house is really cool,
Use your Kinzcash and buy a pool.
Elizabeth Pekar, Grade 3
Burr Elementary School, MI

Puppy/Dog

Puppy
Cute, fun
Playing, running, jumping
Cage, outside, hunting, yard
Big, strong
Dog
Liam Callahan, Grade 1
Ladoga Elementary School, IN

My Very Own Unicorn

I have a pet, a colorful pet
It is a unicorn under the rainbow
She comes running when I call
She means the world to me.
Kelsey Dehanke, Grade 3
Emerald Elementary School, MI

Butterflies

I like butterflies.
Butterflies are such pretty colors.
Flapping their wings up and down.
Blue, green, orange, red, and purple.
Pink, black, and turquoise blue.
Such colorful wings.
They look like a rainbow in the sky!
Mallory Mills, Grade 1
Rock Ledge Elementary School, WI

Crocodiles

Green
Dangerous
Scales
Crocodiles
Noah Mangeri, Kindergarten
Northfield Elementary School, OH

How I See Spring

I see spring in the air.
I see spring in my hair.
I see spring in trees.
I see spring in the leaves.
Miguel Ruiz, Grade 3
H. R. McCall Elementary School, IL

The Fly

He is flying as fast as he can through the damp, wet forest.
What's that…a camping site?
People…and they have food. YUM!!!
Oh no…flypaper, sap, bug spray, and a fly light.
PHEW! I made it through.
Hot dogs, corn, oh no. A fly swatter.

Caleb Swanson, Grade 3
Emerald Elementary School, MI

Petal Meadow

When the sun goes up it's a nice sunny day!
I get out of bed and excited to play…in the petal meadow!

I see so many flower petals like orange, white,
blue, yellow, purple, and red.

I feel the sunshine upon my face.

I find an apple tree.
I sit under the shade eating an apple from the tree.

Up comes a friendly bee offering honey to me.
Its sweet aroma smells so good.
So I take it home for my family and me.

The sun goes down and time to sleep! Zzzzzzzzzzzz.

Christopher Guerra, Grade 3
Henry W Longfellow Elementary School, IL

Family

Family is love is sharing and caring
Family's love is pretty like a flower and it has a lot of power
Family's love is sweet like honey when the days are sunny.
When families and friends sit together next to trees they think of sweet dreams.
Family's love is a heart that can never tear the family apart
I feel so happy and safe when I spend time with my family.
On family nights me and my family spend time happily.
My family gives me love no matter what I've done.
Remember love doesn't come from presents
it comes from the heart always from the start

Maha Ikram, Grade 3
Aqsa School, IL

Football

Quarterback hut, hut
Hike, run, tackle
Touch down Colts and Bears
They are the strongest ones.
Alberto Sauceda, Grade 3
Levan Scott Academy, IN

Puppy/Mika

Puppy
Snuggle, furry
Playing, cuddling, barking
I love my puppy
Mika
Anna Keagler, Grade 2
Coy Elementary School, OH

Hockey

Hockey is
awesome,
exciting,
fun,
fast,
hard hitting,
unfriendly,
difficult,
upsetting,
lots of pressure,
injurious,
You must be
TOUGH!
Hugh Brady, Grade 2
Queen of All Saints School, IL

Girls and Boys

Girls
Pretty, smart
Singing, dancing, acting
Dresses, dolls, trucks, ties
Boxing, racing, repairing
Strong, tough
Boys
Katie Halwachs, Grade 3
St Clare Catholic School, IL

Hate

Hate is when I get mad at the devil.
I hate when I get sent to my room.
Hate is when I lose my temper.
Hate is getting frustrated with my brother.
Hate is when I scream out of control
I feel hate in bad strangers.
I feel hate in nightmares.
I hear Ethan say, "I hate you."
Hate is just like the devil in you.
Hate is when someone calls me a name.
Hate is when Justin holds me upside down
and all the blood goes to my head so…
I get mad and punch him in a bad place.
Hate is when you get mad.
Aidan French, Grade 2
Michener Elementary School, MI

Pigs

Pigs peee-you
Strong stinky smell
When you feel them
It's a furry feeling
Big noses
Spots
Brown, black, white
Peee-you!
Peee-you!
Caitlin Taylor, Grade 2
Country Meadow Elementary School, IN

Dogs

Dogs, dogs, dogs,
black and white,
Dogs, dogs, dogs,
like to play,
Dogs, dogs, dogs,
like to jump,
Dogs, dogs, dogs,
like frisbee,
Dogs, dogs, dogs,
like to smell,
I love dogs!
Taylor Stickan, Grade 1
Hamilton Community Elementary School, IN

Shamrock

S hamrock cakes are good to eat.
H omes have shamrocks.
A re shamrocks real?
M oms like shamrocks.
R oar! Dinosaurs attack shamrocks.
O utside it is fun to find shamrocks.
C lover is shamrocks.
K aty likes shamrocks.

Luke Staley, Grade 2
Woodford Elementary School, OH

Basketball History

My teammates are sweating,
30 seconds left in the game!
One more point and we win!
We might make basketball history.

It's down to 20 and we're all running...
I'm open! I'm open!

My teammate sees me,
And before I know it's trapped in my hands.
I run down the court dribbling the ball,
I shoot...

The basketball goes in with a swish,
We won!
The crowd is shouting, hurray! hurray!

You won!
You made basketball history!
Chanted the fans in the stands!

Dana Egelhoff, Grade 3
MacArthur Elementary School, WI

Lions

Lions are cool and they're king of the jungle
The have sharp teeth
They eat meat like Gazelle,
Water buffalo, and other things
Lions have manes

Kyle Feller, Kindergarten
Ramalynn Montessori Academy, MN

Baby

Baby
I have been

waiting
and

waiting
and

waiting
for this
happy
moment
Melissa Grusczynski, Grade 2
Orchard Lane Elementary School, WI

Puppy/Dog

Puppy
Soft, fun
Cute, sleepy, playing
Drinking, swimming, jumping
Mom, couch, eating
Big, strong
Dog
Autumn Leonard, Grade 1
Ladoga Elementary School, IN

What Can It Be?

Funny
Happy
Wonderful!
What can it be?
Joyful
Silly
Special
It's easy
To see
Helpful
Respectful
Caring
A friend can be!
Taylor Wilson, Grade 1
Carriage Hill Elementary School, NE

Frosty/Blizzard

Frosty
The storm is bad
Horrible icy storm
The storm is horrible and cold
Blizzard
McKenna Frappier, Grade 3
Midkota Elementary School, ND

Legos

I like to build with Legos.
I know that I have over 100.
They are very cool.
I can build a building.
I can build a ship.
I can build anything!!!!
Collin Anderson, Grade 1
Ramalynn Montessori Academy, MN

Autumn Walks

Leaves crunch as you walk
The crisp breeze blows by smoothly
Beautiful leaves fall
Alicia Lawyer, Grade 3
Jefferson Elementary School, MI

School

School is for playing
School is for making friends
School is for making things
School is for fun
School is for me
Jesse McCutcheon, Grade 3
Henryville Elementary School, IN

Molly

Molly
blue eyes
loves to climb
my sister is Kirsten
volleyball is my favorite sport
has a cat named Baby Girl
Molly Pfeiffer, Grade 3
Barhitte Elementary School, MI

If I Were a Food I Would Be

I would be a fruit
The fruit I would be is an apple
I would be a sweet apple
Because I am sweet
I want to be a fruit because they are sugary
I want to be a food that matches my characteristics
Apples are also cherry red
Red is one of my favorite colors
Apples are very juicy
I love juice, especially apple juice
Apples are my favorite kind of fruit

Anusha Ebrahim, Grade 3
Decatur Classical Elementary School, IL

Spring

S un in the sky while the horses run in the grass and the wind blowing
   and newborn horses growing up.
P lants eaten by horses and baby horses while children play in the spring.
R eindeer hop and look for food in the forest
   and fathers getting their antlers sharp.
I nsects flying in the air and crawling in the ground.
N o more winter only spring drops, rainbows and leaves that are green
   and fresh air.
G rass ran over by horses and baby horses growing up.

Tabitha Camacho, Grade 3
Peck Elementary School, IL

Rilla's Homework Excuses

I don't have my homework because my fat fish ate it.
After half the sheet was gone, my pencil split!
No speak English, me!
My fingers got stung by a bee.
The subject is so boringly political.
That is not so very, very, critical!
I couldn't concentrate because of that loud talk show.
It wouldn't stop because it didn't have "pause" like a video!
My nephew made me look at his tooth, so white and pearly.
My mom made me go to bed oh, so early!
So, if these excuses are a bore,
I could come up with a lot more!

Rilla McKeegan, Grade 3
Decatur Classical Elementary School, IL

The Ghost
Night. Scary.
My mind
Thinks
Monsters.
Footsteps
I
Think
Are not mine.
A door
Opens
CCCRREEEAAAKKKKK.
A ghost!!!!
AAAAHHHHH!!!
I give my cat food
And run.
Peter Stelter, Grade 3
North Intermediate School, MN

I Can't
I can't have marshmallows for dinner?
No s'mores?
No cake?
No rootbeer?
No popsicles?
No ice cream?
How come?

No chocolate pie?
Or gum?

Just like in the past.
I never get the good stuff.
I just thought I'd ask.
Dominic Shamblin, Grade 1
Northfield Elementary School, OH

Slipped on My Behind
I went in the pool
But then I drooled
I went blind
And slipped and fell on my behind
Jonathan Coleman, Grade 2
Arbury Hills Elementary School, IL

Rain
New life

Falling from the sky
Perfect for birds
As they hunt for worms
You're tiring to watch
Tiring to see
But you don't get tired
While you make
Swimming pools for worms
Just listen
Cla cla cla cla
Lauren Meyers, Grade 2
Orchard Lane Elementary School, WI

Bowling
Bowling
Fun bowling
Roll the ball
To hit some pins
Bowling is exciting
Bowling's cool
Bowling
Michael Resk, Grade 2
Webster Elementary School, MI

Soccer
Kick, kick, kick
My sister kicks the ball to me
And I kick to Martin.
The ball went in!
Yeah, yeah, yeah!
Don Taft, Grade 1
Strange Elementary School, WI

My Friends
Anna has a banana.
Savannah has a bandanna.
Susanna has a last name Montana.
Miranna has a sister Hannah.
And they're all my friends.
Kendra VandenHeuvel, Grade 1
Rock Ledge Elementary School, WI

SpongeBob

S pongy
P erfect TV show
O cean animal
N ice
G reat
E xcellent friend to Patrick
B ikini bottom
O ften causes trouble
B est TV show ever

Katelin Escamilla, Grade 1
James R Watson Elementary School, IN

Baseball

Fun
Cool
Bats
Bases
I like baseball

Cooper Wilson, Grade 2
McKenney-Harrison Elementary School, IN

Spring

S unny days are coming
P urple tulips are jumping.
R ed flowers are blooming fast.
I nsects are getting big.
N eat kids are playing at the park.
G iant hills of dirt are getting bigger.

Tayton Lierman, Grade 2
Stanton Elementary School, NE

Shapes

circle
square
triangle
rhombus
trapezoid
rectangle
oval
Shapes are cool!

Kayden Hall, Grade 1
James R Watson Elementary School, IN

Dogs

Dogs are very amazing creatures
They follow your command
Some lend a helping hand
They fetch and play
Almost every day
Some are big
Some are small
But I love them all.

Alexandra Hoye, Grade 3
Noonan Academy, IL

Snowmobiling

We go
Vroom
Vroom.
We ride.
We go all day.
We ride
Ride
Ride all day
And night.

Kelsey E. Kurylo, Grade 1
Bristol Elementary School, WI

Breakfast

I see a pancake breakfast today.
I hear my friends talking to me.
I smell pancakes and sausages.
It tastes good, yummy, and delicious.
I feel fine.
I'm full.

Kurt Rogers, Grade 1
Eastside Elementary School, MI

Grass

Green
Soft
By my toes
I like it
Straight
Grass

Owen Licht, Kindergarten
Northfield Elementary School, OH

Birthdays

Cake
Ice cream
Balloons
Party hats
Party horns
Birthdays

Kara Freyhauf, Kindergarten
Northfield Elementary School, OH

My Hickery Dickery Shoe

My hickery, dickery shoe,
If you sniffed it, P.U.!
My hickery, dickery shoe,
It's magical!
Woo Whoo!
My hickery, dickery shoe,
It's a nose plugger!
Whew!

Karlee Boldin, Grade 2
Patterson Elementary School, MI

Books Are Fun

I like long books
I like short books
I like in-between books
I like to read with my mom
I like to read with my dad
I like to read with my friends at school
Books are fun!

Christa Daniel, Grade 1
Webster Elementary School, MI

I Am...

I am a girl
Who likes soccer
And nice toys.
I love doing girl things,
Except makeup.
I don't like makeup.
But my sister does,
I am a girl!

Alyssa Brito, Grade 2
Mentone Elementary School, IN

When Fall Comes

When fall comes the leaves change colors.
When fall comes there are no more bees.
When fall comes I can't play ball, and I can't make bird calls.
When fall comes all the costumes are sold, when fall comes you always get a cold.
When fall comes it gets really chilly, when fall comes you want to be silly.
When fall comes I wear my hood, when fall comes everything is good.
When fall comes the grass isn't green, when fall comes you can't be mean.
When fall comes the nights are cold, so you have to be bold.
When fall comes I run home, to put out the Halloween gnome.
When fall comes I wear my coat, when fall comes I'll make a leaf moat.
On fall nights I turn on the light, and the mosquitoes bite.
When fall comes the leaves change colors.

Claire Marie Embil, Grade 3
JFH Educational Academy West, IL

Spring

S ounds of wind chimes fill the sweet flower scented air. Flowers fill the air
with candy scents as the nose can smell.
P ets walking on the sidewalks with the owner. People being glad that spring
is finally here.
R ings, rings you hear them everywhere because the ice cream truck is here.
I nsects come by more often. Butterflies are as pretty as the eye can see.
N o coats, mittens, hats or scarves that's what I like the most about spring.
G entle kites and birds sore in the sky.

Jennifer Chavez, Grade 3
Peck Elementary School, IL

Crazy Mice

There are some mice in my house.
My mom thinks mice are nice,
But my dad thinks they have head lice.
When they come to my house,
My mom gives them rice,
But my dad tries to stick them to ice.
I gave them a game of dice.
I tried to convince my dad that mice are really nice.
But my dad still doesn't like mice.
But there is a mouse wearing a blouse.
I saw mice slice
some cheese twice.

Ellie Thein, Grade 2
MACCRAY West Elementary School, MN

Skating Rink

Skating rink
Bright, slippery
Dancing, moving, twirling
Place to skate at night
With lights
Ice plaza
Maggie Malone, Grade 3
St Michael School, OH

Fireworks!

We wait, wait, wait, then…
BOOM! CRACKLE!
O-o-o-o-ah! Look at that!
Again! Again! Again!
BOOM! Sis-z-z-z-le!
More! More! Lights flash!
Then it's dark again.
And the grand finale!
It's all over…bye.
Sally Ming, Grade 3
Holly Elementary School, MI

The Rain

The rain goes pitter patter
I wish I was in Spain
I wish I wasn't in the rain
It drives me insane.
It is cold.
I smell the mold.
Ryan Peterson, Grade 3
St Timothy's School, MN

Summer

Summer summer,
I love summer,
Swimming in the sun,
You never need to run,
Playing in the park,
Watching the dogs bark,
Playing with your friends,
Wishing summer never ends.
Ciara Joyce, Grade 2
Queen of All Saints School, IL

Happiness Is…

Playing on the swings,
Playing on the merry-go-round,
Playing with the basketball,
Playing on the ropes,
Playing on everything!
Richard Clark, Grade 1
Hamilton Community Elementary School, IN

Chocolate Dogs

I love dogs!
How about you?
Do you love dogs?
Well, I do.
They listen.
They are friendly.
They are white or brown.
Some even look chocolate colored.
I love chocolate!
How about you?
Kendall Sizemore, Grade 2
McKenney-Harrison Elementary School, IN

Pain Is Rain

Pain is rain falling down the window frame.
You sit there wondering why.
But, all you want to do is cry.
No place to go.
No place to play.
You might wonder if this rain will ever go away.
Britney Schuetter, Grade 3
Emerald Elementary School, MI

Ski Racing

Through the gates, past the wand
Speeding like a bird, fast, fast, fast,
Feeling a little cold but don't really care.
You hear people hooting for you.
Glide through the icy snow
G-O G-O is all around you!
Hands frozen to poles.
YES! Flying through the gates!
Wondering what time I got.?.?.?.?.?.?.?
Andrea Thurnheer, Grade 3
Greenvale Park Elementary School, MN

Manning Brothers

Eli plays for the New York Giants
He
Played
In
The Super Bowl this year
XLII, which was this year!

Peyton plays for the Indianapolis Colts
He
Played
In
The Super Bowl last year
XLI was last year!
They can both throw a mile high
So it looks like a crystal where the ball went!

They both play football
TOUCHDOWN!!

You rock, Manning Brothers!

Brandon Burggrave, Grade 2
James R Watson Elementary School, IN

Rain

Rain feels like leaving your family
I know how it feels
It keeps on haunting me
When I left my dad
It feels sad
I hope this nightmare goes away
It feels like
Clouds
When I go outside
It's just like tears.
When
Will
The
Rain
Go
Away?

Lilli Hanes, Grade 2
James R Watson Elementary School, IN

Grave Stone

You grow to a baby
Have fun when you are a kid
You work as a man
Now your time is up for living
You got to get buried
Now you're in heaven
Hope you have fun

Kyle Guzdziol, Grade 2
Patterson Elementary School, MI

Snow!

Snow is beautiful when it falls,
it's fun to play in it.
It feels cool and cold when it falls,
snow is awesome!!!

Nicholas Hoffman, Grade 3
Houdini Elementary School, WI

Sun

Rising sun
moving up
lighting the day
brighter and brighter
bringing life to us
warming our bodies
letting us eat
we will live

Nick Charlton-Perrin, Grade 3
Greenbriar Elementary School, IL

Isaac

Funny, Video games
Happy, cool
Cats, pool

I like to wrestle with him
and play basketball with him.

Sometimes I go to his house
and we play dart guns and football
together.

K.C. Reschar, Grade 3
Henryville Elementary School, IN

Miasaura

Miasaura
means good
mother lizard.
Miasaura is a
dinosaur on
Dinosaur King.
It was in
Switzerland.
It laid eggs
if it's a mother.

Daniel Fuelling, Grade 2
Waterloo Elementary School, IN

Springtime

Spring is here.
Now we can play
In the wonderful earth.
Birds are singing.
Grass is growing.
Flowers are blooming.

Everyone is cheering up.
Spring makes everyone happy.
Spring is the best season!

Leema Kalayil, Grade 2
St Robert Bellarmine School, IL

My New Puppy

I have a new puppy.
His name is Trevor.
He is black.
He is soft.
He is playful.
I love my puppy.

Haley Burnett, Grade 1
Henryville Elementary School, IN

Snow Race

Let's watch the snow race.
Let's have some hot cocoa too.
We had lots of fun.

Devan Di Grado, Grade 2
Ramalynn Montessori Academy, MN

Iditarod

I cy path
D on't want ice to break because you will fall in
I must take breaks
T errible if you fall in the ice
A musher controls the sleigh
R eally fun for the dogs
O h no! Too much snow
D on't want it to be hot

Paulina Linares, Grade 2
Central Elementary School, IL

Winter

Winter looks like snow and people sliding down the hills.
Winter feels cold, bare, and freezing.
Winter smells like the warm cookies.
Winter sounds like birds chirping loudly and kids laughing.
Winter tastes like hot cocoa and gingerbread cookies.

Serena Williams Gareau, Grade 2
Coy Elementary School, OH

Dogs

Dogs, dogs, dogs. Dogs are lots of colors
Brown,
Black,
White,
Tan,
Yellow.
Dogs, dogs, dogs. Dogs can be lots of names.
Buddy,
Oreo,
Cammy,
Jake,
Alley,
Daisy,
Spot.
Dogs, dogs, dogs. Dogs can have lots of markings.
Polka dotted,
Spotted,
Striped.
Dogs, dogs, dogs. Dogs are *awesome!*

Morgan Spade, Grade 2
Country Meadow Elementary School, IN

Spring Is Fun

Spring is here
And school is almost out
Now everyone is going to shout
I watch the sun
And I like to play and run

Abby Hooley, Grade 2
Ladoga Elementary School, IN

Husky

Husky
Smart, fast
Running, dashing, pulling
Powerful sledding
Companion
Snow dog

Dominique Capparuccini, Grade 3
St Michael School, OH

Camp

I'm going to camp!
Climbing!
Running!
Bugs!
Lots of fun!

Parker Ellis, Kindergarten
Ramalynn Montessori Academy, MN

Imagine Me

Imagine me, a football.
Flying,
Kicking,
Spinning around the field.
Waiting to be tackled.
Thrown to another player.
Slamming.
Waiting to be kicked off.
Making a touchdown.
Flipping
Sliding
Flying up in the air.
Imagine me, a football.

David McNeil, Grade 2
Michener Elementary School, MI

Dream

I dream…
of a place
that kids play and play
we sing, we run
but when I wake up…
it's all back to normal!

Peyton Ottersbach, Grade 3
Henryville Elementary School, IN

Birds

I like birds.
They are my favorite animals
They fly in the sky.
Baby birds try to fly but
they can't they're too small.
Some birds don't even have wings
to fly with.
Mother birds teach baby birds
to fly in the sky.

Tabitha Pedraza, Grade 2
Peck Elementary School, IL

Spring

S unbathing
P arty
R un
I ce cream
N ap
G ame

Makayla Bechtold, Grade 1
Southwood Elementary School, IN

What If…

If I were a balloon I'd fly up to the sky.
I'd fly around the world and back
and into outer space
and around the moon and back.
And I'd fly through a cloud
and all around up and down
and all around side to side.
I'd say "We-ee-ee-ee-ee!"

Sarah Charles, Grade 3
Holly Elementary School, MI

Puppies

Puppies, silver, black, and brown.
To me they are a gold crown.
Puppies are so cute they should wear a suit.
Some are playful and sleepy.
But some are just plain creepy.

Vinnie Fanning, Grade 3
Atwood Elementary School, MI

The Sea

The blue sparkly
Crystal sea
Is beautiful at sunset
But it is deep
Too deep
I could drown
Oh, wait, I forgot
I'm in the shallow part of the sea!

Landon Myers, Grade 2
James R Watson Elementary School, IN

Pigs

Pigs like to play in mud
Pigs walk very slow
Pigs sleep in the mud
Pigs sleep all night
Pigs!

Heath Meschberger, Kindergarten
McKenney-Harrison Elementary School, IN

Bulldogs

Walking into the field
All the fans yelling, "Let's go Bulldogs!"
"Let's go and win."
I'm up to bat
It was terrifying
When the ball was thrown
It was like lightning
The end of the game
It is over, we win!
We won the championship!

Justin Parks, Grade 2
Country Meadow Elementary School, IN

Grasshopper
grasshopper jumps high
looks for some food in the grass
finds food and goes home
Timothy Grant, Grade 3
Phillip May Elementary School, IL

Books
I love books.
Big books
Little books
Long books
Short books
Any kind of book.

A book in a car
A book in a house
A book with the teacher
A book with a mouse
I love books.

Baby books
Adult books
Soft books
Rough books
I love books.
Sydney Metallo, Grade 2
Stocker Elementary School, WI

School
Learn
Play
Math
Smart
Cool
Spelling
Friends
Language
Test
Reading
Science
This school is for me and you
Summer Sandlin, Grade 3
Henryville Elementary School, IN

Water Horse
I am a water horse
who lives at the golf course.
I might look a little mean.
I like the color green.
I swim under the sea
so the sharks can't catch me.
Tyler Casotti, Grade 1
Trinity Lutheran School, IA

Wrestlers
Wrestlers are big
Wrestlers are small
Wrestlers have big muscles
Wrestlers fight, fight, fight
Who will win the belt?
Ryan Goad, Grade 1
Webster Elementary School, MI

Polly
P layful
O ne bad mess
L ittle ball of fun
L azy
Y ou would love this dog!
Jordan Bailey, Grade 3
Henryville Elementary School, IN

Dance/Ballet
Dance
Twirl, swirl
Jumping big leaps
Happy, fun, hard
Ballet
Roweena Kennedy-Cobb, Grade 3
Burr Elementary School, MI

Rabbits
I love rabbits,
Fur on their feet,
Stomp, stomp, stomp!
Here they come!
Hayden Wege, Kindergarten
Ramalynn Montessori Academy, MN

Teachers

T eachers are great
E ither nice or mean
A lot of fun
C hristmas parties with teachers are really fun.
H ers or his can be fun
E ither like them or not
R you ready for spring break
S orry for the people who get two weeks off for summer

Taylor Bingley, Grade 3
Woodford Elementary School, OH

Brown

Brown feels like hair flapping in the air.
Brown looks like the mane on a running horse.
Brown looks like a crayon the color of a penny.
Brown feels like dead grass.
Brown sounds like an owl who makes loud noises in the night.
Brown smells like bread in the toaster.
Brown tastes like bread.
Brown sounds like flipping a coin.
Brown looks like mud or cement on the ground.

Carli Harrington, Grade 2
Will Carleton Academy, MI

Crocodiles

I see crocodiles swimming in the water.
They have long, green spiky tails and sharp teeth.
I hear them eat fish and fighting with each other.
If its mouth was tied shut
I would like to ride it!

Matthew Goorhouse, Grade 1
Eastside Elementary School, MI

Raindrops

Raindrops, raindrops falling so fast!
If there was a hard raindrop, it would have gave me a cast.
I want to get the raindrops with my fist.
Sometimes I wish raindrops were mist!
Raindrops, raindrops are very wet.
If a raindrop hits you, the raindrop and you just met!

Andrew Hauncher, Grade 3
Deerfield Elementary School, MI

Squirmy
little guinea pig
fast at eating
always makes a cute face
fuzzy
Madeline Morrow, Grade 3
Noonan Academy, IL

The Storm
I looked up up
Into the yellow sun.
It was bright.
I looked down down
At the grass.
The grass shook.
The wind blew.
The tree shook BOOM!
The thunder rumbled.
The tornado twisted.
I looked up up.
I looked down down.
It's all right.
Valerie Gabel, Grade 2
Norris Elementary School, NE

Spring
Blue birds are singing,
spring has come,
flowers are blooming,
spring has come,
blue birds are hatching,
spring has come.
Kaitlyn Galbreath, Grade 2
Hyatt Elementary School, MI

Frog
Frog
Spotted, colorful
Croaking, hopping, swimming
Swiftly grabs insects
With its long tongue
Amphibian
Annie Davis, Grade 3
St Michael School, OH

The Horse That Did Not Like to Golf
I am a horse.
My friends forced me
to golf on the golf course.
I told my friends, I did not want to,
but they said I had to
so I did but I was mad too.
So I cried, "Boo hoo hoo," to school,
because school is not cool.
So I went to the pool
where it is nice and cool.
That is why I go the pool instead of school.
Kailee Roskens, Grade 2
MACCRAY West Elementary School, MN

Baseball
Hit a ball.
It is fun!
Before you know it…
Home run!
Brandon Doehrman, Grade 2
McKenney-Harrison Elementary School, IN

The Day I Got Thrown into the Wash
Hi, my name is Josh.
I got thrown into the wash.
The water started to rise,
So I got soap in my eyes.
I shrank to one inch.
Then my clothes started to pinch.
My mom started to yell,
And she fainted and fell.
Joshua Gribble, Grade 1
Rock Ledge Elementary School, WI

Shelby
Racing stripes
spoiler
back trunk
hood
engine
gas
Vrooooooooooooom!
Aidan Friedel, Grade 1
James R Watson Elementary School, IN

Spiders
Spiders do live in the web.
They have eight legs.
They can make webs.
Spiders.

Brandon Kasinger, Kindergarten
McKenney-Harrison Elementary School, IN

Fireworks
Bright fireworks
Light fireworks
It's going to crack
    B   O
    O   M!
I can smell the repulsive gas from it
Bright fireworks
Light fireworks
Oh, I smell it again
        C
        R
        A
        C
        K!
Repulsive, repulsive, repulsive!
Bright fireworks
Light fireworks
        I
      Love
F   R   W   R   S!!!
    I   E   O   K

Ashlee Allen, Grade 2
James R Watson Elementary School, IN

Pink
Pink is ice cream.
Pink is a pig.
Pink is the sunset.
Pink is the bow.
Pink is lipstick.
Pink is a rose.
I love pink!

Lauryn Marshall, Grade 1
James R Watson Elementary School, IN

Winter

The trees are bare,
The leaves fall down,
Under the snow,
It gets all brown.
Time to play,
And have some fun,
Throw the balls
One by one,
Under the footprint,
Of yours and mine,
It's dirty with mud,
All over our shoes,
Now it's fall,
So,
The trees are bare,
The leaves fall down,
Under the snow,
It gets brown.

Joy Chung, Grade 2
Orchard Lane Elementary School, WI

My Cat

Cats,
Sharp teeth,
They can bite too,
When they get mad at you!

Paigey Thaler, Kindergarten
Ramalynn Montessori Academy, MN

Winter

I see winter snow
    falling from the clouds.
I hear the winter
    wind blowing.

I smell hot chocolate!

I feel the winter snow.
I taste a snowflake.

Mom calls…time to go in.

Jayce Dippel, Grade 1
Woodford Elementary School, OH

I Am…

I am a dreamer
I have all sorts of dreams
Filled with creatures so crazy it seems
From tiny fairies
To huge dragons
To scary goblins
To little elves
Even to…singing pigs
I am a dreamer

Lillian Dwyer, Grade 2
Mentone Elementary School, IN

Spring

Spring is here
It's time to cheer
Breeze is flowing in the trees
Wind is blowing
Dad is mowing
The flowers are growing
It's time for gardening

Jaylie Klusty, Grade 3
Suffield Elementary School, OH

Spring Days

I like the spring days.
There are many ways.
I like to run in the sun.
It will be so much fun!
You can laugh and play,
ride your bike.
I think this is the season I like.
Play with your friends all day long
or maybe just sing a song.

Andrea Flores, Grade 2
Peck Elementary School, IL

Spring

Spring is fun
Spring is for children
Spring is here
Spring is for everyone

Stacie Young, Grade 3
Henryville Elementary School, IN

Sun

We went out to play, it was OK.
The sun was shining, the dog was hiding,
We went in to eat our meat,
When we went back out to play,
The sun went away.
It was soft, sweet rain and gave no one pain.
I walked outside where the soft, sweet rain falls on my head.
And when I go to sleep,
I know a new day is on the way by the next day
It will become today.

Madison Wisen, Grade 2
Jackson Center Elementary School, OH

Colors All Around

Red is like the big red sun
Blue is a pool that is very fun
White is like the snow
Without orange you couldn't put on a show
With yellow you can come alive
With purple you can do the hand jive
Without green I bet there wouldn't be spring
Without aquamarine there wouldn't be any dancing
Gold is like a diamond ring
Silver is like a doorbell that goes "Ring, Ring"
Baby blue is the color of the sky
Magenta is the color that makes you cry

Alisha Scantlin, Grade 3
Kate Goodrich Elementary School, WI

Colors

Pink is so cool.
Purple makes me want to duel.
Blue is the beautiful sky.
Red is a robin that I watch go by.
Brown is a teddy bear.
Grey is so rare.
Yellow is my bright light.
Orange is sometimes bright.

Some of these colors are in the beautiful rainbow!!!

Isabella Lehrer, Grade 3
Atwood Elementary School, MI

Black Dajuanna

Black is beautiful
Black is great
Black is never a mistake
Black is everything you should be
Especially if you are one like me
Black is people in a race
Black is never a disgrace
We once were slaves
But now we are free
We hold the key gratefully
And thank the Lord
That we are free
As everyone can plainly see
Being black inspires me
To be the best that I can be
Dajuanna Lockett, Grade 3
Martin L King Elementary School, IL

Yeah for Spring

It's a great day
for spring.
Spring is nice.
This day will be as
good as me with
the trees and everything.
It's a hot day and
people are having
tons of fun.
Spring is tons of fun!
Tyler Howard, Grade 3
H. R. McCall Elementary School, IL

Today

Today I was stomped on by ants
Who tried to get me
But they missed me and
Then they hit the wall behind me and
They missed me again and
It hit them and
So poor little old ants
Are dead.
Tanner Cartner, Grade 2
Patterson Elementary School, MI

Pirates of the Caribbean

Pirates
Stealing, hunting
Fast, quiet, sneaky
Killing, shooting
Sao Feng
Devin Bebar, Grade 3
Wilton Center Elementary School, IL

Winter

Sledding
throwing snowballs
snowboarding
on little jumps

I love winter
Megan Andersen, Grade 2
Pathfinder Elementary School, MI

Scared

I'm scared in the night.
I'm scared in the day.
So scared of everything in my sight.
No matter where I go there's a
Scary thing in my sight.
Allison Blaszczyk, Grade 3
Atwood Elementary School, MI

My Cat

My cat is exploring,
So much to explore,
Sniffing, jumping, running,
Fun
Madison Doonan, Grade 2
Parkwood-Upjohn School, MI

Gum

Gum
Chewy, fruity
Blowing, popping, tasting
It is so good
Sour
Matthew Gassel, Grade 3
Atwood Elementary School, MI

Dogs Bark a Lot

My dog and I go to the park.
My dog's name is Mark.
My dog likes my toy ark.
And he barks.

My dog likes to play
With frisbees all day.
When I tell him to stay
He does it, and that's ok.

Ethan Moe, Grade 2
MACCRAY West Elementary School, MN

Wolves

Hoooooowwwllll!
Night!
Hoowll!
Grrrrrr!
Howl!
Bark!
Sniff!
Wolves howl at night!
Hooooowl, ho hooowl!

Sheila P. Facklam, Grade 2
Country Meadow Elementary School, IN

Cream Corn

"Dinner's ready," says Dad.
Audrey asks, "What are we having?"
"Cream corn, mashed potatoes, and pork."
Mom answers. My stomach turned...
queasy at the thought of...
the slimy...disgusting...juicy...
shriveled up bodies of the yuckiest...
food on the face of the earth!
I scream in terror at the sight of
yellow monsters that crawl down
your throat and make a terrible taste
in your mouth! Mom says...
"Bed time!" I drop my fork...
and run upstairs to get ready for bed.

Lucas VanMeter, Grade 3
Henryville Elementary School, IN

Global Warming

As you sit
While your light is lit
You can stare
At a rare bear.
Some of the ice may melt
But you still felt
Some below our feet.
As you think
About how they're almost extinct.
You watch as a sploch
Drips from an icicle above.
When you use
Your hairspray you abuse
The polar bears.
Also your garbage
Sits and looks like a mirage
Inside your garage.
You think it's not there
But to a polar bear
That's just not fair.
Emily Karrels, Grade 3
Houdini Elementary School, WI

Tennis

Boom, boom, boom.
The ball hits the racket,
and the racket hits the ball.
The ball goes over the net,
and it goes back again.
Boom, boom, boom.
Sophie Dimoff, Grade 2
Meadowbrook Elementary School, IL

Tadpole/Frog

Tadpole
Tiny, fast
Swimming, jumping, eating
Outside, wiggling, yard, creek
Hopping, hunting, sleeping
Jumpy, fun
Frog
Tommy Garrett, Grade 1
Ladoga Elementary School, IN

Hunting Time

Gun shots, horses trotting
Hunting time
Middle of day
Dogs barking, four-wheelers driving
Dead deer, clear blue sky, fallen trees
Driving, logging
In summer
Sad and mad
Joel VanDyken, Grade 3
Coulee Region Christian School, WI

Soda

Fizz, fizzle, moan,
I gurgle as I groan!

Glug, glug burp and belch,
Mmm, Mmm soda.

Chuckle as I drink!
Mmm, Mmm soda.
Sarah Burnham, Grade 2
Meadowbrook Elementary School, IL

Horses

Clippity clop, clippity, clop,
Here comes the mare.

My heart racing
it can't stop until he's really here.

He's tall and proud
He stands above the crowd

I wish he was mine!
Annamarie Charmoli, Grade 2
Cedarcrest Academy, MN

Waterfall

Pouring waterfall
So smooth, rich, and clean
Then reflections appear
Avery Dean, Grade 3
Mable Woolsey Elementary School, IL

Imagine Me, a Leaf

Imagine me, a leaf.
Brown and crunchy
Flying in the sky
Landing on the green grass.
Lost and all alone
Bored and freezing, trying to find a friend
Trying to find home.
I am really sad and I wish I had a friend.
Would you want a friend if you were a leaf?
I would.
I hope I don't turn into an icicle.
I would try to fly, but I am too cold.
It is almost Halloween and I don't want to get stepped on.
I think I'll be all right, but I need a plan.
I found a plan! I won't get stepped on.
Now I can go trick or treating.
Imagine me, a leaf.

Madison Overton-Randall, Grade 2
Michener Elementary School, MI

What Bugs Me

My teacher yells at us.
My brother keeps singing on the potty.
My dad kisses me all the time.
My brother keeps sitting on a whoopee cushion.
My brother keeps riding his motor cycle into a tree.
My brother chases me with a lawnmower.
My mom won't let me get a Wii.
My brother acts like a super baby.
My dad spanks me.
My teacher makes me do stuff.
My dad yells at me.
My mom doesn't let me bungee jump off the house.
My dad drives 90 mph.
My teacher won't let us bungee jump off the school.
My friend John says he has a squad car.
My teacher makes us go potty.
My teacher gives us short recess.
My brother breaks everything.
My brother goes to the bathroom every 5 minutes.

Sebastian Nalls, Grade 2
Pope John XXIII School, IL

Hot Chocolate

Hot chocolate
Tasty, delicious
Sharing, drinking, warming
Drink it on a cold snowy day
Cocoa beverage
Jack Jeffries, Grade 3
St Michael School, OH

Ice Fishing

Ice fishing
Careful, patient, safe
Sitting, watching, waiting
I'd bring a chair
Winter fishing
Abby Roy, Grade 3
St Michael School, OH

Basketball

B all is orange
A nytime we can play
S weat a lot
K eeps you motivated
E at a lot
T all to play it
B all is round
A ll the time I play it
L ong arms to play
L ong games to play
Peter Ragen, Grade 3
Noonan Academy, IL

Playing Football

Quarterback threw
I ran
I caught
I twisted
Touchdown!
Who's gonna beat them
Raiders?
Nobody!
Devin Lintz, Grade 1
Bright Elementary School, IN

Rain

Rain can be cold, rain can be hot;
It rains a little, it rains a lot.

It rains here, it rains there,
It rains almost anywhere.

It can be wet, it can't be dry;
It rains so much, my oh my.

Rain may seem bad, it's a help though;
For when it rains, it helps the plants grow.

And if you look, you may see,
A rainbow high above a big tree.

So see, it is not bad at all
And if you're outside, you'll have a ball.
Lana Howell, Grade 3
Zanesville Christian School, OH

Friends

There was a puppy
Who I called Fluffy
She was a Beagle
She had a friend
Named Scruffy
Because he was so fluffy
Who was also a Beagle
They also had a friend
Who was a seagull
His name is Trevor
They all were never
Nappy because they
Were all were so happy
They played and played
Then they had a big charade
They made up
Then they played a game called stage up
Then they had lunch
After they were done
Then they played
In the sun
Julie Kurian, Grade 3
Forest Park Elementary School, OH

Puppies
Puppies are cute.
Puppies are funny.
Puppies are fun.
Puppies are fast.
Puppies chase birds.
Puppies swim fast.
Puppies like hiding.

I love puppies!

E'va Lindemann, Grade 1
James R Watson Elementary School, IN

The Spring Garden
Dewy day in the spring garden,
Rose is all in dew.
Oh rose! Poor beauty,
As red as truthful lips
Sitting by her friend poppy.

Anna Feldman, Grade 2
Shorewood Hills Elementary School, WI

Camp
C ome to have fun
A time to be outdoors
M ake new friends
P eaceful place to be

Erin Sukala, Grade 3
James R Watson Elementary School, IN

My Great-Great Grandfather
My grandfather
Was
So
Sweet,
Loving,
Nice,
Darling,
Fantastic,
Grandfather
I love my grandfather!

Caitlynn Parker, Grade 2
McKenney-Harrison Elementary School, IN

The Same

Every day the same
School is very lame
The same I wish would change
We never rearrange the seats
She never gives us treats
Every day the same
I wish I never came
Same, same, same.

Kaitlyn D. Tyson, Grade 3
Elmhurst School, MI

If I Were a Flower...

I would hear the wind.
I would see everything.
I would smell the fresh air.
I would taste the sweet food.
I would feel the bees on me.
I would spin around when it is windy.

Brianna Delaney, Grade 2
Stocker Elementary School, WI

Sweet Little Butterfly

Sweet little butterfly
floating on the wind
Sweet little butterfly
going to the zoo
Sweet little butterfly
going home.

William Kelley, Grade 3
Weymouth Elementary School, MI

My Mom

My mom is really crafty.
To her sometimes I'm sassy.
I will try to always be nice.
My brother and I can be quiet as mice.
My mom is so smart.
She loves me with all her heart.
My mommy is so funny.
She is as cute as a bunny.
I love my mommy!

Emma Woodward, Grade 1
Strange Elementary School, WI

Short and Tall

I am short.
I am tall.
Am I the small one?
Am I big?
Am I a mouse?
I don't know.
Are you?
Are you a cow?
Moo!

Danica Ehlers, Grade 2
Midkota Elementary School, ND

Jake

Always
in
trouble
always
looking
for
mischief
always
going
to
the
bathroom
lazy
lazy
bad
bad
Cat!!!

Erin Davis, Grade 2
Pathfinder Elementary School, MI

Summer

School is out
We're all out and about
We're having fun
And everything is done
It's all about summer
But when it's over
It's a bummer

Nolan Potts, Grade 3
Suffield Elementary School, OH

Nights Glory
At night I can hear my covers rustling
and stuffed animals flipping off my comfortable bed.
A car's light is shown to me.
I also can hear my tired dog whining and whimpering.
I feel restful and peaceful and I always get a good night's sleep.

Yaasi McHerron, Grade 3
North Intermediate School, MN

Summer
I love summer and it's a bummer it's winter right now.
I like winter, but summer is fun because you get to play in the sun.
You eat popsicles, they drip off your tongue.
You eat and eat 'til the day is done.
The sun is shining and no one is whining because summer is the best.
All the fresh fruits are growing.
It is summer, it is not snowing.
The flowers are growing in the dirt and I'm wearing my bright green skirt,
Because summer is here.

Hannah Streeter, Grade 2
Greenbriar Elementary School, IL

My Feelings About Blue
My eyes are blue.
If my favorite football game broke, I would feel blue.
Blue smells like the ocean.
Blue feels as soft as the pillow at my house.
Blue water has a splash sound when I jump in the pool.
When I look at a blue crayon it looks round and straight.
Blueberries taste dull.

Keegan Carpenter, Grade 2
South O'Brien Elementary School, IA

My Brother
Dylan
1 year old
Not potty trained
Crawls on stuff
Slobbers
Drools
That's all I know!

Ayn Jividen, Grade 1
South Monroe Townsite Elementary School, MI

Spring

Flowers start to bloom,
As spring comes.
There are so many
Different colors,
So many different
Types of flowers,
And so many
Colorful butterflies
As spring comes
Animals come out
From the long winter,
And birds start to chirp
Spring is beautiful.

Mallika Brar, Grade 3
Detroit Country Day Junior School, MI

Snowboarding

I'm riding on the snow
It feels so good gliding back and forth
It feels so good riding up and looking down
But when I get off I feel so much better
I go back down gliding makes me even happier

Kylie Buckna, Grade 3
MacArthur Elementary School, WI

Spring

S omething is in the air that smells good
P lanting flowers in the garden
R ain falling from the sky
I love the smell of fresh air
N ice, long, rainy days
G ardening with my grandma

Annika Huston, Grade 3
Montrose Elementary School, MN

I Built a Robot

I built a robot that could do my homework
he can do my chores and wash the dishes.
He can clean my room and take out the trash,
but I forgot one thing...the batteries.

Brendan Lewis, Grade 3
Henryville Elementary School, IN

Holidays

Halloween is the holiday where we like to trick-or-treat.
Halloween is the holiday we get candy that is so sweet.
Thanksgiving is the holiday where we really feast.
Thanksgiving is the holiday we feast on turkey and roast beef.
Christmas is the holiday where we get lots of treats.
Christmas is the holiday the Wise Men came to greet.
Good Friday is the day the red flowed from His hands.
Good Friday is the day people were sad throughout the lands.
Easter is the holiday happiness rose from faces.
Easter is the holiday news came from faraway places.
St. Patrick's Day is the day the rainbow flows from the pot.
St. Patrick's Day is the day where gold we try to spot.
4th of July is the day they wrote the Declaration.
4th of July is the day we have lots of celebration.
Now my poem is at its end
But I will say it next time, my friend.

Riley Sanderson, Grade 3
Oak Ridge Elementary School, MN

Never Kill

People should never kill
because it can ruin people's lives
and because it can start things that you don't want to happen.
It can also hurt someone's family.
Most importantly never try and hurt, kill, threaten
or try and get revenge on your family.
That's why you never kill.

Patrick Michael, Grade 3
Weymouth Elementary School, MI

Space

Space.
The Milky Way one of many others,
Our galaxy!
All the gas giants
And the dwarf planet
All combined and Earth of course!
Our planet!
The beautiful stars of gas rule this place of darkness.
Space.

Seamus Conway Scanlon, Grade 2
Onaway Elementary School, OH

Spring Is the Best

Spring time is the best
time of the year.
Where you see butterflies
and robin eggs.
You hear bees buzzing
and geese honking.
Children playing
and whispering winds.
You smell the flowers and BBQs.
You feel playful and joyful,
fresh and in shock.
This is why spring is
the best time of the year.

Skylar Murphy, Grade 3
H. R. McCall Elementary School, IL

Spring

S inging birds
P retty flowers
R ed robins
I think spring is nice.
N ice temperature
G reen grass

Jackson Miller, Grade 1
Southwood Elementary School, IN

I Can't

I can't have gum for dinner?
No pop?
No popcorn?
No licorice?
No cookies?
No M&M's?
How come?

No cake?
Or Pepsi?

Just like in the past.
I never get the good stuff.
I just thought I'd ask.

Madison Kiernan, Grade 1
Northfield Elementary School, OH

LeighAnna

LeighAnna
She is nice
She runs fast
I am fast too!
LeighAnna is a good friend
I really care about her
Even though
I don't act like it
I still care about her
I don't act like it
because I'm waiting
for something to happen
so I can tell her…
That I care about her.

Carlos Carranza-Baker, Grade 1
Webster Elementary School, MI

Spring

Spring is fun
Flowers are pretty
Boys and girls run
I see my new kitty

David Clark, Grade 2
Ladoga Elementary School, IN

Timers

Timers
with a soft
deserty sand
pouring like…
dry rain

Ray Glass, Grade 2
Orchard Lane Elementary School, WI

My Happy Horse

My happy horse
Happy running,
Happy eating,
Happy kicking,
Happy neighs,
Happy horse.

Shayleigh Shriver, Grade 1
Mentone Elementary School, IN

Snowflakes
Shiny
Smooth
Cold
Pretty
Neat
White
The twinkle
They sparkle

I love it when they fall down to the ground!

Jordan Stayer, Grade 1
James R Watson Elementary School, IN

Rain
Rain
rain
rain
is
cold
oh, no
lightning
falling
thunder
roaring it stops
All is wet
Muddle puddles
fun

Boone Bacon, Grade 2
Country Meadow Elementary School, IN

Sunshine and Sky Light Blue
Sunflowers are yellow
And the ocean is light blue
I make the sunshine
You make the sky light blue
I fly over the ocean as you make the ocean blue
You make me feel like I should be with you
I have opened your eyes as you open mine
All I have to do is make the sun shine
High, high, high in the light blue sky

TeAngela Henderson, Grade 3
Martin L King Elementary School, IL

Snakes

Snakes have heat sensors
on their nose.
Eat mice, red eyes.
Six foot long.
Killing machines.
Snakes are cool
but they wrap around you.

Evan Ford, Grade 3
Henryville Elementary School, IN

Snowflake

I am a snowflake.
I start like rain,
but as I get closer to the ground,
I get a little flaky!
I start to stretch and freeze!
Then, when I touch the ground,
I'm a little patch on someone's yard.
I am a snowflake!

Olivia Mikel, Grade 3
Mentone Elementary School, IN

Snowballs

Snowballs
Hard
Ouch!
Who threw that?
Trey!
Snowballs
Back at you
Gotcha!

Branden Rael, Grade 1
Carriage Hill Elementary School, NE

Ocean

water rolling
fish swimming
shells coming
up to the shore
it is cool
to see this.

Eryn Belleman, Grade 2
Pathfinder Elementary School, MI

Cats

I love cats
Gray cats
Blonde cats
Fun cats
Crazy cats
Any kind of cat.

A cat at the ocean
A cat that can jump
A cat at the pond
A cat that went bump
I love cats.

Silly cats
Funny cats
Furry cats
White cats
I love cats.

Darian Lott, Grade 2
Stocker Elementary School, WI

Bunny

I know a bunny
who is very funny
and likes money

A bunny who is very, very funny
and likes to play
and likes May.

Michael Lee, Grade 2
Meadowbrook Elementary School, IL

Buddy

Buddy
Friendly, Golden Retriever
Jumping, running, playing
He does tricks.
Laying, drinking, eating
Trouble maker, serious
Dog

Riley McKee, Grade 3
Nishna Valley Community School, IA

My Spring

I see birds flying around.
I see bees making the honey inside the beehive.
I smell flowers and fresh air.
I smell wet wood.
I hear birds chirping.
I hear geese honking.
I feel happy and excited.

Juliet Mojica, Grade 3
H. R. McCall Elementary School, IL

Sea Monsters

Terrifying
Eat, eat, eat
They hunt
In groups
Eat, eat, eat
Whales and sharks.

Gavin Willett, Grade 1
South Monroe Townsite Elementary School, MI

Spring

Spring is loving
Spring is nice.

You can camp,
You can plant,
Sometimes you can fish.
You never know if it's going to be warm or cold this spring,
But you do know there will be a nice day coming soon.

Makayla Tuck, Grade 3
Lorain Community School, OH

Tacos

Tacos, tacos
Juicy
Crunchy
Mushy
Lettuce
Cheesy
Tacos, tacos
I love tacos!

Austin Spence, Grade 1
South Monroe Townsite Elementary School, MI

Colors

The sun is yellow like
the flowers.
The moon is white like
the light.
The pig is pink like
the flowers.

Katya German, Grade 1
Peck Elementary School, IL

Football

Football
is fun
and
awesome
dirty
and
rough
and
so, so
much fun!

Timmy Dare, Grade 2
Queen of All Saints School, IL

Polar Bears

Polar bears live on ice
but it's not very nice.
Polar bears eat fish
but not on a dish.
Polar bears slide down hills
when it chills.

Jonathan Sanchez, Grade 3
Peck Elementary School, IL

Fireplace

Fireplace
Hot, cozy
Warming, comforting
Snuggle up while
Drinking hot chocolate
Burning logs

Sophia Fallieras, Grade 3
St Michael School, OH

Gummy Bears

G ummy and yummy!
U nited States makes them.
M r. Bear and…
M other Bear love each other.
Y ummy in my tummy!

B eing yummy is dangerous!
E ating them is the right thing to do.
A ren't they good?
R ed, green, orange, and yellow bears.

Jesse Elkins, Grade 3
Woodford Elementary School, OH

What Is Yellow?

Yellow is a nice cool drink of lemonade
Yellow is a shooting star and a nice fast car
Yellow is a banana and the sun rising
Yellow is mustard on a hot dog

Tanner Larkee, Grade 3
Kate Goodrich Elementary School, WI

First Days of April

April's first days are here.
There will be flowers and showers everywhere!
When April's showers go on harder
There will be flowers,
And flowers that will grow on farther!
There will be leaves growing on trees
And bees buzzing by.
It looks like summer, but
It's really spring!

Gerard-O'ahu T. Soriano, Grade 2
St Robert Bellarmine School, IL

Tick, Tock, Time!

Tick, tock, *TIME*!
Time to rhyme!
Tick, tock, *RING*!
Time to sing!
Tick, tock, *BEEP*!
Time to sleep. Zzz.
Tick, tock, time!

Darby Easterday, Grade 2
James R Watson Elementary School, IN

Freedom

The Statue of Liberty,
You who stand so great,
You lift your torch
beside the door to freedom,
Your torch guides us all
Who are yearning to be free in America,
Your greatness signifies
the freedom and justice of America,
You…are the Statue of Liberty.

Ryan Corrigan, Grade 3
Detroit Country Day Junior School, MI

Swim

When you dive in the water
you hear the crowd cheer
when you get to the top of the water.
When you work hard your legs go boom
and your arms are splashing.
When you win a race
you feel real proud.

Megan Meyer, Grade 2
Meadowbrook Elementary School, IL

Spring Is Near

We've been waiting for the weather to change.
Will it ever be spring?
Will it ever be nice again?
We can't wait 'till it's Spring this year!
Spring is the time for friendship.
Birds are chirping in the air,
Spring, oh spring is near.
Time for playing outside with our friends,
Time for camping out,
Time for flowers in the garden,
Time for Easter.
We can't wait for spring.
Spring is early this year.
Spring is almost here.
Time for bike riding with friends.
It's time for SPRING!

Cierra Mitchell, Grade 2
Ashland Park/Robbins School, NE

Guitar Girl

Peyton says a pop star
Is what she wants to be.
Jason would be a Red Wing player,
And Lauren would be a teacher.

I'd like to be a guitar girl
And make the children smile
I'd toss my guitar up in the air
Singing while I do it.

I'd make a million CD's
As many as I could.
And I would give free CD's
To everyone who's good.

Cassidy Lemanski, Grade 3
Atwood Elementary School, MI

Baby Doctor

Jessica says a nurse
Is what she wants to be.
Sydney would be a vet,
And Mrs. Strait would go to Hawaii.

I'd like to be a baby doctor
And make the babies smile.
I'd give them to their mommies,
And hold them for a while.

I'd make a million babies smile,
As many as I could.
And I would give stuffed animals
To every baby who's good.

Hunter Poser, Grade 3
Atwood Elementary School, MI

Waterfall

A waterfall is pretty.
It's like a rainbow in the pretty sky.
It has lots of pretty sparkles,
In the pretty water sky.

Mariah Brown, Grade 3
Lorain Community School, OH

The Sand Macaw

The macaw is the sand.
I feel the sand in my heart.
The macaw is fast as my heart
Racing through me.
The sand is as quiet as the crab.

Jaclyn Heinrich, Grade 2
Norris Elementary School, NE

Puppies

Puppies
Cute and playful
Feel so soft and fuzzy
Love to run around and play with you
Loving

Emma Dickman, Grade 2
Loveland Elementary School, OH

I Am Hummer

I am Hummer.
Drive me,
play video games in me,
and watch TV in me.

I am Hummer.
Drive me through rocks.
Drive me through the desert.
Drive me through water.

I am Hummer.
Drive me as you please.

Jameson Baker, Grade 2
Mentone Elementary School, IN

My Dog

Brown
And white
I like my dog
Bow wow bow wow
Bogey
My dog

Luke Jackson, Kindergarten
Northfield Elementary School, OH

Birthdays

B right and early, ready for fun!
I n the kitchen the cake waits,
R ight away people start to come.
T ogether we crack open the piñatas.
H ow yummy the cake tastes!
D ances to funny music,
A t the pool we play tag.
Y ells and laughter fill the air,
S aying goodbye to partygoers.

Jocelyn Ting, Grade 2
Onaway Elementary School, OH

The Waterfall

Hiking up to the cave
In between the rocks
Bats were hanging on the wall
When the water hit the ground
It splashed on the rocks
When we got to the edge
It splashed me
My other brothers got so close
They were wet all over
Up so high I didn't want to go in the cave
Mom and Dad helped me go inside
I was very scared to go in
I'm always glad that I listen to my parents.

Ben Matthews, Grade 2
Broken Arrow Elementary School, KS

Spring Goes Pop!

One day,
Out of the blue
I hear from you,
"It's raining!"
I look
Mother says
"Spring goes pop!"
Out of the clear air
My dog barks,
Hello, it's spring here!
Hello, it's spring here!
And so it is!

Anne Nietling, Grade 2
South Boardman Elementary School, MI

The Candle

As the candle goes
Up and down
It shines the room all around

Now watch the teacher
Blow it out
And then the light won't shine!

Lauren Kunz, Grade 2
Orchard Lane Elementary School, WI

The Messy Room

My room is very messy,
I do say so myself.
My sister has to clean it,
She's as tired as an elf.

When she has to clean it,
She whines and whines all day!
I'll say she has to clean it.
Well, that's really all I say!

Juliet Rowe, Grade 2
Onaway Elementary School, OH

Flowers

Flowers tingle with spacious gleam
   like gems sparkling at noon
with courageous beauty
   like butterflies shining
   like beautiful stars at night
and multicolored red
            blue
            or green
any color a flower can be
more beautiful than the sunset
or even the ocean in the sparkling sand
more valuable than gold
waving in the wind
growing and dying
you plant them in April
and they die in September

Sam Six, Grade 2
Hillcrest Elementary School, KS

Diesel

Dog
feisty, cute
laying, jumping, digging
learning to be obedient
Diesel

Macee Wiles, Grade 3
Smithville Elementary School, OH

Crystal

C aring
R eally sweet
Y o yo's well
S wims very well
T all
A lways nice
L oving

Crystal Farris, Grade 3
Atwood Elementary School, MI

Spring Fever

Flowers bloom, birds sing,
It's spring!
Let us go outside to play,
Maybe on a Saturday.
Thunderstorms boom,
Sending winter to its room.
I have spring fever, that's for sure,
I'll bet your pet will shed its fur!

Brody Flynn, Grade 2
Campbell Elementary School, NE

Pink

Pink as pink flowers
Pink is pretty princesses
Pink is juicy bubble gum
Pink is for cotton candy
Pink is for pink balloons
Pink is for a pink heart
Pink is a love color
I love Pink!!!

Paige Armbruster, Grade 2
Bristol Elementary School, WI

Jake the Snake
Jake the snake
baked a cake with a rake
during an
E
a
r
t
h
q
u
a
k
e.

Jackson Norton, Grade 2
Country Meadow Elementary School, IN

Chubby Pig Named Gig
There was a chubby pig.
His name is Gig.
He had a very big wig,
That he wore to the jig.
I know he's very chubby,
But he still needs a buddy.
While on his high heels with wheels,
He met a friend named Keels.
The next day the sky was gray.
They went to Greenbay to sleep in the hay.

Hannah Carlson, Grade 3
Florence Elementary School, WI

Midnight
Small
Cute
Black
Likes sports
My favorite
Go on the computer
Sleep with her every night
Will stay with me forever
I love her.

Olivia Marsh, Grade 2
McKenney-Harrison Elementary School, IN

Corvettes

Corvettes
Fast, sporty, cool
Sliding, rolling, spinning
Smooth, shiny, sporty, detailed
GM
Tyler Ignash, Grade 3
Atwood Elementary School, MI

Basketball

Basketball, basketball
Orange and black stripes
Round
In the hoop
10 scores
You win!
You win a trophy!
Basketball makes me feel excited
Taylor Krueger, Grade 1
Rock Ledge Elementary School, WI

Star

Dancing in the night
A beautiful sight to see
Magnificent
Around the moon
Everybody loves them
Great and twinkley
Joseph Prostko, Grade 3
Somers Elementary School, WI

I Am a Puppy

I am a puppy.
I love to jump and play
with the paws on my feet!!

I am a puppy.
I love my owner and I don't
really like cats!

I am a puppy!
Lexie Ault, Grade 2
Mentone Elementary School, IN

Spring

Spring pops in
With flowers booming
And the sun shining
On a warm happy day
With sweet-smelling flowers
And birds chirping
Rachel Lenz, Grade 3
Hanover Elementary School, MN

What Is Christmas?

C is for charity and giving.
H is for home for the holidays.
R is for relatives we love.
I is for icicles.
S is for snow.
T is for togetherness.
M is for many blessings.
A is for a gift for everyone.
S is for saying I love you.
Brittany Stone, Grade 3
Valentine Elementary School, NE

My Grandpa

Fun!
Always teasing!
Watching the football game!
Saying I have stinky feet
Laughing
I *love* my grandpa.
Riley Sweet, Grade 2
Pathfinder Elementary School, MI

Pegasus and Unicorn

They are all different kinds of horses
Some can disappear
And some can fly
And some can run fast
I wonder if they are the last?
The Pegasus says, "Hi"
And the Unicorn says, "I'm shy"
Honey Nilson, Kindergarten
Sleepy Hollow Elementary School, IL

Winter/Spring

Winter
dark, gloomy
snowing, hailing, sledding
snowmen, cold, rain, babies
weeding, planting, smelling
flowers, birds
Spring

Abigail Paige Maxson-Stabile, Grade 3
Pickaway Elementary School, OH

Free Flying

F lying high, a bird
R ushes to your flame,
E legantly lands on an
E mber, gracefully
D arting to the
O cean, blissfully
M orning shines on her wing

F lying in the
L ovely sun, she happily
Y ells in joy as the
I mmigrants come to
N avigate through the big crowd
G radually the shy bird flees

Elizabeth Obermaier, Grade 3
Detroit Country Day Junior School, MI

Feeding Snowmen

Don't feed snowmen chicken noodle soup.
They will melt with just one scoop!
So, don't feed snowmen chicken noodle soup.

Lane Hilgenhold, Grade 2
Perry Central Elementary School, IN

Spring

S unshine is the best thing for gardens.
P ink is the color in the rainbow.
R abbits are the cutest things in the world.
I ce cream is the sweetest thing.
N ip of cold wind in the air.
G rass these days are just so green.

Amanda Schmidt, Grade 2
Stanton Elementary School, NE

The Rain

It makes the sky gloomy
and
It ruins your baseball game.
Chloe Willer, Grade 1
Holden Elementary School, IL

Soccer

Soccer
Black and white
Kicking, moving, jumping
Automatic pains all around
Futbol
Nathan Gryspeerd, Grade 3
Burr Elementary School, MI

My Grandparents

She has horses.
She has a farm.
She lives in England.
Grandma Sue

She makes cookies.
She works at a hospital.
She lives in Prairie City.
Grandma Sharon

She makes noodles.
She makes pies.
She lives in Bussey.
Grandma Rose

He has a truck.
He has a John Deere.
He was a teacher.
Grandpa Gordon

He lives in England.
He has a farm.
He has tractors.
Grandpa Steve.
Coady Cambage, Grade 1
Anita Elementary School, IA

What I Love About Delays

More time to sleep.
My brother doesn't make a peep.
Then my sister shouts,
"It's time to go out!"
Andrew Bennett, Grade 1
James R Watson Elementary School, IN

Model Trains

Fast
Slow
Up and down
Controller
Oh no!
Press red button!
Train wrecks
CRASH!
I like model trains!
Graham Seiler, Grade 1
James R Watson Elementary School, IN

Basketball

Scoring
Shooting
Rebounding
Stealing
Traveling
Dribbling
Winning
Losing

I love basketball!
Addison Cruz, Grade 1
James R Watson Elementary School, IN

Ethan

E xcellent kicker
T oo fast
H e is nice
A wesome kid
N ot funny

I like Ethan
Daniel Brown, Grade 1
Hamilton Community Elementary School, IN

Bugs
Creeping
Buzzing
Crawling
Pinching
Biting
Stinging

OUCH!

Noah Mondor, Grade 1
James R Watson Elementary School, IN

The Easter Bunny
The Easter Bunny is so funny.
The Easter Bunny is not crummy.
The Easter Bunny gives Easter egg hunts.
On Easter we set out carrots for him to munch.
He gives us candy eggs
And hops on his legs.
The Easter Bunny is so nice.
Maybe, I should pay him a good price.

Jeremy Struckel, Grade 3
Woodford Elementary School, OH

Cars
Cars
Misty
Lightning fast
Noisy

Cars
Colorful
Awesome
Racers

Cars
Spin out
Burn out
Drag racer

Cars

Kyle Davis, Grade 3
James R Watson Elementary School, IN

Sea Horses

Sea horses have tails.
They're a lot smaller than whales.
They cling onto sea weed.
They travel in a slow speed.
Food and water is what they need.
To learn more read, read, read!
Hannah Gardner, Grade 1
Rock Ledge Elementary School, WI

Friendship

F un
R eally funny
I ce cream
E ating
N ice friends
D ogs to play with
S leepovers
H ide and seek
I ce cream
P ajamas
Caitlin McGrorty, Grade 3
Chaska Elementary School, MN

Spring

S ummer is coming
P ool is getting ready
R iding my bike
I ncredible time
N o more snow
G rinning because I had a fun day
Aryston Terry, Grade 2
Stocker Elementary School, WI

Uncle Frank

My uncle Frank's hugs
Are so gentle and sweet
I wish I could still feel it
With my hands
But I can still feel them
With my heart
Riley McLeod, Grade 2
Orchard Lane Elementary School, WI

Sun

The sun
Orange and yellow
Shining bright

Steaming
With lava inside
Bursting out

Made out of gases
All around
It melts anything

Fire
Flames falling
Hotter than anything
On Earth
Katie Crockford, Grade 3
Greenbriar Elementary School, IL

Pinolio

Pinolio is a chocolaty drink from
the country Nicaragua.
It is so tasty it's the pleasantest thing
I've ever dreamed of having.
I get to drink pinolio at my family's
house on Saturday. Our family gathers
all together to share in God's grace
and blessings. I sure hope pinolio
is at the table waiting for me in Heaven.
Samuel Guerrero, Grade 2
Cedarcrest Academy, MN

My Bedroom

When it's sunny and hot,
I like to be there in the afternoon,
To hear music and see the sun
Through the window,
While I play my games.
I will be back each day,
And that makes me feel happy inside!
Carlo Fontaine, Grade 3
St Robert Bellarmine School, IL

Ruby

Ruby is so cute
She jumps on me a lot
She makes me laugh when she licks me.
She's always by my side
She's there when I need her
She knows when we get home.
I love Ruby so much
Ruby is my friend.
Ruby is the best.

Bobby Mueller, Grade 3
Noonan Academy, IL

Fat Cat

I have a pet who is a cat.
My cat's name is Matt.
Matt wears a hat that's very fat.
Matt sleeps on a mat.
Matt plays with a ball.
Matt goes to the mall.
Matt is tall.
He was walking in the hall.
And, that is all.

Jacob Gould, Grade 2
MACCRAY West Elementary School, MN

School

School is fun
School is cool
Art is creative
Gym is exercise
Music is cool
Library is really cool books
Office is bad!

Dion Urbina, Grade 2
Country Meadow Elementary School, IN

Grandma's House

You take one step into Grandma's house —
the cinnamon bread baking in the oven.
It smells so sharp and sweet.
Grandma's baking is like heaven's angel
cooking in the kitchen.

Zeke Lee, Grade 3
Emerald Elementary School, MI

Fish

Fish in the ocean
Clown fish, jelly fish
Jelly fish can sting you!
Anika Aadalen, Kindergarten
Ramalynn Montessori Academy, MN

Monster Truck

Always crushing
Old cars and trucks
Jumping spinning
Flipping over on the side.
Hoods always flying off
Tires on the go
Cab roofs falling off.
Andrew Redder, Grade 2
Pathfinder Elementary School, MI

Turtles

Big and Little turtles
With hard shells
Some snap.
Some don't.
Some are green.
Some aren't.
Big and little turtles
With hard shells
Drake Doll, Grade 1
Woodford Elementary School, OH

Friendship

F air
R espect
I ntelligent
E ncouraging
N obody is left out
D ifferent
S hare
H elpful
I nfinite friendship
P assionate
Michael Sholtz, Grade 3
Lorain Community School, OH

Gold

Gold looks like really dark gold coins.
Gold smells like pretty gold blossoms.
Gold sounds like a little star.
Gold tastes like pineapple fruit snacks.
Gold feels like little golden roses.
Gold feels like happiness.
Kiera Bordner, Grade 2
Will Carleton Academy, MI

Spring

S unflowers are growing high.
P ink petunias are smelling good.
R ainy days will be nice.
I ce is melting.
N ice weather will be moving in.
G reen grass should be coming.
Lacey Lanz, Grade 2
Stanton Elementary School, NE

Apples

Sour
Yummy
Red
Circle
Apples
Kyle Smith, Kindergarten
Northfield Elementary School, OH

Kylee

Beautiful, crazy
enjoy, sidesplitting
animals, friendly

What I like about Kylee
is to talk on the phone
and go to movies with her

Kylee is my friend
because she is
the first one I met
Callie Mansfield, Grade 3
Henryville Elementary School, IN

The Guardian Light

After going through horror,
Big waves, strong winds,
Only for the worst…deportation…
So I, the Statue of Liberty
Welcome all of you
To the land of the free,
Through all your good times and bad.
We are all one family now.
One family of the land of the free.
And so, I stand here to welcome thee
I, the Statue of Liberty.

Brendan Dolan, Grade 3
Detroit Country Day Junior School, MI

Steelers

Steelers rock,
Steelers rule,
Steelers rock and
Colts drool!
They won the
Super Bowl
Five times.
They are the
BEST!

Jared Reutebuch, Grade 2
James R Watson Elementary School, IN

The U.S.A.'s Guardian

She's my hopes and dreams,
When I'm in bed as I think about her,
And say to myself,
"What a wonderful world!"
This statue helped so many people,
And she continues to guard my friends and I…
Along with the United States of America.
I love you Statue of Liberty…
For protecting me from harm,
For inspiring me to succeed in my dreams,
And for teaching me not to give up.

Grant Rinke, Grade 3
Detroit Country Day Junior School, MI

I Can't

I can't have M&M's for dinner?
No pop?
No chocolate pie?
No cake?
No gum?
No cookies?
How come?

No s'mores?
Or chips?

Just like in the past.
I never get the good stuff.
I just thought I'd ask.

Brooke Tyukodi, Grade 1
Northfield Elementary School, OH

A Duck

I see a duck in the pond.
I hear the duck quacking.
I smell the dirty pond water
that the duck was in.
I feel the duck touching me.
Soft feathers feeling me.
Happy little duck.

Jamie Matheson, Grade 1
Woodford Elementary School, OH

Softball

Running bases
Going places
Throwing balls
Yelling calls

Christine Follenweider, Grade 3
Noonan Academy, IL

Daisies

They blow outside,
Yellow, pretty, in the grass
Shine in the springtime.

Nanci Hernandez, Grade 2
J C Hoglan Elementary School, IA

Snowflake

S nowflake Bentley
N egatives for pictures
O wned a camera
W ilson Bentley
F lakes falling
L iked taking pictures
A s the crystals formed
K ing of winter
E xperimented

Jade Boote, Grade 3
Midkota Elementary School, ND

Mr. Pig

Mr. Pig
Nice, furry
Play, eat, sleep
He is my friend
Furry-wurry.

Lindsey Eastabrooks, Grade 3
Somers Elementary School, WI

Egg

Round egg
Cold
Brown
A snake
inside
Waiting
to hatch
Crack
"Mama!"

Alexia Siefken, Grade 1
Carriage Hill Elementary School, NE

My Five Senses

I see my mom cooking pancakes.
I hear birds humming and singing.
I smell butter.
I taste delicious pancakes.
I feel so happy.

Logan Lambdin, Grade 1
Eastside Elementary School, MI

Flowers

When the rain comes down the flowers grow,
There are many kinds of flowers,
Some are big,
Some are small,
Some are pink, red, white and even yellow!

DeAndre Brown, Grade 2
Gen George Patton Elementary School, IL

Ice Cream

Ice cream smells sweet,
and it's a nice treat.
Sometimes it's a little too cold for me.
I am glad the freezer doesn't have a key.
I'm as hungry as a cow
cuz I want to eat it right now.

Jordan Zesch, Grade 1
Trinity Lutheran School, IA

Spring

Spring looks like rain storms.
Spring smells like melting snow.
Spring feels like wet icky water in mud puddles.
Spring tastes like warm tomato soup.
Spring sounds like splashing muddy water.

Adam Castaneda, Grade 2
C W Neff Elementary School, MI

Balls

You hit them
You catch them
You bounce them
You throw them
You kick them
But most of all,
You have FUN with them!

Noah Fike, Grade 2
McKenney-Harrison Elementary School, IN

Alex the Alligator

Alex likes to go swimming in the river.
He likes to stay in the river for two hours.
Alex, are you watching those fish?

Connor Radovan, Grade 1
Stocker Elementary School, WI

Green

Green is the
Color of grass
And tree tops
But the snow
Is SO beautiful
I wish that
I knew
Which one
Was better.

Brendan Davis, Grade 2
Norris Elementary School, NE

Killer Whale

Killer whale
Big, glossy, black
Meat eating, attacking
Twelve teeth on each
Jaws are dangerous
Large dolphin

Nate Meyers, Grade 3
St Michael School, OH

Isabelle

I s made well.
S uper
A wesome
B avis
E ats
L ouisa
L ove
E vanston

Isabelle Bavis, Grade 2
Pope John XXIII School, IL

Spring Is Fun

Spring is fun
In the sun
Running, laughing, having fun.
This is why my spring is fun,
Running, laughing, in the sun.

Lyric Atkinson, Grade 3
Bentley Primary School, KS

Spring

S mells like spring is here.
P retty butterflies flying in the sky so high.
R inging bells birds chirping and fresh air.
I ce cream with topping for kids to eat.
N o coats no hat we're free at last.
G reen leaves growing in the trees so high.

Adrian Ortega, Grade 3
Peck Elementary School, IL

Trees

Trees are important,
They help us breathe,
Trees are also homes to the animals,
They also give us food that we eat,
Trees are so special to me,
On Earth Day I will go out and plant a tree.

Dashawn Hall, Grade 2
Gen George Patton Elementary School, IL

My Family

We love to play games with each other
We go many places with each other
We love each other very much
We are the best!

Marissa Lane, Grade 2
Springfield Boys and Girls Club ABC Unit, IL

Pets

Cats
Dogs

Pets, Pets, Pets

Hamsters
Birds

Pets, Pets, Pets

Hermit crab
Crabs

Pets, Pets, Pets

Taylor Miller, Grade 1
James R Watson Elementary School, IN

Friends

Friends are nice.
Friends are sweet.
Friends are very nice to meet.

When I'm feeling
Down in the dumps
They're always there to cheer me up.

Friends are nice.
Friends are sweet.
Friends are the only thing that keep me ME!

Desiree Thomas, Grade 3
Woodford Elementary School, OH

Sad

Sad, sad, sad,
is not my heart.
Sad is not my glad.

Sad hurts my heart.
It is not my glad.
It breaks me apart.

Ronnisha Tolbert, Grade 3
Cityview Performing Arts Magnet School, MN

I Am Ice Cream

I am ice cream.
You eat me on a hot, summery day.
Please don't let me drip!

I am ice cream.
You lick me, lick, lick, lick,
and lick me, lick, lick, lick,
and lick me, lick, lick, lick,

I am ice cream.
I am yummy and delicious and my flavor
is vanillicious.

I am ice cream.

Bryce Cudney, Grade 2
Mentone Elementary School, IN

Pizza

Pepperoni
Cheese
Sauce
Pizza
Taylor Prospal, Kindergarten
Northfield Elementary School, OH

Cars

Cars
Cars, fins
Cars have wheels
Have windows and rims
Have a belt
Play music
Cars
Tristin Smith, Grade 2
Webster Elementary School, MI

My Favorite Sport

Soccer is the best game
Better than all the rest
I've been taught from a great master
It's all I want to do
Every year I practice
And get better every day and night
I even play in my house
I don't think I'll ever stop
At least not tonight
It makes me feel very happy
Nick Matthews, Grade 2
Broken Arrow Elementary School, KS

I Love My Aunt

I love my aunt
she is cuddly
and the reason I pick her
because I love her
and she is in the hospital
we do not get to go in to see her.
I really really hate that.
Breanna Robertson, Grade 3
Henryville Elementary School, IN

Tyler R.

good friend, cool, gives hugs, kind
related to his mom and dad
cares deeply about people
who feels happy
who needs friends
who gives hugs
who fears friends, fighting
who likes to see friendship
resident of the school Weymouth
Collin Wendel, Grade 3
Weymouth Elementary School, MI

We Like Spring

Spring is fun
Spring is good
I like spring
No matter what.
The storm is warm
I would like to be reborn
Now 5, 4, 3, 2, 1,
Spring is fun.
Billie Pickle Jr., Grade 3
H. R. McCall Elementary School, IL

Stars

S tarlight
T oo many wishes
A steroid
R are
S un related.
Maddy Bloomer, Grade 3
Henryville Elementary School, IN

First Pet

B lack, brown, and white
U p and down he jumps
S it and begs
T ug of war
E ats dog food
R uns a lot
Zack Gillespie, Grade 3
Kyle Trueblood Elementary School, KS

Sun
Sun is
BRIGHT,
Sun sun!
Sun is
LIGHT,
Sun sun!
Sun is
SHINY,
Sun sun!
Sun is
HOT,
Sun
Sun
Sun!

Grace Wallace, Grade 2
James R Watson Elementary School, IN

My Fish
My fish swims.
My fish dives.
My fish eats.
And my fish dies.

Kerstin Price, Grade 1
James R Watson Elementary School, IN

Sweet Sunshine*
You are my sunshine.
When you rain and cry,
It makes me cry, my sunshine.
Without you I'd fall out of place,
My sunshine.
When you set it puts a twinkle in my eye.
When the moon comes out,
Coyotes howl for you.
When you get darker you feel bad,
But pretty soon you get bright again.
When I play under you,
It makes me smile.
You are so important.
You heat the earth and you heat my heart.
Love, Mia

Mia Marrocco, Grade 2
Switzer Elementary School, MI
*Dedicated to my mother

Hulk Hogan

H e has money!
U nleashed man
L oves his family
K ind to his family

H onesty
O ptions
G ood friend
A merican guy
N ever stopped wrestling.

Dakota Bostock, Grade 3
Henryville Elementary School, IN

When They Give Me...

When they give me a cat,
I want a turtle.

When they give me a turtle,
I want a horse.

When they give me a horse,
I want a dog.

When they give me a dog,
I want a kitten.

When they give me a kitten,
I want a puppy...
AND when they give me a puppy
I Want A Puppy Right Now, Please!!!

Kayla Merley, Grade 2
Mentone Elementary School, IN

My Two Greedy Dogs

My two greedy dogs fight a lot,
They fight in the mail slot.
I get them a giant tasty bone,
I'll give them an ice cream cone.
I opened the door and saw my dogs,
Then I found some silly frogs.

Abby Millis, Grade 1
Monroeville Elementary School, OH

My Mommy

kind like a flower
loving and caring
and best of all
she loves me
I love my mommy

Maddie Wosinski, Grade 2
Pathfinder Elementary School, MI

Taco! Taco!

Taco, taco
I love you a lot,
You're soft and yummy,
Meaty and small.
I make you and love you,
Oh, I can't get enough,
Taco! Taco!
You're big stuff!

Mitchell Sisky, Grade 1
Northfield Elementary School, OH

Dog or Cat?

Dog
fluffy, black
running, barking, chasing
little, cute, fast, curious
creeping, rolling, pouncing
smart, orange
Cat!

Zachary Roberts, Grade 3
Normandy Elementary School, OH

My Silly Poem

I see a bus,
I see a bug.
I see my mom,
I give her a hug.
I shake my cake,
I see a mouse.
I give my dad,
A big house.

Taylor Greilich, Grade 1
Monroeville Elementary School, OH

Things I Love
I love my pet.
I love my mom.
I love my dad.
I love my grandpa.
I love my grandma.
I love my home.
I love my cat.
I love my family.

Steve Baker, Grade 1
James R Watson Elementary School, IN

Happiness Is…
When you do not have to get a shot,
When you can read books,
When you are in class,
When you are with both of your cousins,
When you can play outside,
When you can do stations,
School is cool!

Amber Lichtsinn, Grade 1
Hamilton Community Elementary School, IN

Hershey Kiss!
I'm a dark brown tasty snack,
I look like a pointy pyramid.

I'm a bomb blowing up in your mouth,
I'm wrapped in a blanket of tin.
I'm gooey sweet and thick…

I'm a Hershey Kiss!

Abbey Chase, Grade 3
Gwendolyn Brooks Elementary School, IL

Rain
Pludge, pludge, pludge
The rain pludged on the window.
It tries to tell us something.
It just seems like you can guzzle it down.
Pludge, pludge, pludge.

Jacob Haberly, Grade 2
Country Meadow Elementary School, IN

A Gloomy Day on
Capitol Parkway

It's a gloomy day on Capitol Parkway.
The trees are white,
and the ground has a blanket of snow.
Jack Frost is nipping at your nose.
Some people are in, and some are out.
People who are out
are dressed like Eskimos.
It's a gloomy day
on Capitol Parkway.
Makenzie McNemar, Grade 3
Beals Elementary School, NE

Friendship

Nicholas
Kind, caring
Kickballing, drawing, running
Very nice to me
Nick.
Kaelyn Bencs, Grade 3
Somers Elementary School, WI

Summer

Summer is hot with
hot brutal days
and very sunny skies
on very burning days
with kids wearing shorts
and shirts.
Connor Weyrick, Grade 3
Northfield Elementary School, OH

Mermaids

Sea
Beautiful
Seaweed
Swim
Fish
Human
Mermaids
Danielle Demko, Kindergarten
Northfield Elementary School, OH

Shocking Sky

Clouds are coming
Sunset going down
Rain colorful rain
Cars drive by the sky

Dark blue and gray
More lightning
Lights up the nasty sky
With colorful light
Luke DiNanno, Grade 3
Greenbriar Elementary School, IL

My Mom

My mom
Loves me
No matter
Who I am
Sarah Howell, Grade 2
Orchard Lane Elementary School, WI

Moving Day

I felt bad
I left Fremont School
I went to Grant School
And sometimes I cried
My teacher said
Why are you crying
I said I miss the other school
I'm glad I'm back
Felicity Bradley, Grade 2
Pathfinder Elementary School, MI

Friends

F un to play
R un down a hill
I love to laugh
E at together
N ice to each other
D ance to cheer up
S leep over
Calista Kloepfer, Grade 2
Meadowbrook Elementary School, IL

The Butterflies

The butterflies fly in the sky.
When I see them they fly by.
I'm so happy to see them.
They're happy to see me.
We fly together in the beautiful blue sky.

Yuliana Guzman, Grade 3
Peck Elementary School, IL

I Hate the Dark

I hate the dark
Because it is too late
I hate it because
I'm not used to it.
I hate the dark.

Addison Stallard, Kindergarten
McKenney-Harrison Elementary School, IN

Me

Justin
Cool, awesome, funny
Son of Jason, Angela and Shawntele
Much loved by my parents
Sibling of Erica, Nikole
Wishes to be a movie star
Wants to be a doctor
Who is afraid of nothing
Who feels good
Who gives greatness
Who would like to go to Michigan University
Who enjoys sleeping
Resident of Wyandotte
Valeri

Justin Valeri, Grade 3
Jefferson Elementary School, MI

Flowers

You can plant flowers,
You can pick flowers,
Flowers are pretty.
They come in many colors,
They can be big or small,
Short or tall.

Angel Clark, Grade 2
Gen George Patton Elementary School, IL

Snow Day

Shining snow,
Making snowmen,
Building forts,
Throwing snowballs,
Going ice-skating
Amazing fun.

Victor Alex, Grade 2
Queen of All Saints School, IL

The Lion

I have a lion that's nice
and does not hurt
He is harmless
He's good not bad
He eats meat not people
He lives in the world not here
He screams like this ROOAAR!

Miguel Perez, Grade 1
Peck Elementary School, IL

Northern Lights

Northern lights
Arcs, clouds, streaks
Twinkling, sparkling, stunning
Natural display for
Thousands of miles
Aurora

Marjorie Sayers, Grade 3
St Michael School, OH

The Wilderness

Wilderness,
Beautiful,
Lots of
Animals,
Plants,
Things to learn,
and find,
Beautiful,
Wilderness.

Tony Spallone, Grade 2
Queen of All Saints School, IL

Cats and Dogs

Cats are white
Dogs are brown
I play with them
All over town.
We run and play.
Right to the park.
We swing and teeter
Until it's dark.

Autumn Hinrichs, Grade 2
MACCRAY West Elementary School, MN

Happiness

Happiness is a circus
I see big and large toys
I hear the pretty elephants blowing
I smell the pink delicious cotton candy
I touch the pony's mane
I taste the yellow popcorn

Faith Williams, Grade 3
Litchville-Marion Elementary School, ND

My Dog

My dog is smart.
It sniffs if there's strangers.
If my dog barks
We don't let them in.
If my dog doesn't bark
We let them in.

Drew Stoy, Kindergarten
McKenney-Harrison Elementary School, IN

Sojourner Truth

Sojourner
Brave, honest, forgiving, kind
Who lived from 1797 to 1883
Lover of freedom for slaves
Who fears war
Who needs peace on Earth
Who gives her life to save us
Who would like to see the world in harmony
Resident of Battle Creek
Truth

Sophie DeRango, Grade 3
Parkwood-Upjohn School, MI

Katelin

K ind
A mazing
T errific
E xcellent
L ikes me
I s my friend
N ice

Alyson Kain, Grade 1
James R Watson Elementary School, IN

Colors

Yellow is happy like the sun.
Black is boring like midnight.
Green is relaxing like peace.
Red is made when your heart is broken.
Blue is sad, like a lonely girl.
Orange is caring like a mother.
Pink is normal like me.
What is your normal color?

Madison Potts, Grade 3
Atwood Elementary School, MI

Candy

Candy is sweet
It is a tasty treat
Chocolate is the best
For Easter, I had a chocolate bird in a nest
I would love to go to a chocolate factory
And it would all be for me

Jo-Ann Salwierak, Grade 2
Arbury Hills Elementary School, IL

The Jumpy Rabbit

I knew a little rabbit
Who liked to jump a lot
He liked to eat carrots but
He liked to hop a lot
He liked to run but
He liked to sleep a lot…
But he loved his mother more.

Billy Allen, Grade 3
Holy Redeemer Christian Academy, WI

Cub/Bear

Cub
Soft, cuddly
Playing, eating, crawling
Cave, mom, wild, Antarctica
Hunting, swimming, sleeping
Large, brave
Bear

Hunter Chadwick, Grade 1
Ladoga Elementary School, IN

My Stupid Stitches

I hate my stupid stitches.
They hurt, and the doctor
Had to give me a
Shot to numb my nose.
I hate my stupid stitches
A lot, and I have a
Stupid bandage on.

Abdurrahman Seraj, Grade 2
Hillcrest Elementary School, KS

Baseball

B eginning the game
A thletes hitting the ball
S arcastic teammates
E liminating teams
B ases loaded
A ll cheering
L iving to win
L osing to nobody

Kyle Phillips, Grade 3
Kyle Trueblood Elementary School, KS

Virginia Beach

Long coast line
Salt water mist
Sand in my toes
Tasty fresh shrimp
Loud waves crash
In the morning

Kendra Stepp, Grade 3
Smithville Elementary School, OH

Spring

Spring is fun.
Spring is when you ride bikes.
I like to run.
I like the color of the flowers.
Some are yellow, red, and orange.
I can see the steam
and the bell rings.
When spring comes
my dreams come true.

Edgar Soto, Grade 3
Peck Elementary School, IL

Running

Thump, thump, thump,
Running through the woods.

Thud, thud, thud,
Whizz, whoosh!

Faster, faster through the trees
Pitter patter, pitter patter
Through a pile of leaves.

Ping, plunk, bang,
whizz, whoosh,

Running through a pond.

Lindsey Masterman, Grade 2
Meadowbrook Elementary School, IL

Amazing red clouds
Rest on an ocean of white
Seem like huge monsters
Hunting the buildings in the ground

Buildings walk past
The blackberry tree
To reveal the baseball batter
In the clouds

Mateo D'Agaro, Grade 3
Greenbriar Elementary School, IL

Grandpa Jon/Grandma
Who is the one that watches the race with me?
Grandpa Jon
Who is the one that lets me help with dinner?
Grandpa Jon
I love my grandpa!!

Grandma, grandma
Do you love your grandma?
Grandma, grandma,
My grandma reads to me,
Grandma, grandma
I love my grandma!!

Ashlee Comment, Grade 1
Hamilton Community Elementary School, IN

Skateboard
I like
to do skateboarding
Well, I'm not that good
My brother is good
But I know some moves
My brother could do a grind
And when I ride my skateboard
I like the sun on my face
Well I sometimes
fall down to the ground
And sometimes my brother
falls down to the ground
And sometimes my brother and I are good

Billy Phiavilayvong, Grade 2
Hillcrest Elementary School, KS

My Name
Julianne is my name.
I have long hair
and a dot on my nose.
Freckles everywhere.
Long eyelashes.
Kind of tall and
I love to draw.
I found out yesterday
My name is a way they cut French fries!

Julianne Steinman, Grade 2
McKenney-Harrison Elementary School, IN

Click Clack

Click, Clack, Click, Clack
I play on my computer
with a slack.
Click Clack
Click Clack
I have a virus
I call him Jack.

Click Clock
Clock Click

Jack is gone.
Click Click
Clack Clack
Jack is back
in black.

Nick Fischer, Grade 3
St Paul's Lutheran School, MN

Snow Pictures

S now pictures
N ice
O ld scientist
W ent in a blizzard
F un pictures
L iked snow crystals
A scientist
K ind
E xciting

Daniel Gleason, Grade 3
Midkota Elementary School, ND

Swimming

Fun, wet
Hot, summer
Athletic, cool
Teams, strong
Diving, sunblock
Jumps, flips
June, July, August

Shea Caylor, Grade 3
Henryville Elementary School, IN

Grace

Grace
Smart,
Caring,
Beautiful,
Sister of Katelyn,
Loves Dad,
Loves Mom,
Loves pandas,
Feels sad about getting hurt,
Needs water, food, and clothes,
Gives clothes, food, and toys,
Fears storms, dark and thunder,
Who'd like to go to China,
Who dreams of panda bears,
Princess Grace

Grace Garlick, Grade 1
JFH Educational Academy West, IL

My Crazy Brother

My brother
is
a
monkey
he is
always causing
trouble
double
trouble.
He goes in
my
room   when
he's   not
supposed
to   and   steals
my
stuff   my
brother
is   always   causing
trouble
double   trouble

Holly Kortge, Grade 2
Pathfinder Elementary School, MI

Dogs

Dogs can sniff,
Dogs can bark,
Dogs can jump,
Dogs can attack.
I love dogs.
Dogs can fight,
Dogs can fetch,
Dogs can do tricks.
I love dogs.

Abby Ferrell, Grade 2
James R Watson Elementary School, IN

Yellow

Yellow tastes lemony and a little squishy too.
Yellow reminds me of my Smiley.
Yellow is my favorite color.
Yellow reminds me of the sun.
Yellow comes in all sorts of things.
Yellow reminds me of sunflowers.
Yellow is the color of Pac Man.
Yellow is slippery like a banana peel.

Berg Kuhn, Grade 2
Bristol Elementary School, WI

Happiness

Happiness is a family reunion
I see lots of handsome and beautiful people
I hear funny laughing
I smell tasty homemade ribs
I touch their new furniture
I taste the delicious pie

Anthony Capistran, Grade 3
Litchville-Marion Elementary School, ND

A Clown

A clown is funny.
A clown can juggle.
A clown can blow up balloons.
A clown can do tricks.
A clown can make me laugh.

Cady Conrad, Grade 1
James R Watson Elementary School, IN

When They Give Me...
When they give me a TV
I want a camera.

When they give me a camera
I want a MP3 player.

When they give me a MP3 player
I want an iPod.

When they give me an iPod
I want a Game Boy.

When they give me a Game Boy
I want a DS

When they give me a DS
I want a DS
NOW!
Travis Shull, Grade 2
Mentone Elementary School, IN

The Monkey's Job
There once was a monkey named Bob
Who really needed a job.
He got a job to make pie
When he got fired, he began to cry
And hit his head on a log.
Emma Gochnauer, Grade 3
Smithville Elementary School, OH

Snowy Day
S nowflakes
N ice snow
O utside there is beautiful snow
W ow!
Y ou can have fun

D elightful
A ngel in the snow
Y es! I get to go outside
Katelyn Romaninsky, Grade 3
Midkota Elementary School, ND

My Baby Brother
My brother gives me kisses.
He loves, loves, loves
Me, me, me.
I love him.
Kaylee J. Bernardy, Grade 1
Bristol Elementary School, WI

Haiku
Five, seven, and five
Captures a moment in time
Beautiful haiku
Dustin Kasser, Grade 3
Mable Woolsey Elementary School, IL

Spring
Spring here
Spring here
Everywhere spring!
Birds hatching
Flowers blooming
Everywhere spring!
Rithika Dandeboyina, Grade 2
Stocker Elementary School, WI

Skateboarding
Skateboarding is lots of fun.
Especially in the hot, hot sun.
In the day and in the night.
Oh, I love skateboarding,
It is so much fun!
Andrea Pearsall, Grade 3
Atwood Elementary School, MI

Jacket
Jacket
Winter, fluffy, heavy
Insulating, containing
An outer covering
To keep you warm
Cozy coat
Katrina Wierzbicki, Grade 3
St Michael School, OH

Candy

You can eat it.
It is sour or sweet.
It is good.
It is just like you!

Anna Johnson, Grade 2
McKenney-Harrison Elementary School, IN

Summer

It is cool when
That hot, steaming sun
Glares on you.
Oh NO!
I am burnt.
Ow — that hurts!

Kelsey Wilson, Grade 2
James R Watson Elementary School, IN

Lindsay Gardner

Lindsay
Talks a lot, funny, and really cute
Daughter of Phil and Debbie
Much loved by family and friends
Sibling of Haley Gardner my sister
I wish I was the oldest out of me and my sister
Wants to be a teacher
Who is afraid of my dog if he bit me
Who feels sleepy
Who gives the hardest work
Who would like to go swimming
Who enjoys my friends
Resident of Wyandotte Public Schools
Gardner

Lindsay Gardner, Grade 3
Jefferson Elementary School, MI

Spring

S unshine is warm and hot.
P uddles are wet and sometimes deep.
R ainbows are colorful and pretty.
I nsects are cool and awesome.
N ight raindrops knock on the window.
G iant worms come out to play.

Tanner Krusemark, Grade 2
Stanton Elementary School, NE

Colors

Peach reminds me of people's skin.
Gold is a trophy when I win!

Orange means there is a mango.
Yellow makes me do the tango!

Green is the color of money.
Bronze makes me think about honey.

Indigo is my favorite color.
Purple is my favorite other.

Light blue makes me look up in the sky.
White is something in my eye.

What do colors mean to you?

Kian Bral, Grade 2
Detroit Country Day Lower School, MI

Rain

Drip, drop
Drip, drop
Sprinkling
Now it's raining hard
Drip, drop
Drip, drop
Muddy puddles at my house
Drip, drop
Hear the thunder and the lightning
Drip, drop

Madison Ring, Grade 2
Country Meadow Elementary School, IN

Sharks

Sharks like to attack
And they never let go.
People will die.
Sharks like to swim.
Sharks will eat anything.
Sharks are monsters.

Evan Goodman, Kindergarten
McKenney-Harrison Elementary School, IN

Colors

Gray is when it's a rainy day
Green is when it's time to pay

Blue is when you look at the sky
Black is a color that makes me sigh

Gold makes beautiful autumn leaves
Silver is really nice to receive

White is the snow
Purple just makes me glow

Red is sometimes the color of your cheek
Pink is the color that makes me want to peek

Jessica Hillstrom, Grade 3
Hanover Elementary School, MN

My Mom

My mom is great no matter what date.
She'll share a smile not just for a while.
She's sweet and kind not just in my mind.
We laugh and play not just for a day.
She's lots of treasure not just a measure.
She's got love and care in her heart to share.
She's just like a dove on the cloud above.
All of this states that she is quite great!
I love my mommy!!!

Olivia Weidenbenner, Grade 3
St Clare Catholic School, IL

My Poor Grandpa John

My poor grandpa John
He died in 2004
All the love is gone.
He was funny.
I really miss him.
He was the best of them all…my greats!
Now all my greats are gone.
They will always be in my heart.
I will never forget them, Great Grandpa John.

Christian Warren, Grade 3
Henryville Elementary School, IN

The Sun

When the sun speaks to us
It says
Wake up
When the sun goes down
It says
There's going to be another
Day

Mitchell Vang, Grade 2
Orchard Lane Elementary School, WI

Bright Moon

The bright moon spins too
It makes lots of tracks
And shines in the night

Kalleigh Clevenger, Grade 3
Mable Woolsey Elementary School, IL

Sincere Glider

A sea turtle glides
through the ocean

It goes deeper
and deeper into
the ocean
but the turtle
will make it

Seeing a shark
the turtle pretends to be a rock
the shark
gets closer and closer

A noise reaches the shark's ears
and it is scared away

The turtle
has reached
its hunting grounds
and it makes
it safely home

Jenna Weszt, Grade 3
Greenbriar Elementary School, IL

Shea

Smart, Funny
Silly, Weird
Nice, Friendly

Shea is my friend
because she makes
me laugh, smile, and
feel good about myself.

My friend and I like to
play school at recess.
We like to play together
at school and at home!

December Skelton, Grade 3
Henryville Elementary School, IN

Spring

Spring
Colorful, rainy
Blowing fast winds
Spring comes so fast
Wild

Bailey Campbell, Grade 3
Suffield Elementary School, OH

I Can't

I can't have Scooby snacks for dinner?
No gummy bears?
No pop?
No cookies?
No popsicles?
No gum?
How come?

No Pop-tarts?
Or cake?

Just like in the past.
I never get the good stuff.
I just thought I'd ask.

Kathryn Burns, Grade 1
Northfield Elementary School, OH

Green
Green is my favorite
The color of the grass…
Green.

Dalton Parker, Kindergarten
McKenney-Harrison Elementary School, IN

Ants
Red, brown
Ant farm
Two antennae
Six legs
Three body parts
One thorax, abdomen, and head
Queen ant
Ants are cool insects.

Abby Glenn, Grade 1
James R Watson Elementary School, IN

Houses
A pink house,
A green house,
A red house,
A purple house,
A blue house,
A black house,
I like my house.
Do you like your house?

Colton Carper, Grade 1
James R Watson Elementary School, IN

Daddy/Mommy
D ad is funny
A lways loves me
D rinks coke
D oes work a lot
Y ells, "Jacob come here!"

M y mom talks a lot
O ften watches TV
M uffin lover
M om wants the house clean
Y ells, "Cody come here!"

Jacob Pattee, Grade 1
Hamilton Community Elementary School, IN

All About Spring

In the spring I see Canada Geese.
In the spring I see puddles.
In the spring I see bright clouds.
In the spring I hear airplanes.
In the spring I hear the wind.
In the spring I smell flowers.
In the spring I feel hot.
In the spring I feel coldness.
In the spring I smell the fresh air.
In the spring I hear the wind chimes.
In the spring I feel relaxed.
In the spring I feel happy.
In the spring I feel hyper.
In the spring I hear birds chirping.
In the spring I feel good.
In the spring I feel glad.

Niquera Short, Grade 3
H. R. McCall Elementary School, IL

Candy

Candy is red
Candy is blue
Candy is colorful
And sour and sweet.
Candy is bad
It hurts your teeth.
Candy is good
It tastes sour and sweet.

Brendan Rogghe, Grade 3
Atwood Elementary School, MI

Dad

My dad has brown hair
He loves baseball
My dad is tall
He always plays
baseball with me
and my brother
He hits us ground balls
and pop flies

Derek Hall, Grade 3
Henryville Elementary School, IN

Buckeyes

B e the winner.
U se the ball to throw.
C atch the ball.
K ick the ball to start.
E veryone has fun.
Y ou are going down.
E verybody wins and loses.
S ay "good game" when it is over.

Samantha Perrin, Grade 2
Woodford Elementary School, OH

Color Poetry

Hot pink is a flower bloom.
White is the taste of snow.
Green is like the grass in spring.
Black is a hole in the forest.
Yellow is the sun burning on me.
Blue is a lonely day.
Red is a rose given to you.

This is how I describe colors.

Carli Gable, Grade 3
Atwood Elementary School, MI

Skate

S weet
K ool
A fun sport to do
T ubular
E xciting

Josh Bartold, Grade 3
Floyd Ebeling Elementary School, MI

Dogs

Dogs are cute
They are so cute.
Dogs are fun to play with.
I love dogs.
My dog's name is Lucky.
She is fun to play with.

Jakenda Short, Grade 2
Midkota Elementary School, ND

Freestyle
Freestyle makes me wiggle and squirm.
Can't catch my breath.
Tricks and backflips.
Motorcycles being ridden fast and zooming.
Can't wait to watch again and again!

Samuel Jon Aldea, Grade 3
Atwood Elementary School, MI

Cats
Tiger cats
Black cats
White cats
I love cats.
Gray cats
Yellow cats
Too
Many
Cats!

McKenzie Dufresne, Grade 1
James R Watson Elementary School, IN

Baseball
Baseball is fun, fun, fun.
I like baseball
To hit the ball and run!
Outfield is fun, fun, fun.
I like the outfield
To catch the ball and throw
And hear the umpire call
Out, out, out!!

Erik Young, Grade 2
Shorewood Hills Elementary School, WI

The Sea
It's a beautiful blue.
I feel so alive.
Listening to the sound,
I feel like I am going to die.
I feel like I am time.

Catherine Thiltgen, Grade 1
Madison Central Montessori School, WI

Pencils

I am a pencil
I HATE being a pencil
You would too if you were a number 2
People throw you away,
They leave you in their book-bags
I might be a pencil,
But I have feelings!

I am a pencil
Being a pencil is hard work
You have to write,
Even if you don't want to!
People are harsh!
They use your erasers,
It hurts!
I am a pencil,
A proud number 2,
But I
HATE BEING A PENCIL!!!

Carlee Conrad, Grade 3
James R Watson Elementary School, IN

The Wonderful Earth

The Earth is a very wonderful thing to have
because when you wake up in the morning
you see all the flowers growing out of the grass.
Wow! The Earth has a lot worth showing!
It gives us trees and it grows us food
and it puts us all in a happy mood!
It has all of the creatures that fly,
and hide, and some are very shy.
But, best of all, we all live on the Earth
and I am so glad that we do…
how about you?

Murfee Cook, Grade 3
St Columbkille School, IA

Cats

Funny
Cool
Colorful
I love cats!

Eric Schild, Grade 1
James R Watson Elementary School, IN

One Beautiful Morning
When the beautiful sun rises high
It reaches up to the morning sky

The waves are pretty foamy blue
It even shines like morning dew

The children swim in the ocean
With a great joyful motion

The flowers nodding on the green grass
The parents watch and never pass
Emily West, Grade 3
Krambrooke Academy, MI

I Am Ice Cream
I am ice cream.
I come in many different flavors.
Vanilla,
Chocolate,
Strawberry.

I am ice cream.
Mix me in M&M's and take a bite.
Mix me in apple pie and
THEN take a bite of me!

I am ice cream.
Michael Paseka, Grade 2
Mentone Elementary School, IN

Index

Index